ST EDMUND'S BURY:

also a View of ST EDMUND'S HILL, RUSHBROOK and HARDWICK.

Grafton this Plate is most humbly Dedicated,

most Obedient Servant J. Kendall

Angel Hill, in St Edmunds Bury, December 1774. J. Kendall's engraving, first state, with 2-horse gig, and the Angel Inn before refronting. At St Edmund's Hill, on the extreme left, the Frenchmen stayed 8 months with Mr Symonds; see p. xxii.

A FRENCHMAN'S YEAR IN SUFFOLK

French impressions of Suffolk life in 1784

SUFFOLK RECORDS SOCIETY

General Editors
Norman Scarfe (post-medieval)
R. Allen Brown (medieval)
G. H. Martin (medieval)

Secretary
Peter Northeast

A FRENCHMAN'S YEAR IN SUFFOLK

French impressions of Suffolk life in 1784

including a preliminary week in London, brief visits
to Cambridge, Colchester, Mistley and Harwich
and a fortnight's tour of Norfolk

The *Mélanges sur l'Angleterre* of
François de LA ROCHEFOUCAULD,
supplemented by the *journaux de voyage* of
Alexandre de LA ROCHEFOUCAULD
and the *lettres à un ami* of
their companion, Maximilien de LAZOWSKI

Translated and edited by
NORMAN SCARFE
and with a Foreword by Edmée de LA ROCHEFOUCAULD

The Boydell Press

Suffolk Records Society
Volume XXX

A Suffolk Records Society publication
first published 1988 by The Boydell Press
an imprint of Boydell & Brewer Ltd
PO Box 9, Woodbridge, Suffolk IP12 3DF
and of Boydell & Brewer Inc.
Wolfeboro, New Hampshire 03894–2069, USA

ISBN 0 85115 508 1

British Library Cataloguing in Publication
La Rochefoucauld, Francois de
A Frenchman's year in Suffolk : French impressions of
Suffolk life in 1784 : including a preliminary week in
London, brief visits to Cambridge, Colchester, Mistley
and Harwich and a fortnight's tour of Norfolk : the
Melanges sur l'Angleterre of Francois de La Rochefoucauld,
supplemented by the journaux of Alexandre de La Rochefou-
cauld and the lettres a un ami of their companion,
Maximilien de Lazowski.   (Suffolk Records Society; v. 30).
1. Suffolk. Social life 1784. Biographies. Collections
I. Title   II. La Rochefoucauld, Alexandre de   II. Lazowski,
Maximilien de   IV. Scarfe, Norman   V. Series
942.6′4′0922

ISBN 0-85115-508-1

Library of Congress Cataloging-in-Publication Data
La Rochefoucauld, François, duc de, 1765–1848.
[Mélanges sur l'Angleterre.   English]
A Frenchman's year in Suffolk : French impressions of Suffolk life
in 1784 : the Mélanges sur l'Angleterre of François de La
Rochefoucauld / translated and edited by Norman Scarfe.
p.   cm. — (Suffolk Records Society ; v. 30)
"Supplemented by the journaux of Alexandre de La Rochefoucauld."
ISBN 0-85115-508-1 (alk. paper)
1. Suffolk—Social life and customs.   2. England—Social life and
customs—18th century.   3. England—Description and
travel—1701–1800.   4. Country life—England—History—18th century.
5. French—Travel—England—Suffolk—History—18th century.   6. La
Rochefoucauld, François, duc de, 1765–1848.   I. Scarfe, Norman.
II. La Rochefoucauld, Alexandre de.   III. Title.   IV. Series:
Suffolk Records Society (Series) ; v. 30.
DA670.S9L313 1988
942.6′4—dc19
                                                            88-14532
                                                            CIP

♾ Printed on long life paper
made to the full American Standard

Printed in Great Britain by
The Camelot Press PLC, Southampton

Contents

List of Illustrations

Jacket painting: Mistley across the Stour from Brantham, painting by
    Elias Martin, 1776

Credits

Dr John Blatchly for front endpaper and Pl. 28
St Edmundsbury Museums Service for rear endpaper
The La Rochefoucauld family for Pls. 1, 3, 4, 10
Sir John Ruggles-Brise and the Paul Mellon Foundation for British Art for Pl. 2
The Beauvais Archives for Pl. 5
Librairie Plon, Paris, for Pl. 8
Suffolk Record Office for Pls. 13, 15, 29
National Portrait Gallery, London, for Pl. 19
Sir John Soane's Museum for Pl. 23
Stockholm National Museum for book-jacket and Pl. 24
Essex Record Office for Pl. 25
Ipswich Museums and Galleries for Pl. 27
Norfolk Record Office for Pls. 30, 43
Norfolk Museums Service for Pls. 33, 34, 38, 44
Holkham Estate and Courtauld Institute of Art for Pl 40
National Trust, Blickling Hall, for Pl. 41
The editor is responsible for Pls. 6, 7, 9, 21, 22, 31, 32, 36, 37

Translator's Note

Professional writers are self-conscious about using the same adjective twice in as many sentences, unless for emphasis. François de La Rochefoucauld, at eighteen, concentrated more on accuracy of description than on a literary effect. Such words as *beau*, or *agréable*, or *prodige*, are sometimes used more readily than they would have been by Proust. In translating, I have not hesitated to repeat adjectives in this slightly unsophisticated way. François made his meaning exceptionally clear, and I hope I have allowed him to do so in English. I have not thought it necessary to try to re-create some notional 1780s English: where 'it is' seemed too formal, I have invariably preferred 'it's' to ' 'tis'.

ix

To Mlle Françoise Marchand
and in admiration and tribute
to Jean Marchand, 1894–1988,
Croix de Guerre, Chevalier de la Légion d'Honneur,
artist and scholar,
Librarian to the French Chamber of Deputies and National Assembly

Foreword

On ne saurait être que sensible à l'aimable évocation d'un personnage de sa famille faite par un écrivain étranger. Et lorsque ce portrait et le récit d'une période intéressante de sa vie sont accompagnés par une documentation remarquable, le plaisir est complet.

C'est le sentiment que j'ai éprouvé et qu'éprouveront tous ceux qui liront l'introduction que M. Norman Scarfe a consacrée à la réédition du voyage nouvellement traduit par lui-même du *Voyage de François de La Rochefoucauld en Angleterre* (1784). Ce jeune homme, âgé de 18 ans, et son frère Alexandre avaient été confiés par leur père, le Duc de Liancourt, à Mr de Lazowski, venu de Pologne en France avec le roi Stanislas, et bien capable d'accompagner deux français, intéressés par l'agriculture anglaise. François, qui connut Arthur Young, le célèbre agronome anglais, a laissé impressions et description de Bury et des différentes étapes de son voyage, comme il devait plus tard écrire les *Souvenirs du 10 Août 1792* et de la nuit passée aux Tuileries avec Louis XVI et la famille royale, avant leur tragique journée à l'Assemblée.

M. Norman Scarfe, historien de classe, a réuni toutes les informations possibles concernant les La Rochefoucauld de l'époque et leur action à la fois réformatrice et fidèle au Roi.

Je ne puis que le remercier et le féliciter pour son travail admirable.

Edmée de LA ROCHEFOUCAULD

Preface and Acknowledgements

My first obligation is acknowledged in the dedication of this book. The late M. Jean Marchand's studies of the observant young La Rochefoucauld travellers, François and Alexandre, with their tutor, Maximilien de Lazowski, were responsible for their being published in the 1930s – the French travels, in French, in 1933 and 1939, the *Mélanges sur l'Angleterre* in English in 1933. M. Marchand had already published (1929) François' *Souvenirs du 10 Août 1792 et de l'Armée de Bourbon*, poignant as de Vigny, with a long Introduction outlining the lives of the La Rochefoucauld–Liancourt family; before the Revolution, during its critical early stages, in exile, and on their return to France. Theirs is an engaging, significant, and at times very moving, story; and one of the freshest and most vivid chapters is this one, the *Mélanges*, written of their first year abroad, in Suffolk – mainly by François but with reliable factual assistance from his younger brother, Alexandre, and additional material keenly observed by Lazowski. All this I have collated much more fully here than was done either in 1933 or when the *Mélanges* appeared in its original French in Paris in 1945, as *La Vie en Angleterre au XVIIIme Siècle*. (In 1933, the late S. C. Roberts was the translator.)

Meanwhile, in 1940, M. Marchand brought out for the Institut Français de Washington the *Journal de Voyage en Amérique et d'un Séjour à Philadelphie, 1794–5*, written by the duc de Liancourt, the father of François and Alexandre: the horrors of a rough Atlantic crossing under sail can never have been more graphically, or sympathetically, recorded, and one wishes that more of the duke's autobiographical writing had survived the Revolution: it apparently included, before they were confiscated, three volumes of his own experiences as a young man in England, in 1768–9 (Pl. 3).

Early in 1987, I decided that a new translation and edition of his sons' description of their year in Suffolk was needed. With the permission of the present Librarian of the National Assembly in Paris, I started work, in that handsome room, on the transcription of the four volumes of manuscripts in which François described their travels from Bury St Edmunds through much of midland, northern and western England in 1785. While I was working in Paris I was most kindly received by Mlle Françoise Marchand, whose father was already gravely ill. With great generosity, she presented me with copies of her father's transcripts of those four volumes of travels in 1785, and I hope to produce an edition along much the same lines as the present one. Mlle Marchand informed me of the duchesse Edmée de La Rochefoucauld's interest in my work, and introduced me to her. Herself a remarkable writer, the duchess gave me an enchanting tour of her family's portraits in her Paris house: her late husband was directly descended from François, and their son is the 14th duc de La Rochefoucauld and 8th duc de Liancourt. Alexandre's direct descendant, the 7th duc d'Estissac, President of the Jockey Club, with equal kindness suggested that I should make use of Alexandre's eighteen notebooks and made them available in his room in perhaps the most exclusive club in Europe. I felt greatly honoured, and not least when he, and the duchesse Edmée, and her daughter, the writer Solange de La Rochefoucauld, visited me in that august chamber. The eighteen cahiers of Alexandre will be especially useful when I come to the travels in Britain, in 1785–6, which I think will make a single volume. During my Paris visits, my old friend, M. Georges Ausset, patiently accompanied me to the La Rochefoucauld places.

The writings of Lazowski, the tutor and friend on these travels, are equally indispensable to this work. The originals were in the possession of the late Jacques Ferdinand-Dreyfus, who wrote a life of François' father in 1903, *Un Philanthrope d'Autrefois*. He made transcripts available to M. Marchand; and Mlle Marchand has made available to me all those she could find; fortunately, those that appear (from gaps in the pagination) to be missing are not vital to the job of supplementing the record of the La Rochefoucauld brothers. The original Lazowski writings now seem to be untraceable. A few original letters of his are among the collections of Arthur Young in the British Library, which is where the main document reposes on which this present book is based. It appears to be a manuscript by François himself of the *Mélanges*, written for his father. It is Add. MSS 35108, and all that is known of it is that it came from the Phillipps sale and was bought from Quaritch on 13 April 1896 (not 1869, as was stated in 1933). It was Phillipps MS 23868. Whenever I have checked the published transcript against my microfilm of the original, I have found the transcript immaculate. The hand is cramped but fair. A facsimile page was published in the 1933 English edition.

My obligations, then, are first to Mlle Marchand, and to the duchesse Edmée de La Rochefoucauld and the duc d'Estissac, for their very kind help and encouragement. Among my friends over here, Margaret Statham has shared her knowledge of Bury St Edmunds topography and history, and John Bensusan-Butt readily tackled problems of the Essex–Suffolk borders. Over illustrations, Sir John Ruggles-Brise has let me use Russell's lively portrait of Arthur Young. John Harris suggested the splendid painting of Mistley from the Stockholm National Museum. Vic Gray, Essex's County Archivist, arranged for me to use the detail of the Bernard Scalé survey of Mistley. John Blatchly and Chris Reeve respectively enabled me to have for front and back endpapers the two states of J. Kendall's *Angel Hill in St Edmund's Bury*, which might have been drawn and engraved with this book specially in mind! In Norfolk, Robin Emmerson of the Castle Museum and Paul Rutledge of the County Record Office have been extremely kind: likewise John Maddison's assistant at Blickling and Mr F. C. Jolly at Holkham. Judy Egerton of the Tate Gallery has been generous with advice. Mr N. Cotterell of Ipswich did wonders with the photography of the endpapers: Geoff Cordy of Felixstowe did marvels in making my own nine photographs acceptable: Trevor James of the Suffolk Record Office's Photography Unit was helpful as always. Peter Northeast and David Dymond have patiently helped as usual with various questions. Finally, I must thank Paul Fincham and Pru Harrison and the Boydell Press, our publishers, for all their customary care, and Ken Shiplee especially: in forty years of book producing, I have not met with more accurate and accomplished type-setting. My friend Frank Collieson has very kindly lent an expert hand in reducing those of our slips and inconsistencies that remained.

Introduction: Suffolk and the French Revolution

ENGLAND, TO ITS OWN dismay, beheaded Charles I in 1649; and in 1688 it sent James II packing, to lodge for the rest of his life with the Bourbons at St Germain, overlooking Paris. In 1793, the French beheaded Louis XVI. The connection between these desperate political events in England and France (though in 1784 the formation of the *Assemblée Nationale*, and the storming of the Bastille, lay five years in the future) is never far below the surface of this otherwise cheerful book, which is about English provincial life in a good year (only the weather was bad: almost incessantly). It is about great landlords, tenant farmers, servants and labourers; about manners – when to remove hats and wear slippers – and beliefs, Roman catholics, the dreadful English sabbath, Gretna Green (and other) marriages, road transport, local justice, town water-supplies, cloth-making and silk-making, Lowestoft porcelain, horse-racing at Newmarket, and an unusually lively general election; it is about grand houses, parks, 'the English garden', the meaning of the word 'saloon', and about amazingly clean and neat smaller houses and cottages and *their* gardens; it is about drawing-matches and field sports and Friendly Societies (or 'Box Clubs'); it is about every detail of improved methods of agriculture and stock-breeding. On Box Clubs, a very perceptive general point is registered (p. 190): 'it is always at table that the English do business'.

The three men savouring all these English things, with detailed notes expressing frequent surprise and rueful expressions of envy, were the two elder sons – Alexandre (16) and François (18) – of the duc de Liancourt, later La Rochefoucauld-Liancourt (who was a leading 'liberal' and at the same time close to Louis XVI – Grand Master of the Wardrobe at Versailles: Pl. 1) and their 40-year-old bear-leader (précepteur, companion and friend), Maximilien de Lazowski, whose father had been a court official of King Stanislaus at Lunéville, in Lorraine: so far I have not traced a portrait of Lazowski. During their

1. The duc de Liancourt, the father of François and Alexandre: detail from portrait attributed to Baron Gros.

2. *Arthur Young: pastel by John Russell, RA.*

year in Suffolk, the three quickly came under the wing, and the spell, of Arthur Young, already a famous advocate of every kind of improved husbandry: they themselves caught his enthusiasm. They had already spent much of the time from late-1781 to mid-1783 on similar travels through France.[1] Already they were indefatigable sightseers of the useful in preference to the picturesque. (They loved the picturesque at Blickling.) But their five-day tour with Arthur Young on the Essex border and in East Suffolk, in July of 1784, was something of a turning-point in their lives. Despite the rain, it was a resounding success. They enjoyed it so much that they resolved on another such tour, as soon as possible, round the neighbouring county of Norfolk, before setting out on the more serious venture they had intended into the further parts of England. Not only does Arthur Young's company seem to have added zest to the July tour, it was the true beginning of the staunch, immensely fruitful, friendship between Young and Lazowski and the duc de Liancourt and his family.

If this friendship had not formed, one of the most extraordinary, and influential, travel books ever written would perhaps never have been undertaken – certainly could never have included such astonishing first-hand and eye-witness accounts of Paris and Versailles during the critical, formative, opening days of the Revolution. Arthur Young's *Travels* (in France and Italy) were first published at Bury St Edmunds in 1792.[2] When a French translation appeared in 1793, the *Convention* ordered 20,000 copies to be printed and distributed, free, in each commune. In 1801, the *Directoire* went further, and published a translation of Young's select agricultural works in eighteen volumes, entitled

[1] Jean Marchand, ed., *Voyages en France de François de La Rochefoucauld*, 2 vols, 1933, 1939, Société de l'Histoire de France.

[2] There are two 'modern' English editions, neither complete, for Young wrote copiously. One was for Bohn's Libraries, in 1892, by the delightful Miss Betham-Edwards, a Suffolk woman who knew Young's descendants and their family papers and who spent fifteen years in France, in Young's footsteps and going her own way. Leslie Stephen justly commented 'Here and there the notes might be a little fuller' (*Studies of a Biographer*, 1898). Of Young, Stephen wrote: 'He was not a walking blue-book, but a highly sensitive, enthusiastic, impulsive, and affectionate man of flesh and blood, whose acquaintance every sensible man would have been glad to cultivate.' In the more 'recent' edition, by Constantia Maxwell of Trinity College, Dublin, the notes are fuller. Young's abundance leads to editorial difficulties. Miss Maxwell's edition (CUP) was published in 1929.

Le Cultivateur Anglois. It was a tribute to Young himself but also to the duc de Liancourt, to whom Young's ideas were profoundly sympathetic (Pl. 2).

This being so, it has long seemed to me a most lucky chance that 'Mr Walpole', who turns out to be Horace Walpole's cousin, the Hon. Thomas Walpole of Lincoln's Inn Fields, a banker with business and other interests in Paris,[3] should have met Lazowski and the boys in London. There they arrive, near the beginning of this present volume, and are deflected by him away from Bristol (where they would *not* have met Arthur Young) and in the direction of Bury St Edmunds (where they very soon did). François does not include the proximity of Arthur Young's house at Bradfield Combust, very near Bury, as one of Mr Walpole's reasons for their going to stay at Bury. But Young himself gives it as one of Lazowski's reasons. The passage in Young's *Autobiography*[4] is worth quoting at some length, as it contains the best description of Lazowski written in either language:

'At this period commenced a most agreeable acquaintance with a French gentleman who came to Bury, and I must dilate a little on the origin of his journey. The Duke of Liancourt was Colonel of a French regiment, the quarters of which were at Pont-à-Mousson, in Lorraine, to which he went every year according to the regulations of the French army. At that place he accidentally met Monsieur de Lazowski, son of a Pole, who came to Lorraine with King Stanislas. The Duke was so struck with his manner and conversation that he resolved to cultivate his acquaintance. About that time he was in want of a tutor for his two sons – not for the common purposes of education but to travel with them. He accordingly engaged Lazowski to make the tour of France with these lads, the Count de La Rochefoucauld [François], and the Count Alexandre de La Rochefoucauld. The Duke thought it an important part of education to become well acquainted with their own

---

[3] W. S. Lewis, ed., *Horace Walpole's Correspondence*, Vol. 27, p. 1070, indexes the references to Hon. Thomas. So does Vol. 36 (1973), where (p. 248) on 9 Dec. 1787 Horace wrote: 'My elderly cousin Mr Thomas Walpole has espoused . . . Mme de Villegagnon at Paris who is no infant neither . . .' The proof that 'Mr Walpole' was Thomas Walpole is contained in Alexandre's *tome* VIII, where, on p. 81, he wrote simply: 'Mr Walpole demeure à Londre où il est banquier.'

[4] Ed. M. Betham-Edwards, *The Autobiography of Arthur Young*, 1898, pp. 119–21. It is a most engaging book.

country. During two years they travelled over the greatest part of the kingdom on horseback. The Duke was so well pleased with the conduct of Lazowski on this journey that, having determined to send his sons to England in order to acquire the language of the country, and generally in compliance with the Anglomania which then reigned in France, he continued Lazowski in his situation and sent them all three to England.

'Among other objects in France, Lazowski had given some attention to agriculture, particularly in its connection with political economy. On his arrival in London, he made enquiry who could most probably give him information relative to agriculture, manufactures, commerce and other national objects. Among others, I was named to him by some person who was so partial in his representations that he at once determined to fix at Bury for a short time, which he understood was the nearest town to my country residence. He and the two young men went to the Angel Inn, from thence hired convenient apartments,[5] and enquired where I resided. At that time I was absent, and Mr Symonds,

---

[5] The endpapers show the Angel Hill, Bury St Edmunds, in 1774. J. Kendall published two states of this fine engraving, both dated 1 December 1774. The front endpaper shows *the 1st state*. A coach-and-four are entering the Cook Row (now known as Abbeygate Street). Above the coach, two inn-signs mark the site of the Angel Inn, where the French spent the first day or two before finding apartments – possibly in the house immediately south of the Angel (we are looking south). The three-storey building facing us is the Assembly Rooms (now the Athenaeum, and much altered). Above the Assembly Rooms, on the skyline, is Hardwick House, the many-gabled seat of the Rev. Sir John Cullum, author, in 1784, of a valuable *History of Hawsted and Hardwick*, but already stricken with the 'pulmonary complaint' of which he died, at 52, the following year. The Cullums are the only local gentry who do not appear in the recollections of the French, and one understands why. The farther church-gable and tower are St Mary's, the nearer tower is the great Norman bell-tower of St James, formerly serving as the main gate leading to the abbey church, once one of the greatest buildings of its kind in Christendom. Its ruins were much more considerable in 1774 than they are in 1988. The great 14th-century gatehouse led to the abbot's courtyard. To the right of it is a good representation of a 2-horse gig, known as a curricle: a gig was like this but drawn by one horse. On the skyline, left of the 'abbeygate', is Rushbrook, the home of the Davers family. On the skyline at the left edge of the print is St Edmund's Hill, the new house designed by Robert Adam for Professor John Symonds, where the French made their home from the end of May 1784 till they left on their tour of England the following February.

The principal difference in *the 2nd state* (back end paper) is that the front of the Angel Inn has assumed its present three storeys and pediment, and the gig has given way to more, and finer, pedestrians – drawn, apparently, by the local artist Henry Bunbury (see *Catalogue, The John Greene Collection of Prints of Bury*, 1934, No. 27).

understanding that two young men of fashion from France were at Bury, introduced himself and showed them various civilities, and when I returned brought them over to Bradfield. From that time, a friendship between me and Lazowski commenced, and lasted till the death of the latter.

'Lazowski was about 40 years of age, and in every respect a most agreeable companion. He soon made rapid progress in the English language, which he spoke not only with fluency, but often with extreme wittiness. There was not in his mind any strong predominant cast; but the grace and facility of his manner, with suavity of temper, made him a great favourite; and being also highly elegant and refined, he often produced impressions which were not easily effaced. From his general conversation in mixed society, it was not readily concluded that he could or would attend with great industry and perseverance to objects of importance. But this would have been erroneous, for he exerted the greatest industry in making himself a master of all those circumstances which mark the basis of national prosperity, and he formed in his own mind a very correct comparison of the resources both of Britain and of France. He often expressed to me much surprise at what he thought on this subject in England, and declared that the ignorance of the French relative to their great rival was most profound.'

We need to get the origin of this very valuable friendship straight. It has sometimes been suggested that it was in existence at least five years earlier. Jacques Ferdinand-Dreyfus, in 1903, and Jean-Dominique de La Rochefoucauld, in 1980, in two admirable full-length biographies,[6] base themselves on the first *Vie du duc*[7] in the matter of his first visit to England in 1768: 'At 21, he felt the need to travel, but usefully, to learn, and went to England, where he was serious and curious, which always pleases the English.' M. Dominique de La Rochefoucauld rightly wonders, though, what justified Dreyfus's assertion that 'he crossed the Channel in search of freedom of government and to see how machines worked, and dairy-farms and stock-breeding'. That might be antici-

---

[6] J. Ferdinand-Dreyfus, *Un Philanthrope d'Autrefois: La Rochefoucauld-Liancourt 1747–1827*, Paris 1903, pp. 13, 30. J-D de La Rochefoucauld, C. Wolikow and G. Ikni, *Le Duc de La Rochefoucauld-Liancourt*, 1980, p. 63.

[7] *Vie du duc de La Rochefoucauld-Liancourt*, Paris, 1837, by the youngest of his three sons, Frédéric-Gaétan, 14 years younger than François.

pation, based on hind-sight. Gaétan quoted Mme du Deffand's letter of 24 May 1769 to Horace Walpole, saying that she had now met M. de Liancourt, that 'everything good you told me of him made me want to meet him: I found him very natural, and very simple'. Gaétan omitted the passage in which the young nobleman told Mme de Deffand how *infiniment content* he was with Horace Walpole, and what a good account he had given her of a *fête*, presumably at Strawberry Hill.[8] We are far from political freedom and factories. It does appear that the 21-year-old Liancourt made three volumes of notes on his first English journey, but as they were appropriated by the government in 1793, and not since found,[9] we had better stick to Gaétan for his father's motives. Both Ferdinand-Dreyfus and M. Jean Marchand manage to involve Arthur Young with Liancourt and with his aunt the duchesse d'Enville at this time, 1769. The long passage from Arthur Young's *Autobiography* effectively belies his involvement with them before 1784.

Apart from Horace Walpole's correspondence with Mme du Deffand, there is another very agreeable record of Liancourt's English visit in 1768/9.[10] It is the perfect conversation-piece of the period, painter not known, but as it were by Zoffany, or Henry Walton, and hangs in the Paris house of the duchesse Edmée de La Rochefoucauld (Pl. 3). The future duc stands with a piece of muffin in his left hand, the teacup and saucer in his right, as he discusses the newspapers with his slightly older cousin and lifelong friend, the duc d'Enville (25). In September 1792, this gentle student of natural science, d'Enville, was arrested: as he was being driven through Gisors with his mother and his wife, he was hauled from the coach by a howling mob, and stoned to death.

---

[8] W. S. Lewis, ed., *Horace Walpole's Correspondence: Mme du Deffand*, II, (1768–1770), 1939, p. 240.

[9] Ferdinand-Dreyfus, op. cit., p. 14, n. 2. J-D de La Rochefoucauld, *et al.*, loc. cit.

[10] A more precisely dated scrap of evidence for Liancourt's visit, Mme la duchesse Edmée allowed me to transcribe from the original in her possession: it is a most interesting autograph letter, dated at London on 16 March 1769, from the future duke, as Colonel, to the Lt.-Colonel of his Regiment, thanking him for the state of the regiment at the end of February, pleased that there were no vacancies in the ranks, and going on to show an intimate knowledge of individual personal problems. He ends the letter: 'Now that the time has come to resume exercises, don't exact too much of the first class: as for the awkward ones and the recruits, an hour and a half morning and evening; *and* for messieurs the officers, above all for those back from their 6-months furlough, to get them back into trim as soon as possible.'

3. *François' father, the future duc de Liancourt at 21 (left) in London with his cousin the duc d'Enville, c. 1768–9. It may have been painted by Henry Walton, who was influenced by Chardin.*

Liancourt, in England by the skin of his teeth, wrote of his cousin: 'He professed his belief in liberty long before the word was uttered in France.'

It is known, then, that Liancourt and his cousin were in England in 1769; but that they met, or even knew of, Arthur Young, is utterly improbable. One must similarly dismiss, for lack of evidence, the notion that Young resided (let alone 'often') with the duc at Liancourt between 1773 and 1784, and that 'in 1779 the two sons of Liancourt, François and Alexandre, one 14 and the other 12, went with their tutor Lazowski to spend some time at Bury St Edmunds at Blackfields Hall' (clearly Bradfield was meant).[11]

So much for 'earlier visits'. What is unquestionable is their father's devotion, at least by 1780, to political economy and good works – over and above his military rôle. The print by H. Mauperché (1654, Pl. 4), shows the huge ducal palace (of *c.* 1580–1610) at Liancourt that he inherited on the death of *his* ancient father who lived from 1695 to 1783. It had already been 'improved' in the 'English picturesque' manner by his grandfather. He himself made a new garden *à la mode anglaise* on the hill to the north-east, and his wife, François' mother, built a beautiful creamery, sumptuously decorated, not far from the château: it is the one ducal building (apart from obelisks and garden ornaments) that survived the Revolution and all the dislocations of the 20th century (Pl. 6).

Nowadays, Liancourt lies among beautiful woods just to the right of the main road from Paris to Amiens. It is no longer a picturesque village, but half-way up the street, in a mean little square named the *Place La Rochefoucauld*, is a bronze statue of 1861 commemorating the duc. It records his foundation of the '*Ecoles d'Arts et Métiers*' in 1780, and he stands with his back to an anvil, a set-square and other tools. His introduction of vaccination in France in 1800 is noted, and his co-founding of the Savings Banks, the *Caisses d'Epargne*, in 1818, after the Napoleonic Wars and the Restoration. It is dedicated *Au bienfaiteur de l'Humanité.*

---

[11] Such statements are puzzling in a book based on such thorough research: J. Ferdinand-Dreyfus, op. cit., p. 30. Unluckily, he led M. Jean Marchand into believing in the boys' 'first' visit to Bury in 1779, which is certainly against all the evidence of the three writers here in 1784. (J. Marchand, ed., *François de La Rochefoucauld: Souvenirs du 10 Août 1792 et de l'Armée de Bourbon*, Paris, 1929, p. xii.)

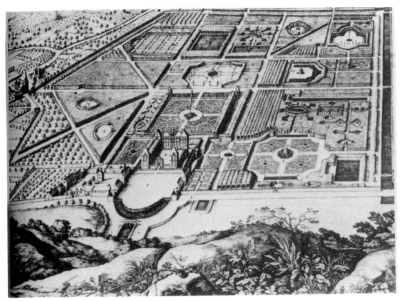

4. *The ducal château at Liancourt, 1654: engraving by H. Mauperché.*

5. *Wheat dibbling at Liancourt, c. 1802: the duc (with lorgnettes) shows the prefect of the department of Oise how it's done.*

At the top of the hill to the north-east of the town, at a cross-roads, a modest obelisk of 1881 commemorates the *Ferme de la Faiencerie*, cradle of the '*Ecoles d'Arts et Métiers*' ('Arts and Crafts' does not quite translate it, in English, though it should). 1881 was celebrated here by pupils (we would now have to say students) from Aix, Angers, Châlons, etc. The stone is carved to show a training ship, a steam engine and a beam engine. On one of the remaining buildings of the *Ferme de la Faiencerie*, which looks distressingly shuttered in my photograph (Pl. 7), the funeral monument of the duc himself has been fixed to a wall defended by a ferocious guard-dog: it was brought here from the *jardin anglais* he created on the slopes of the hill near by, where he was buried. The circumstances of his funeral in 1827 we will return to, also those of the Terror and the exile of the La Rochefoucauld family, between 1792 and the closing of the 'list' of emigrés on 25 December 1799. Here in Liancourt, he wrote, on 26 March 1802, to Arthur Young to tell him he had become a farmer again, even 'an English farmer', and as all his goods had been sold he was a poor farmer. But the park at Liancourt had survived and been given back to him. He had felled the woods, all the trees, and put in the plough 'where you saw garden-walks and cascades and fountains'. He worked at it continually, and in two years had made good progress.[12] He had pulled down much of the château, and lived in one wing. A remarkable sketch of that time shows him with lorgnettes, demonstrating to M. Cambry, the prefect of the department of Oise, the new way to plant wheat, the farmer with a dibbling iron in each hand, and four children following, to pop the seed-wheat into the four rows of holes (Pl. 5). It is precisely the method Lazowski had noted on the old road from Norwich to Yarmouth in October 1784, and described in his 'letters to a friend', the 'friend' being undoubtedly the duke (see p. 211 below).

François was born in 1765 in their Paris house, the Hôtel de Liancourt, in the rue de Varenne which runs west, and parallel with the Seine, to the Invalides. (Its present number is 58: almost opposite the Hôtel de Matignon, the Prime Minister's official residence, it has gained a whole front storey (Pl. 9) and has lost much of the grandeur

---

[12] BL Add. MSS. 35128, fol. 425. Quoted by Guy Ikni, in La Rochefoucauld, Wolikow and Ikni, op. cit., p. 285.

6. *Liancourt: the* laiterie, *built for François' mother.*

7. *Liancourt: Ferme de la Faiencerie: the cradle, in 1780, of the Ecoles des Arts er Métiers.*

shown in Pl. 8. The family was well known for its general Enlighten-
ment and this probably prepared him a little for the very different
society and politics he found in England in 1784. But before that, at
fifteen, he followed his father into the La Rochefoucauld dragoons. For
him, service was limited to four months a year – June to September. We
may be sure he took them seriously, and should not be too surprised at
reading his rather professional appraisals of British defences at Harwich
and his friend Lazowski's at Yarmouth. He later described the miserably
half-hearted use to which his army training was put from September to
November 1792: in the hopelessly incompetent army of the duc de
Bourbon against the 'instant' revolutionary army of France.

But meanwhile, after his first spell of training in 1780, he set off with
his young brother and Lazowski on their first French travels. These
covered much of the time before their departure for England, and some
readers of the present book, and of Arthur Young's celebrated *Travels* in
France, and who know France, may want to read Jean Marchand's
edition of the *Voyages en France de François de La Rochefoucauld 1781–1783.*[13]

By the time they reached Suffolk, much of France was fresh in their
minds, and its shortcomings were often tempered and counter-balanced,
one region by another. Yet there is a constant refrain of admiration
running through their experiences in East Anglia. Indeed, it seems to
start at Dover: 'I first noticed the air of contentment. I felt myself
transported into another world.' In post-Roman London, 'the Franks
were already envious of its growth'. St Paul's rebuilt by voluntary
contributions: 'that wouldn't have happened with us'. 'One notices
here, and in everything, the English love of the public good.' In London
clubs and taverns, 'all the men have to defend their liberty, as we have
not'. And so it goes on: 'Those who don't believe that that government
is best under which people live most happily should travel in England.'
Two centuries later, one has to confess this makes refreshing reading to
an Englishman!

Stern as they were in the pursuit of 'political arithmetic', the guard is
often down: most notably at the end of the July tour with Arthur
Young. 'This little tour gave me the most enormous pleasure: it was not
merely that all I saw was new and interesting, but every single thing
was agreeable, and I was quite discontented on the sixth day to get

[13] In 2 vols, 1933 and 1939, Paris, Société de l'Histoire de France.

8. Hôtel de Liancourt, Paris, late 17th century.

9. Hôtel de Liancourt, Paris, today.

back home.' Soon after that, he wrote a vignette on 'English Farms and some Agricultural Details'. In the winter, when the cattle were brought in, all of them together in the open farmyard, it truly delighted him to walk about among them. 'You see a great quantity of oxen, cows, horses, foals and pigs, all there together, *and in separate attitudes.*'

This would be a good moment to hand over to François, and some readers may slip over to him and return later to the last part of this introduction, to read a brief sketch of the lives of the main characters after 1784.

Lazowski and the boys made a tour of the midlands, the north and west country in the first half of 1785, and then probably returned to France for François' military duties. In 1786, Lazowski and Alexandre were over here again, but apparently without François: they toured Scotland and crossed to Ireland. Alexandre's notebooks are full of detail, though Lazowski writes in his audible English with a touch of disappointment to Arthur Young from Glasgow, 6 May 1786:[14] 'We run instead of travelling. My companion wishes only to move from place to place. He counts every day how many miles we have done, and his satisfaction is all wais in proportion to the number . . . I was of opinion of shortening the travel and not go to Ireland but we shall, and to his great disappointment he will not very likely get to the regiment – but all that is childhood . . . I write four hours at least every day. I leave the highlands with which I have been much entertained . . . They deserve more than any people to be free.'

The following May, 1787, Young was in Paris at the beginning of his three years' of incomparable experiences of France: staying at the Hôtel de Liancourt, meeting the duke's mother and wife (his kind hostess), breakfasting in the duke's apartments in Versailles, meeting the duke's ill-fated cousin d'Enville, whose prowess in the natural sciences he knew of, and setting out for the Pyrenees with François and Lazowski: back in Paris that September.

François had transferred to a regiment of *chasseurs-à-cheval de Champagne* at Schlestadt, in Alsace. There he served till the beginning of the Revolution, in which his father played so central a rôle, and part of which Young saw and accurately described. For an agronome, an

---

[14] BL Add. MSS. 35126, fols 338–9.

agrarian economist, his political judgement seems remarkably mature. On 27 June, seventeen days before the Bastille fell, he wrote:[15] 'The whole business now seems over, and the revolution complete: the king has been frightened by the mobs into overthrowing his own act of the Royal Session . . . and with that I shall leave Paris.' And off he went to Reims, and Lunéville to meet Lazowski's old father, and Burgundy and Auvergne, and Toulon, to make more observations on French agriculture!

Liancourt's part in the Revolution began on the night of 14 July, the troubled night after the Bastille had fallen. It is fairly well known that, while most of the deputies tried to get some sleep on benches and tables in the chamber, Liancourt, as Grand Master of the Wardrobe, walked into the heart of the château of Versailles, to the alcove where the king slept, woke him, told him about the storming of the Bastille and, when the king exclaimed 'Quelle révolte!', replied 'Ah, sire, dites "révolution".'[16]

Gaétan's explanation of his father's actions is that he wanted the king to adopt freely the principles of the revolution, 'so that it was made with him and by him, who was the sole means of its being done against him'. He took Liancourt's advice, and sent the troops away from Versailles and Paris, and came by himself to the National Assembly.

The point of going into these matters here is that when things then went steadily from bad to worse, Liancourt was blamed for his work that night, allegedly making Louis look weak (though he impressed the Assembly). The queen (whose responsibility for the tragedy was not negligible) and the king's emigrated brothers, notably Artois (later Charles X), were implacably hostile to Liancourt. These odious *Ultras* precipitated the ugly scene with the police at Liancourt's funeral at the Madeleine in 1827, in which his coffin was knocked into the gutter and smashed open, ostensibly because the family had, without clearing it with the police, allowed children from the *Ecole des Arts et Métiers* at Châlons to act as bearers.[17]

---

[15] Constantia Maxwell, ed., *Travels in France*, CUP, 1929, p. 159.
[16] There are various versions of this event, given in Appendix III by J. Ferdinand-Dreyfus, op. cit., pp. 509–10. Enthusiasts for the revolution liked to think that he said 'c'est une grande révolution'.
[17] J-D de La Rochefoucauld, C. Wolikow and G. Ikni, op. cit., in their Annexe XXI, give the most vivid description of the duc's funeral, as extracted from Alexandre Dumas' *Mohicans de Paris*, chapters 150 and 151.

What is ironical is that Arthur Young was right in seeing, on 27 June, seventeen days before the Bastille, that the king had ruined his cause and allowed the uniting of the three 'estates' to form the National Assembly. Yet after the events of 1792, with Liancourt escaping from Rouen to England by the narrowest margin, then the September massacres, and in 1793 the guillotining of the royal family, Young came to forget his original diagnosis, and to blame his friend Liancourt for being liberal and therefore responsible! When Liancourt came to Bury, in October, nice (but no great political thinker) Fanny Burney (step-daughter of Young's wife's sister, and a great favourite with Young) had come to think of the duc as largely responsible for the fall of Louis XVI!

Meanwhile François, for whatever reason, had conceived a deep devotion and loyalty to the person of the king, and was in close personal attendance on him while he was forced to live in the Tuileries (from October '89) until 10 August '92, when François walked with the royal family to the *Assemblée Nationale*, giving one arm to Madame Elisabeth, the king's sister, the other to Madame de Lamballe, both doomed. He himself was often threatened that week with cries of 'A la lanterne!' He left Paris, pistol in hand, and reached England soon after his father.

The serious and curious descriptions of East Anglia in this book, François followed with an account of other parts of England and then by *Souvenirs du 10 Août 1792 et de l'Armée de Bourbon*, admirably edited by Jean Marchand. In September 1793 François married at Altona, in Slesvig-Holstein, close to Hamburg, Marie-Françoise de Tott, daughter of the celebrated baron de Tott, writer and French ambassador in Istanbul, where she was born. She was responsible for the drawing of him, apparently the only surviving portrait (Pl. 11). Jean Marchand gives some particulars of life in Altona, where there were thought to be as many as 8,000 émigrés at one time. François and his wife were joined there by his father in 1798. François described her as a remarkably good musician.

There is material for a slender book on the life of the French émigrés in Bury. Mme de Genlis was here with some curious characters in 1792 and made some disobliging remarks about Arthur Young.[18] Fanny

---

[18] Carlyle fairly characterised Mme de Genlis as 'Pretentious, frothy; a puritan, yet creedless, darkening counsel by words without wisdom.'

Burney said that as soon as Liancourt arrived in October, Mme de Genlis 'quitted Bury with the utmost expedition. She did not even wait to pay her debts . . .'[19] Fanny Burney said that Liancourt then occupied the Genlis' house, as no other that was vacant suited him so well.[20] The duc made a strong impression on Fanny Burney, who herself married a French émigré, General d'Arblay, the following year, July 1793. Liancourt was 'very tall, and were his figure less, would be too fat, but all is in proportion. His face, which is very handsome, though not critically so, has rather a haughty expression when left to itself, but becomes soft and spirited in turn, according to whom he speaks [sic], and has great play and variety. His deportment is quite noble, and in a style to announce conscious rank even to the most sedulous equaliser. His carriage is peculiarly upright, and his person uncommonly well made . . . he has all the air of a man who would wish to lord over men, but to cast himself at the feet of women.' Daisy Ashford's Mr Salteena is quite eclipsed!

But many English were, like Arthur Young, revising their views about the Revolution: with England at war with France, Liancourt became uncomfortable, even with his English friends, and sailed for Philadelphia on 1 October 1794. His *Journal de Voyage en Amérique*[21] is intensely interesting: perhaps the most readable of all his family's writings in that late 18th-century generation. In the middle of a horribly stormy voyage, he entered in his diary the *cri de coeur*: 'Ah Cockfield, Cockfield, quand m'y retrouverez-je!'[22] (Pl. 10)

---

[19] *Diary and Letters of Madame d'Arblay*, ed. Charlotte Barrett, 1893, p. 445.
[20] Was it the house next to the Angel, that absurdly bears a plaque merely stating the name Louis Philippe? On 14 February 1793, a 5-bay, 3-storeyed Georgian-fronted house in Whiting Street, now number 84, appeared in the rate book as 'Duc de Lerincourt House – 12 rent, 1.4s rates'. The house was unoccupied the previous August. One wonders if he was living there in 1794? A confused note appeared 20 years later in *East Anglian* I, 1814, p. 44: 'Death: 6 Jan 1814: Aged 20: Alexandre Desoutre, natural son of M. Liancourt (now Duc de Rochfoucault) by his French servant, during his residence in Bury with Madame Gentis, and the ill-fated Pamela, afterwards Lady Edward Fitzgerald.' The bit about Mme Genlis is impossible for many reasons. Peter Northeast noticed this obituary. Dr Jane Fiske notes a reference to his death, as 'de Soustrice', in James Oakes' diaries, which she is editing for this society.
[21] Ed. Jean Marchand, *Institut Français de Washington*, 1940.
[22] One of his close English friends, Lady Blois, whose husband was a disastrous gambler, lived at Cockfield Hall, Yoxford, in Suffolk, when it was not let to recoup gambling debts. Liancourt visited her at Melton, near Woodbridge: see below, p. 133.

10. *Cockfield Hall, Yoxford: home of Liancourt's friend, Lady Blois.*
(T. Higham, in Excursions through Suffolk, *1818)*

Liancourt and François were able to return to France in 1799. François' life, worthy and unadventurous, is fully outlined in Jean Marchand's introduction to *Souvenirs du 10 Août*. Plate 5, the dibbling of wheat at Liancourt, shows the duc's incorrigible determination to improve mankind. In 1968, the 150th anniversary celebrations of the *Caisse d'Epargne et de Prévoyance de Paris* recognised the duc as its co-founder, with Benjamin Delessert, in its handsome commemorative book.

The duc remained true to his liberal principles: François reacted, by moving to the king's personal service in the last months of the old monarchy, feeling perhaps that he might be able to make up for his father's 'liberal leanings'! We can read, in his study of politics while he was in Suffolk, that he had no conception of constitutional monarchy: for François, George III was not a king.[23] For his father, I think Louis XVI ceased to be king in June 1791, with the Flight to Varennes, and the king's abjectness and apathy, a sort of spiritual abdication: yet he dreamt of getting the king to Rouen and the Channel. Young Alexandre cut an

[23] See p. 77 below.

altogether different dash. In 1788, when he was 21, he married Adélaïde Pyvart de Chastullé, daughter of a French Guards officer who was also a rich proprietor in Saint-Domingo *and* connected with the family of Beauharnais and Napoleon's beloved Joséphine. As we saw from Lazowski's comment on his attitude to the Scottish tour, Alexandre's heart was in the army. But when war broke out in 1792, he was as puzzled as his father and brother about which army to fight for. He probably withdrew for a time to Domingo. Back in France in 1797, his wife became *dame d'honneur* to Joséphine. Alexandre became a Napoleonic diplomat, ambassador at Vienna in January 1805, and later took part in the negotiation of the Treaty of Tilsit.[24] Reduced to local government after the war, he died in 1841. François lived just long enough to see the revolution of 1848. He was probably not sorry to see the demise of Louis-Philippe.

Now we return to 1784, and François' spirited letter to his father, telling him not to expect any bright observations, but claiming that all the facts are true!

---

[24] Jean Marchand, 'Un ambassadeur de Napoléon', in *La Revue d'Histoire Diplomatique*, 1934.

Letter of Dedication

For you, my dear father, I've written such part as I think may interest you of what I've learnt in this country. I warn you: all the information gathered here is taken only from Suffolk, and – above all – the prices set out here are those peculiar in this county. So don't base your judgement on what you may know from other parts of England: there may be differences – indeed, there must be. But don't conclude, on that account, that my facts are wrong. I can't pretend to have made any bright observations, but I can claim that all the facts I tell you of are true, and have been checked by various people before being written down.

I have been a bit exercised about the order I should put my findings into. I've given it much thought and – unable to find a form that seemed clear and sensible – decided to impose no order at all, but wrote down everything just as it came into my head. There is only the table of contents to help you find what you may be looking for, for to read it all from beginning to end would be like reading a dictionary in which I've taken no trouble over alphabetical order. It is easy to settle the order of a travel journal, for one writes down each day what one has seen. But, after 13 months in one place where everything was new to me, how could I find any natural order for things that were totally different, and what reason was there for dealing with one thing ahead of, or behind, another?

I present you with this small offering, unworthy to be laid upon your altars; but each of us does what he can, and one day, perhaps, I shall do better: that will always be my aim. Accept this as if it were good, and I ask nothing in return but much indulgence.

I am, my dear father,

Your, etc.

11. François de La Rochefoucauld (1765–1848): the portrait by his wife.

François de La Rochefoucauld began with their arrival at Dover. For completeness we start (as M. Marchand did in his French edition) with Alexandre's very brief notes on the journey from Paris, and the Channel crossing. Between Paris and Bury, there is a discrepancy in their dates. François was writing 'as it came into my head' thirteen months later; Alexandre's notes were scribbled at the time: at sixteen, dates and mileages were his strong point.

Alexandre: We left Paris on 21 December [1783] at 10 o'clock in the evening, in the diligence for Calais. The diligence has 8 places, and is very uncomfortable. The first stage was at Amiens, the town large and well built. I give no details, since we arrived at night and left very early. From Amiens to Montreuil, and from there to Calais, where we arrived in the evening of the next day. We stayed two days in Calais, and left on the 27th at 2 in the afternoon. *Crossing:* we sailed at 2 in a good packet-boat. Weather good, but little wind. When we reached the northern point of the coast of France, the wind rose and little by little reached such a pitch that when we came to try to enter Dover harbour, after a four-hour crossing, we had to wait nine hours at the entrance to the harbour, in what is known in seamen's terms as *une tourmente*, half tempest, half squall. At last, after those nine hours, we entered the harbour at 3.30 a.m., every one very ill.

DOVER

François: We arrived at Dover on the 28[1] after a hard crossing. We had waited two days at Calais as the weather was too bad, and we left only to make one of the roughest sea-voyages possible. For twelve hours we were exposed to the most disagreeable upheavals, which made me ill the whole time. This seasickness is overwhelming: every moment, you think you are going to die, and nothing can help you. M. de Lazowski and my brother – my two companions – and our servants, were as ill as I was. It is a tribute exacted by the sea, and happy are those she exempts.

[1] The manuscript says 'le 2'.

3

The town of Dover is pleasant enough, although quite small. It is situated at the foot of a high hill. All the houses are of a neatness that is pleasing: generally not tall, and brick-built, but some are timbered and plastered. The port is fairly large, and the whole harbour was full of ships when we came through.

Near the hill that dominates Dover, there is another, much taller, shaped like a sugar-loaf, on the top of which is the castle; extremely old and very badly maintained. It commands the whole countryside, and was for that reason very important in former times. All that is left of it is an old building falling into ruin. They look after only those buildings needed for a small garrison in war-time; in peace-time it could hardly be smaller. From the castle there are good views of the shores of France; and if the weather had been clear I could have seen Calais, quite distinctly. A little below the castle, on the slope of the hill, is a battery of six or seven guns, among which I saw a long culverin named 'Queen Elizabeth's pocket pistol'.

At Dover I first burnt coal and found it very inconvenient. I regretted during those first days that we had no firewood, for, when one is cold, warming up – especially one's feet – takes a long time. Coal is much better for warming a room. But I found the smell of coal extremely disagreeable: I soon got used to that, however, and now that I have been in England some little time, I prefer coal to wood, because one isn't constantly having to mend it and it does throw out more heat.

It was at Dover that I first noticed the air of contentment (*l'air d'aisance*) of the country I was entering: I saw that all kinds of people – the neighbouring countrymen, even the servants – were well clothed and, above all, of great cleanliness; that the furniture of their houses was all made of mahogany, even in our inn; that they had those tables which are so dear in France. I saw several charrettes,[2] all harnessed to good horses with good trappings, which entailed an outlay beyond the means of our farmers. I was charmed with all this from the moment I saw it. I felt myself transported into another world.

The weather was extremely bad, freezing and snowing hard, so that I couldn't enjoy a view of the countryside.

---

[2] Literally *carts*, but here perhaps a form of *trap*. The French 'charrettes anglaises' was used to describe 'petites voitures de luxe', 2-wheeled, for 2 or 4 people.

We left for London the moment our baggage had been examined, at about 2 o'clock on 3 January 1784: as we couldn't manage the 72 miles from Dover to London in what was left of the day and as we didn't want to travel by night, we went for the night to Canterbury.[3] There we arrived very late, and next day came to London. I could scarcely see Canterbury and Rochester, but got the same impression of neatness as at Dover. All along the road I saw nothing but houses, and often charming houses, all white and surrounded by fences that gave them an air of the greatest elegance. The whole route was one perpetual village, the houses interrupted only by evergreen trees – often very fine.

POST-HORSE TRANSPORT

The post-carriages are also extremely convenient. There are three kinds: the *stage-coaches*, which are diligences with fixed times of departure and arrival for all parts of England: they hold six passengers and are harnessed to four horses. The *diligences* hold four, are harnessed to two horses, their departure and arrival times are also fixed: they are more expensive than the stage-coach, but more comfortable. The third kind are the *post-chaises*,[1] harnessed to two horses and driven by a postillion, with two or three passengers. They go extremely fast, they charge eleven English shillings a mile, and do at least eight miles an hour. Sometimes they go for twelve or sixteen miles, after which you change both horses and carriage. All are harnessed to excellent horses: in France we have no idea of their quality: all tall, well-made and with their tails docked, and as well turned-out as those of a rich private person in France, and all go at a spanking pace.

[3] Alexandre noted that they travelled from Dover in a diligence, drawn by 6 horses and seating 6 persons comfortably: covering 7 or 8 miles an hour. Alexandre wrote of 'the magnificence of the inns of Canterbury' and 'the beauty of the chairs and the drinking glasses'. Arrived safe and sound in London at 8 in the evening of 28 December. Discrepancy of dates irritating: we have to favour Alexandre's, as being noted down at the time; it is no great matter.

[1] They looked like half a coach – the rear half – suspended midway between four wheels.

As to miles, it is necessary to grasp their length, because in England distance is generally measured only in miles. The French 'league' of 2,400 *toises*[2] is a little under 3 miles: 25 of these leagues make a *degré* or 60 miles.[3]

Postal organisation in England is very different from France's. Everyone here can have horses and carriages: it is no kind of exclusive privilege. Only since the war[4] has it been necessary to pay the government a small tax, which falls merely on the richest class, those who travel. Every postmaster is interested in having good horses in order to provide a better service than others. There is no limit to the routes they must take: a traveller, if he wishes, may take a carriage at Canterbury for a journey to Edinburgh. The postmasters have no restrictions: it is always a good-will bargain they make when they hire out their horses and carriages.

LONDON

We arrived in London at night. We could scarcely see anything on our arrival; but, by what light remained, it seemed beautiful. We lodged in King Street, St James, to be in the fashionable quarter, and convenient for walking.

London is a town of great antiquity: good authorities affirm its existence before Julius Caesar's invasion: the Romans settled in it as the most convenient site for a port and for communicating with all their possessions in the island.

As the Roman colony was not numerous, the ancient Britons attacked and pillaged the town; and it was several times subjected to fire and the sword – successively by the Franks, the Picts, the Scots and the Ostrogoths; again, in 850 it was destroyed by the Danes; but always it rose again from its ashes and became richer than before. The wall of the City was built at about the time of defence against the Franks, already envious of the growth of London.

[2] A *toise* was just under 2 metres.
[3] This calculation is obscure.
[4] American War of Independence, 1775–83.

It wasn't until the year 900, or so, that they began to build houses of stone and brick in London; before that, it was just wooden huts. The town continually received, from successive kings, great privileges and liberties which enabled it to establish a great trade which it has maintained without interruption down to the present day.

William the Conqueror introduced a better form of government, which was perfected as the various peoples of Britain gradually accepted the laws.

The City has always been the principal mainstay of the Crown, when the nation was governed by arbitrary power and since the Revolution. In 1666, London was entirely reduced to cinders,[1] an event that contributed most to its present beauty. Before that, the streets were narrow, badly built. By their jumbled arrangement, they preserved a fetid atmosphere which every year killed off a large number of the population; and the shortage of water added to the unhealthiness. Since then, an entirely new City has been built, avoiding all the disadvantages of the old one. In consequence, London is very well spread out, down the side of a hill and resting on the Thames. Its very convenient position means that it abounds in everything necessary and pleasant in life. Bulky merchant-ships arrive there with the greatest ease; and frigates, without the slightest trouble, although sixty miles from the sea.[2] Ships of the line are obliged to drop anchor in front of Greenwich hospital, two miles downstream, to unload their guns: unloaded they could reach London docks, but they stay at their first mooring.

The shape of London is an oval oblong, 7 miles long, 3 wide and 18 in circumference.[3]

This city is the seat of liberty and of the encouragement of the arts – as it is the centre of the trade – of all England. All religions are practised here: there are 315 different churches or temples, 103 parish churches

[1] The Great Fire of London began on the morning of Sunday, 2 September 1666, destroying all the City within the medieval walls except for a small patch in the north-west: some 13,200 houses, 89 churches and dozens of public buildings.
[2] He must be measuring from the North Foreland.
[3] Unlike most of his observations to his father, which were first hand, many of these London statistics François gleaned from the 1782 edition of *The London Guide*, publ. for H. Fielding. In his mind he was contrasting London with Paris. And what he observed for himself is fresh and interesting.

(not counting St Paul's and Westminster abbey), 69 chapels of the established church, 21 for the French protestants, 11 for the Dutch, Germans, Danes, etc.; 33 for the Baptists, 26 for the Independents, 28 for the Presbyterians, 19 chapels of the papist religions (counting those of the foreign ambassadors), and three Jewish synagogues.

All the London streets are immensely wide and carefully laid out: all have paths on each side for the convenience of pedestrians. Usually, the streets are very clean because the slopes are well managed to carry the water away. The squares, which are very numerous, are of an immense size: I find them even too large, for they have an empty look.[4]

London's shops are decidedly notable: none so magnificent are to be found, surely, in any other city. All the merchants' possessions are displayed through great windows, invariably clean and transparent, and the shops always project a little into the street, so as to present three fronts.

The Thames runs the whole length of London: there is no more beautiful river. It consists of the waters of the Isis,[5] mixed abundantly with its own. The Isis springs on the borders of Gloucestershire, south-west of Cirencester.[6] It flows towards Lechlade, becomes navigable 138 miles from London, and from there goes to Oxford, where it receives the Cherwell: from Oxford to Dorchester, where it enters the Thames.[7] From there the Thames goes on to London, past Wallingford, Marlow, Windsor, Bradford[8] and Richmond: it divides Surrey and Kent from Middlesex and Essex on its way to the sea, and takes in the Medway near its estuary. There are several fine bridges over this river; especially London Bridge, Blackfriars and Westminster, all three in London. The Thames is very broad, and its waters are always high: they are very beautiful, full of excellent fish, and very easy for navigation.

This river at London is so covered with shipping that there is scarcely room for one or two to pass when they need to go up stream. One can hardly see the water for the forest of masts afloat on it.

---

[4] Engravings of e.g. Hanover Square and Cavendish Square show them still treeless: it may be that which made them seem empty to François.
[5] This classical name seems to be maintained only in Oxford!
[6] The true source is 2 miles west-south-west of Cirencester, behind the Thames Head Inn, on the A433.
[7] This curious geography is the result of mistaking the Isis for the Thames proper.
[8] i.e. Brentford.

The Tower of London stands on the east side of the City, beside the Thames. Originally it was the royal palace; it consisted only of what is known as the White Tower, generally believed to have been built by Julius Caesar.[9] In 1076 the Conqueror enlarged it into a place of defence and to receive the respect of the local inhabitants. William Rufus laid the foundations of the castle, which was finished under Henry I, surrounded by a wall and a great ditch, in many places, 120 feet wide.[10] Henry III built the stone gate, Edward III the chapel.[11] Edward IV augmented the fortifications and built the Lion Tower, destined to house the wild animals from abroad presented to various kings of England.[12] In the reign of Charles I, the White Tower was rebuilt and a great many other buildings erected which today give the Tower the appearance of a fortress.[13]

The Tower is surrounded by a moat, filled by opening a sluice to let in the waters of the Thames.[14] It is connected to the river by a little passage, through which all sorts of munitions manufactured in the Tower for the army or navy are sent out or brought back; and by this gate enter the state prisoners who are sent to the Tower. In one small tower that forms part of the fortress, the Crown Jewels are kept. Well: it is so much more remarkable a place for being the only thing in England that shows there is a king. It is here that he comes for a few days when he ascends the throne: in this way he gives the impression of holding the city of London in respect.

The Tower of London has always been important in the various English revolutions: there the executions have taken place that have so often changed the face of this state. Its government is committed to the Constable of the Tower, a post of great importance: he has charge of the

[9] In fact built soon after the Norman Conquest, as François went on to describe.
[10] In fact the 120-ft ditch was made by Edward I;
[11] so was the Byward Tower, the main gate. The chapel is an early Norman work.
[12] In fact the Lion Tower, at the outer gate, was rebuilt as the Middle Tower, again by Edward I.
[13] The White Tower's windows had all been enlarged earlier in the eighteenth century, and in the 1690s Wren had built the handsome Great Storehouse, burnt down in 1841. Its mansard roof and attic dormers may have reminded François of French fortresses. His muddle over Charles I is excusable: plenty of modern guidebooks are just as misleading!
[14] It was finally drained and turfed in 1843.

Crown and the Crown Jewels at the coronation and other ceremonies of state. Under him is a Lieutenant, a Deputy-Lieutenant called the' Governor, a Major, a Gentleman-Porter, a Gentleman-Gaoler, four Gunners and forty Warders,[15] who wear the same uniform as the King's Guard. They are clad in scarlet, with broad bands of blue with gold facings, and on breast and back they wear the royal arms in silver, representing a thistle and a rose with the letters G. and R. Their hats are round, of black material with gold ribbons.

A monument has been raised to the fire of 1666. It is by Christopher Wren – a handsome column of the Doric order, 15 [feet] in diameter, with a base 28 feet square serving as pedestal. The pedestal is 40 feet high, the column with its capital 120, the crown and urn 42, which makes a total of 202 feet. On the pedestal, at the four corners are four dragons supporting the arms of the city and, between them, trophies, emblems of royalty, the sciences and commerce. On the faces of the column are symbols representing England, London and the fire.

All the connoisseurs reckon this column a most noble creation, superior to all modern works of this kind. A few years ago, one could climb to the top by a stair built inside, but it's forbidden because the column leans a little to one side: it is feared that the continual vibration caused by a large number of the curious may bring on its collapse.

Before the Fire of 1666, the Royal Exchange of London was a simple brick building erected by a private merchant.[16] Since the fire it has been rebuilt in Portland stone, which is the most beautiful stone used in England. It is sturdily built, with two fronts, north and south, each with a different portico, and in the courtyard a colonnade of widespanned arches. The south front is the more handsome: [the portico has] Corinthian attached columns supporting a well-designed cornice, and between the columns two niches with statues: Charles I and Charles II in Roman costume, beautifully carved. This front is surmounted by a fine clock-tower, which regulates the whole city.

---

[15] He mistakenly uses the English word 'archers'.
[16] Sir Thomas Gresham's design, modelled by a Flemish architect on the Bourse at Antwerp, was by no means simple: 'one of London's first really civilised buildings' – John Summerson, *Georgian London*. After the fire it was rebuilt by Edward Jerman, whose reproduction of Gresham's arcaded courtyard François clearly enjoyed.

The other front, on Threadneedle Street, has pilasters of a composite order. The interior, being vaulted, makes a good quadrangular promenade for the merchants, sheltering them from the rain. Under the arcade which surrounds a small square are several niches at present vacant except one which is occupied by the statue of the merchant who built the Royal Exchange at his own expense before the Fire.

The merchants have allocated the arcades to different businesses: one for Hamburg merchants, one for those of Amsterdam, etc., so that they can easily find those they want to deal with. At the edge of the court, in niches near the pilasters of the arcades, are statues of a great many kings and queens of England. I forgot to say that those niches which are, with one exception, empty, are reserved for merchants who make a name for themselves either by opening up a new branch of trade or by the services they may render their country.

Close by the Exchange is the Mansion House of the Lord Mayor of London – a fine house, stone-built and with much architectural ornament, but I find it too heavy.[17]

St Paul's is the cathedral of London and the most splendid piece of architecture that I have yet seen.

Originally a temple dedicated to Diana and then built by a Saxon prince, it was destroyed by fire, built again, destroyed six or seven more times, but each time a new building was erected on the ruins of the old. In 1666 – calamitous, or rather fortunate, date for London – St Paul's was burnt for the last time.

The decision was made to build a new cathedral, much more magnificent than the old one. And so an office was opened for the receipt of voluntary contributions. The outcome was that there was not only enough money for the new building, but in the end there was more than was needed – something that does great honour to the English nation, and which wouldn't, I think, have happened with us. Christopher Wren was the architect, he proposed several designs, and of them one was chosen by the taste of the majority.[18]

---

[17] Built 1739–53 by the elder George Dance: Sir John Summerson, too, finds it 'both cramped and over-dressed'.

[18] By great good fortune, he was able to alter it fundamentally as he went along, though he pretended the changes were purely ornamental.

This superb edifice is built of Portland stone. The ground floor is distinguished by a row of coupled columns, with entablatures of the Corinthian order, and on the storey above are various ornaments of the composite order. Between the arcades and windows are a great many architectural features of much variety and beauty.

The west front has the most magnificent portico: two storeys of columns, and a balustrade of black marble along the entire length.[19] The columns of this portico are coupled, leaving spaces for three door-ways – one on each side to provide entrance for the public, the one in the middle for solemn occasions. This last is surrounded by white marble: above it is a carving in low relief showing St Paul preaching to the Corinthians.

Above the principal front is a marble in low relief representing the conversion of St Paul:[20] St Paul with St Peter on his right and St James on his left, the four evangelists with their emblems (the angel of St Matthew, the lion of St Mark, the bull of St Luke and the eagle of St John). The north entrance is designed with an ascent of several steps of black marble: [the transept] has a dome supported by six columns of the Corinthian order, and with an urn festooned.

The south entrance is designed with a taller flight of steps, also of black marble, the portico corresponding to the one on the north side, with a dome supported in the same way. The east end of the church is rounded – apsidal – to frame the altar. At the centre of this beautiful building a tremendously handsome dome rises on columns 20 feet high: it is said that the dome itself is 150 feet high.[21] St Paul's is designed on the plan of a cross, the interior of a most beautiful and simple architecture, extraordinarily vast. It is possible to climb up into the clock-tower above the dome, but it was so cold when we were there that it was impossible to clamber up.

The [British] Museum is a superb collection of a great number of books, prints and antiquities deposited here spontaneously for the instruction or for the curiosity of the public. It is open for three hours a day for the limited number of ten people. It is said that the collection of

---

[19] This balustrade seems to have disappeared.
[20] It is the best known work of Francis Bird who was paid £650 for it in December 1706.
[21] The top of the dome is certainly reckoned to be 366 feet above the ground.

books and the rest of the antiquities cost £100,000 sterling. There are 50,000 volumes, a large number of medals, antiquities, precious stones, agates, a well-furnished cabinet of natural history full of minerals, shells, stuffed fish and birds; also one or two Egyptian mummies. The house that contains this collection is a fine one, well-arranged, an admirable monument bringing together in one place several kinds of collection: but each, individually, is not to be compared with our collections in France. If one brought together the Bibliothèque du Roi, the *Cabinet*, the medals, the engravings, etc., that would be very different from the British Museum. One notices continually, here and in everything, the English love of the public good: a great part of what one sees here has been voluntarily given; and, every day, owners are making them bequests. Parliament has granted the Museum nearly £9,000 a year, sterling.

We didn't forget to go to see Westminster abbey, the burial place of the English kings. I don't know who the founder was. I do know that Henry VII had a great deal of work done and almost brought it to its present form, for since his day no-one has worked there until Christopher Wren, who left it as we see it.[22] The church is cruciform, the nave very grand and the architecture wonderfully light, the west entrance notable.[23]

There are many precious objects that win the admiration of foreigners: the tombs of all the English kings, all marble of different styles; and the tombs of great men who have been granted the honour of burial here. All the chapels of this church are full of very magnificent tombs, but as I was there for only a very short time I didn't take enough note of them to detail them now.

St James's Park is the royal garden: quite large but composed of only an avenue of trees, a big lawn and a patch of water. That was all I saw, perhaps because I was there in winter, in terrible weather.

The palaces of the King and Queen overlook the park and are two brick houses without taste, without ornament and without architecture.

---

[22] After seeing St Paul's, François had Wren much in mind. It is true that in 1698 Wren became Surveyor to the fabric, and that he recommended the composition of the W. towers. But it was his successor, Hawksmoor, who designed them and *his* successor who finished them. Wren proposed a *Gothic* central *dome*, which would certainly have been interesting!

[23] He didn't notice the abbey's Frenchness, but that is probably what he would have expected.

They are said to be very agreeable inside, but from the outside they have none of the appearance of being the residences of a king and queen.

I went once to see a comedy at Drury Lane. The theatre was ridiculously small. I saw Mrs Siddons, an actress of tremendous talent: she gave me tremendous pleasure although I didn't understand a word of English.[24]

In London there are two houses where tragedies and comedies are played: Drury Lane and Covent Garden. The actors of each playhouse are a private company which buys its plays on condition that the other company cannot perform them. That seems an excellent practice, sparking rivalry between the two houses, to get bigger audiences and better plays; also the authors of good plays get better prices and the public get better actors. Finally, London has an Italian opera, but I wasn't able to go: we were dining in town whenever the opera was on.

It was in London that I saw for the first time the way the English lived: altogether differently from our way, but so far I have managed to observe these things only imperfectly. The way an Englishman spends his day in London leaves not much time for work. They rise at ten or eleven and breakfast (always with tea). After that, they go about in the town for four hours or so, until five o'clock, when they dine. In the evening, at about nine, they meet one another, in taverns or clubs, and there spend the night at play or the bottle. That, exactly, is their daily occupation.

The women lead a more restricted life, mostly at home with the children, and sometimes a female friend: a great part of their days is spent thus, while their husbands are sometimes, indeed very often, ruining themselves – for in London one generally plays for enormous stakes.

Everyone, even in England, complains of the way one lives in London; and after hearing what they tell me, I think they do well to complain. It is the custom, when one has people in for a meal, to have the whole town in; so that there is a frightful squeeze, very distressing and exhausting for the mistress of the house. It is easy to see that the

---

[24] It is possible that Foote's *The Englishman in Paris* was on the bill that night. (S. C. Roberts' note, p. 248.)

pleasure of conversation is not very great in such assemblies. On other days they live alone, when they are not at their clubs.

It is largely to these clubs that one attributes the lack of society in London and the ruin of many people: they are so convenient that everyone goes to them. A club has two or three hundred members: usually the number is not fixed. The club's premises are usually large and well furnished, the tables are always covered with newspapers, with tea for those who want it, and with cards and dice for the gamblers: in this way all needs are supplied. The young men go there in their riding boots: no one is bothered about that, and that really suits everybody. Each member pays between five and nine guineas a year according to which club he belongs to. If one wants to eat there, one can. All those who wish to dine together write their names down. These meals, as a rule, are very expensive.

To join one of these numerous societies one has to be proposed by a member and elected by ballot. One black ball and you are not elected: also your name has to be written up a week in advance on the club notice-board so that all members may be informed of the proposal and of the applicant.

The London taverns are good inns where it is accepted that all men go for great, prolonged excesses of wine-drinking. There is a great number of taverns here, where men spend part of the day and all the night.

Those are the two places in which Englishmen mostly spend their time when they are in London. They need, more than we do, to come together in order to discuss together their common interests. All of them have to defend their liberty as we have not, but I couldn't help being astonished that people who have had a good education, and are capable of doing almost anything else, find pleasure – and a pleasure renewed daily – in rejoining other men in order to eat and drink.

When we arrived in London our plan was, after spending a week there,[25] to go on to Bristol to get hold of the language more easily. But Mr Walpole, one of our acquaintances,[26] told us we would have many

---

[25] In fact they seem to have arrived on the night of 28 December and to have left on 8 January. How much they saw and did rules out François' dating.
[26] Hon. Thomas Walpole, Horace Walpole's first cousin, a banker with interests in Paris. See Introduction.

difficulties; we should find a great number of people who spoke French; English was badly spoken in that part of the country; anyway, Bristol was an ugly town, where it rained twice as much as anywhere else in England. He drew our attention to Bury St Edmunds, or Norwich. Suffolk was a province where English was spoken best, and where it was shown by experience that it rained the least. He gave us letters of introduction for both towns; for the second in case we didn't like the first. Several people also gave us letters.

BURY

Our Acquaintances

We arrived at Bury on 7 January 1784.[1] We went out to deliver our letters, and next day all those to whom we had taken them came to see us. Mr Ord, a young and lively clergyman,[2] was the first to arrive. At that time, we did not know a word of English, and he could speak no French; so that we could say only a few words to him, with the help of the dictionary! He stayed a considerable time. Then Mr Symonds arrived, who spoke a little French, so that some clarity was introduced into the conversation![3]

Soon after, we made other acquaintances and were persuaded that we should get on well at Bury. We enquired after a *pension*, where, as paying guests, we could speak English at dinner and supper with our

---

[1] Alexandre's journal, written at the time, says they left London on the 8th, at 10 in the evening, arriving at Bury on the 9th at 7 in the morning. (Cahier I, p. 39, *penes* M le duc d'Estissac.) The first thing we did, Alexandre added, was to go to the inn (according to Arthur Young's *Autobiography*, the Angel). We were tired after the journey, and spent the day writing, without going into the town. Next morning we went out with a guide to deliver our letters of introduction. We were unhappy at meeting no one. We waited till the following day, when Mr Ord came.

[2] The Rev. John Ord, D.D. His family lived at Fornham St Martin, a couple of miles north of Bury, where a great military camp of volunteers was established in a field opposite the church in 1782. His brother Craven Ord (see *DNB*) was a very distinguished antiquarian collector. John was described by Alexandre, in his single-sentence biographies, as 'notre connoisseur dans Bury': our expert (Cahier VIII, p. 54).

[3] Rev. Dr John Symonds (1729–1807), professor of modern history at Cambridge, see later, p. 28 and Pl. 15.

hosts. But Mr Symonds, who was keen to help us find such a place, failed; but he leased us half a house where we did our own catering.[4]

We were the first French who established themselves in Bury: perhaps the first who lived any length of time in Suffolk. And, as the English in general (and, above all, the lower classes) do not like us, they make fun of us, much as we ourselves tend to do by natural inclination, which leads us to laugh at everything. The first days when we went out in the street, they pointed at us and made fun of us, saying, wherever we went: '*Frenchmen, Frenchmen!*' and this I found slightly disconcerting.

We were surprised by all the kindnesses we received. The whole of polite society[5] invited us to dine and sup with them and we spent the afternoons with people who treated us as their friends, who spoke very gently so that we could understand them, who tried sometimes to mix a few words of French with their English and took all the trouble in the world to please us.

Bury is an attractive little town, regularly laid-out on the gentle slope of a hill. It is exposed to the north. There are 7,000 inhabitants. There are several very hospitable houses which we could visit whenever we liked, but in general the townspeople don't greatly care for social activity. So that, although we knew plenty of people, the most we ever saw was one a day – not counting Mr Symonds, whom we saw every day. Some time later, we got to know some people living out in the country, and several who lived in the Bury neighbourhood. So that, after a while, we were as well established as we could possibly be.

THE ENGLISH WAY OF LIVING

The English way of living is totally different from ours. It seems even, in every particular detail that a Frenchman in England has before his eyes, that he must concentrate, reciprocally, on avoiding doing everything he is used to doing. Their physical behaviour shows the effects of this difference.

---

[4] In fact it seems possible that the apartments they hired were rooms let by the proprietor of the Angel immediately adjoining the hotel. (A plaque outside them bears, at present, the entirely improbable name of King Louis Philippe.) See Introduction.
[5] Footnote by François: *Gentilhomme* is an inadequate translation: there is no strict definition of this class in England: what I mean is people of leisure and education.

TEA-DRINKING

(Usage de thé general)

The drinking of tea is general throughout England (see Pl. 3). It is drunk twice a day, and although it is still very expensive, even the humblest peasant will take his tea twice a day, like the proudest: it is a huge consumption. Sugar, even unrefined sugar, which is necessary in large quantities and is very dear, does nothing to prevent this custom from being universal, without any exception.[1] It gives the rich an opportunity to show off their fine possessions: cups, tea-pots, etc., all made to the most elegant designs, all copies of the Etruscan and the antique. It is also the custom for the youngest daughter or lady of the house to make the tea.

The everyday beverage is beer, of which there are five or six sorts. The best known is 'small beer' but even that is dearer than wine in France. I believe it would be possible to grow the vine in England, or so it is said by people who know about agriculture. But it could only be done on the reverse slopes of fairly high hills open to the south. The great winds that blow so often are an insurmountable obstacle to growing vines in other aspects, and as the climate is colder and more variable than ours they would often, even on the better soils, be liable to bad harvests, and they find their land in best use as arable.

In some counties cider is drunk, but it is not as popular as beer. The wine ordinarily drunk is port. The English have exclusive trade-tariffs with Portugal, on the condition that they drink the wine. It is so awful, so thick, that if the English didn't take it as part of a trade deal, the Portuguese would never be able to dispose of it. Bad though it is, it costs three pounds (*un écu français*) a bottle. The Government has put such enormous duties on French wine that only very rich people can afford it. It costs six or eight hundred French pounds (*livres*) import duty per tonne, so that it retails at about 10 or 12 francs a bottle.

---

[1] In 1736, Lord Bristol was keeping an eye on the building of his wife's town-house on Honey Hill in Bury, and wrote to her from Bury: 'I came hither to have talked with Mr Steele your brick-layer, but found him gone to bed with a most violent headache, which his wife tells me he is frequently troubled with to a great degree; at which I told her I was not at all surprised, after she had told me he was a constant drinker of tea.' (*Letter-books of John Hervey, 1st earl of Bristol*, III, 1894, p. 152.)

English cooks are not very skilful, for one fares very ill at table, even in the grandest houses. The great luxury is to have a Frenchman, but few people can go to that expense: apart from the cost of a servant, which is very high what with wages and food, there is also a tax of one guinea on each male servant, which makes it more than dear. There are English noblemen with thirty or forty menservants, but usually it's the women who do the cooking and all the housework that isn't seen, while the menservants are employed only on those duties that have to be performed in front of everyone.

The English have, in general, many more servants than we have, but more than half of those they have are never seen: kitchen and stable-hands, and great numbers of women needed to maintain the extreme cleanliness. Every Saturday, for instance, the general practice is to wash every house from loft to cellar, inside and out. These servants make up the main part of their masters' expenses. They live in, as a general rule, and feeding them is a tremendous business: they never leave the table, and there are always cold joints of meat, and tea, and punch, from morning till night. I have already noticed that the consumption of tea in England is general from the lowest peasant to the highest nobleman: it is in such quantities that it is reckoned that each person, male or female, consumes, on average, four pounds of tea: that is truly enormous.

SERVANTS

English servants, whether of the nobility or of not-very-rich gentry, have almost nothing to do: they are the laziest lot of people you ever saw. They have only to wait at table, and at tea, and sometimes to do their masters' hair, but nothing more. In each [grand] house there is one who has responsibility for the expenses, combining the duties of steward, butler and valet: very often, he is a Frenchman.

Before a servant can enter into service in a house, he must have served his apprenticeship. Parliament has enacted that he must be six years[1] with an employer who will not pay him wages, but only clothe

---

[1] In fact, at least seven: 5 Eliz. c. 4. The Legislature was not in favour of its strict enforcement: Sir W. Holdsworth, *A History of English Law*, XI, 1938, pp. 420–421, but it was not repealed until 1814 (54 Geo. III c. 96). There was an important difference between domestic servants and 'servants in husbandry', who also lived in the house: see p. 55, fn. 4.

and feed him. He is obliged to work from six in the morning till six at night, with two hours set aside for his meals: all that is spelt out by Act of Parliament. If the young man finds a better situation, he may not take it without the consent of his master. He is virtually his slave during those six years. It is only on those conditions that he acquires the right of *settlement* in the parish where he has served his apprenticeship.[2] This right entitles him to be treated, if he has a long illness and cannot pay; to be supported if he falls into poverty; and to find help in his old age – help that goes so far in England that, once they have received it, they no longer have any need to work, and from poverty they go from ease to idleness.[3]

The same Act of Parliament[4] which laid down this wise novitiate for them, also prescribed penalties for those who might not conform to the provisions and who might take on, for example, a servant who has been dismissed from his apprenticeship and is therefore ineligible to be a servant any longer; or those who might turn one of these *boys* (it is the English word) from his duty by taking him into his service.

When they emerge from this apprenticeship, which is hard on them, they are given something between fourteen and twenty guineas a year for wages. They are clothed: boots, spurs, a cap and food. And thus, with no further expenses and little to do, they have the easiest job they could possibly find in England.

---

[2] 3 William & Mary, c. 11.

[3] The responsibility of the parish for its poor, established under Elizabeth I, was being modified in Suffolk by early experiments in establishing poor-law unions: the earliest, at Nacton, 1758, was working well until undermined by rising costs in the 1780s: see e.g. Hugh Fearn, 'The Financing of the Poor-Law Incorporation for the Hundreds of Colneis and Carlford, 1758–1820, *Proc. Suffolk Inst. of Archaeology*, XXVII, 1958, pp. 98–111. There was not much question of going 'from ease to idleness'. But Gilbert's Act, in 1782, did take from the able-bodied poor the need to find and perform successfully their own work; and made the local Guardians of the Poor responsible for finding them work. In an extremely good, thoroughgoing study (*Annals of the Labouring Poor*, Cambridge, 1985, p. 107), K. D. M. Snell concluded that 'to settled inhabitants, rural parishes were indeed "miniature welfare states", and before about 1780, relief policy was usually generous, flexible and humane'. After that, depressions and the Union Workhouses did much heartless and socially divisive damage: cf. Thirsk & Imray, *Suffolk Records Soc.*, I, 1958, chapters III and V. In his chapters 5 and 6, Snell valiantly restores some order to the disorderly study of apprenticeship.

[4] 1563, 5 Eliz. c. 4. *Statutes of the Realm*, IV, 414: it seems doubtful whether François consulted the complicated terms of the Act, but he seemed fairly well informed of its relevance and probably got hold of Blackstone's *Commentaries*: see pp. 40, 79, 89 below.

12. Euston Hall, home of the dukes of Grafton.
(Engraving by R. Acon from T. Higham in Excursions through Suffolk, *1818)*

APPORTIONMENT OF THE DAY

I mustn't forget to mention the ordinary routine of English life; and some curious manners they have; and the length of their meals. So that I can be more precise in these matters, I shall describe the life I have myself been leading, and still lead, daily, while I am staying in an Englishman's home in the country. I lived this way in the Grafton house (Pl. 12). I live the same kind of life every day in Mr Symonds' house.

It is usual throughout England to breakfast together, in the same way that we come together in France for dinner or supper. The favourite time for breakfast is nine o'clock, and already the ladies' hair is done and they are dressed for the most part for the rest of the day. Breakfast consists of tea and various forms of bread and butter. In rich men's houses, you have coffee, chocolate, etc. Invariably, the newspapers are on the table, and those who wish read them during breakfast, so, usually, conversation is not very lively. At 10.30 or 11, everyone goes his own way, to hunt, or fish, or go walking. In all that, one does more or less as one pleases, and so it's very agreeable. That is how it is until 4 o'clock, but, at 4 o'clock precisely, one must be in the drawing-room, and there the formalities are more than we are accustomed to in France. This sudden change of manners is astonishing; I was much struck by it. In the morning you come down in your top boots and a dirty old coat, sit where you like, behave in the room exactly as if you were alone, nobody notices you, nothing could be more relaxed. But, in the evening, you must be very proper, unless you have just that moment arrived. One observes an uncomfortable politeness; strangers go in first to dinner and sit near the lady of the house; they are served in order of seniority with the most rigid etiquette; so much so that, for the first few days, I was inclined to believe they were doing it for a joke.

Dinner is one of the most boring of all things English: it always lasts four or five hours. The first two are occupied in eating, and you have to put your stomach through the whole range of its accomplishments if you are to please the master of the house; for you are asked all the time whether you like the food and will eat some more. I give in, and eat solidly from the moment I arrive until the moment I get up from the table.

The courses are made up much as in France, except that sauces are never used in the English kitchen, and stews very seldom. All the dishes are based on various joints of meat, either boiled or roast, the roast weighing as much as twenty or thirty pounds.

After the *entremets*, you are given small crystal-glass bowls, usually very transparent, for rinsing out the mouth: an improper activity, to my way of thinking. The more refined do not wash out their mouths, but what is even worse, in rinsing their hands they make the water dirty and very disgusting to look at. This ceremony done, the cloth is removed, and you see the most beautiful of tables. It is itself a most remarkable thing that the English make use of such a profusion of mahogany: not only the tables are generally made of it, but even all the doors as well: the balusters of the staircases, and the chairs. And yet it is just as costly in England as it is in France. It is something I don't understand: I'm willing to believe that the English are richer than we are, but I've seen for myself that not only does everything cost twice as much as it does with us, yet they seize every opportunity to use things that are the most expensive.

Their tables, then, are of the most beautiful wood and always as gleaming, as polished as the most lovely glaze. Very soon. it is covered with every kind of wine, for even the gentlemen of modest means always have good wines, and in good quantity. The middle of the table is occupied by some small quantity of fruit, and, to go with the wine, some biscuits and butter, which many English eat with their dessert.

All the servants depart at this time. The ladies drink a glass or two of wine: after half-an-hour, they leave together. Then the pleasure: there is not an Englishman who does not feel contented at that moment. The drinking is sometimes quite alarming, and every man has to drink in turn, for the bottles go continually round the table, and the master of the house makes sure that no one misses a turn. When one has been drinking for some time, and thirst is no longer a sufficient reason for drinking, to provide some incentive to drink, in spite of oneself, the drinking of 'toasts' is begun. The master of the house begins by naming a lady and drinking to her health: everyone does likewise. Another 'toast' follows, and everyone drinks to the health of everyone's lady. Then everyone names a man, and the ceremony is repeated. If there is still need to drink, one can always find new 'toasts': even politics supplies them, and one drinks to the health of Mr Pitt, Mr Fox, Lord North, etc. That's the moment I like best. The conversation could hardly be freer; everyone gives his political opinions with the same ease as his opinions on personal matters. Sometimes the conversation becomes equally free on indecent matters, for one is allowed to speak of everything: I think I have observed that the English don't attach the ideas we do to certain words, for very often I have heard things said here in good company that would be the worst breach of decent manners in France.

The sideboard is garnished also with chamber-pots, in line with the common practice of going over to the sideboard to pee, while the others are drinking. Nothing is hidden. I find that very indecent.

After two or three hours, a servant comes in to announce that tea is ready and to conduct *Messieurs les buveurs* into the drawing-room to join the ladies, who are usually busy making tea and coffee. After the tea, one generally plays whist, and at midnight there is cold meat for anyone who is hungry. During the game, punch is on a table for those who want it.

I have explained with so much detail what I did at Euston, the home of the duke of Grafton, precisely because the same lives are lived throughout England; and because these ways are so different from ours, the details may arouse some curiosity. When one lives in a provincial town, as I have done, and one is asked to dinner, one goes at three and stays till ten; for in no circumstances will the English hurry over drinking and eating. But before passing on to other subjects, I still have to tell you of a grand public dinner that we have had for the Election. It is the custom, the standard custom, for the two elected members of Parliament to give a dinner to the Corporation. The meaning of 'Election', 'Corporation', etc., I shall explain later on: now is not the time.

AN ELECTION DINNER

The elected members, by courtesy, invited us to this dinner, which was extremely polite of them. There were, I think, eighty of us, at two tables, each presided over by one of the new members, each magnificently waited on. Even so, we sat down at table at two o'clock and did not leave it till nine, to go dancing. Three-quarters of the guests were very drunk, and everyone had had rather too much to drink. As we left the table, a great fat farmer asked me to dance a minuet, and leapt about like a twenty-year-old. The duke of Grafton's nephew, brother of one of the members,[1] was so drunk that he was obliged to go to bed for a few hours, and then returned to the ball; and, having asked a lady to dance with him, he couldn't find her again. I have never before attended such a grand banquet, and I was very glad to judge for myself all these good Englishmen who are all very watchful of their rights, but who would give them still, I think, for a few tonnes of their port. You can have no idea of the speed with which they emptied the bottles: I think we had one servant solely employed in bringing us fresh bottles and removing the empties. People smoked, also, at table.

[1] The Hon. George Ferdinand Fitz Roy, later Lord Southampton, was one of nine brothers.

YOUNG PEOPLE IN SOCIETY

Nowhere would you be more at ease in good company than in England. Formalities count for nothing, and for most of the time one takes no notice of them. So it is that, bearing out the received idea in France, the English, and most often the women, seem utterly graceless: they never receive any education in such things; and all the young people that I see in society in Bury appear, as we would say, badly brought up: they hum, they whistle, they sit in the largest armchairs and put their feet up on the nearest chair, they sit on the tables, etc; and do a thousand comparable things that would be ridiculous in France and seem natural enough in England.

Everything I say here is strictly true: I can name ten young people who behave like this all the time, and I say only ten because that is the extent of my acquaintance in Bury, but I believe that the same goes for them all. One should not contrast them with those one has seen in London, because London is another matter: possibly they themselves would not be so easy-going in front of London society; certainly they make themselves at home when they are with their friends.

OUR SPECIAL FRIENDS

Soon after our arrival in Bury we made some new acquaintances. The chief ones were Sir Charles Kent,[1] who lives three miles from the town, and Lady Bristol, wife of the bishop of Derry.[2] She is a woman of fifty, much travelled in France and Italy, and she speaks the two languages very well: they say she is very intelligent. She is tall, of noble bearing and has been a very beautiful woman. From his family name, her

[1] His father, Charles Egleton, took the name Kent in compliance with the will of his maternal grandfather, and was made a baronet in 1782. He lived at Fornham Park, Fornham St Genevieve, just north of Bury, and for a time owned the beautifully-landscaped park over at Holbrook, between the estuaries of the Orwell and the Stour: see below, pp. 126–7.

[2] The old biography, *The Earl Bishop*, 2 vols, 1924, by W. S. Childe-Pemberton, gives a fairly clear picture of the Bristols. More up-to-date but not differing in essentials, Brian Fothergill: *The Mitred Earl: An 18th-century Eccentric*, 1974. François guessed Lady Bristol's age exactly.

husband is Lord Hervey: a man of immense wealth, a notable intriguer, a very lively intelligent character, but he is reproached for lack of stability and failure to carry through a project. He is at present in Ireland, where he is causing an uproar. He wants to change the government of that island. He proposes an alternative form of elections. In defence of the Catholics, he wants them to have a share in liberty and to nominate representatives: all very delicate matters, on which depends the happiness of a great many people. When I say happiness (*bonheur*), I am tending to use a French word for an English idea: their word isn't, properly speaking, happiness, but liberty. The two words are almost synonymous in English usage.

It is generally thought the bishop will not succeed, for he lacks the necessary qualities to inspire complete confidence and carry a scheme through; but he does what he can, and is causing an uproar at present. His lively mind he inherits, they say, from his family who are a little mad; and M. de Voltaire, when he was in England, said he saw here three kinds of people: men, women and Herveys; which shows that there has long been something odd about them.

During all this, the countess of Bristol has been staying in their country house, with her daughter, Lady Louise-Anne,[3] who is perhaps nineteen or twenty and speaks French very well. She has not spent the winter in London, like most of the other gentry of the neighbourhood; but we have gained nothing by it, for we have only been to dinner there once in five months, and called four times. Yet we saw her only twice, although she was at home, which is against the English custom: when they are at home, one expects to be received. I imagine Lady Bristol found such a custom very convenient during her own travels in France, but she herself has not evinced much hospitality towards travellers.[4]

---

[3] Her name was properly Theodosia Louisa, and she was 17; and very nice-looking, according to her later portraits.

[4] François naturally felt aggrieved, but it would be surprising if he had not heard something of the background. Louisa was the Bristols' youngest child. Her two elder sisters, adored by her parents and extremely beautiful, were by 1784 estranged from their husbands, as Lady Bristol had been from hers since 1782. One sees why she might be keeping a rather careful eye on Louisa in the presence of a slightly *épris* young French nobleman two years her senior. When she was 28, she married Lord Liverpool, Prime Minister 1812–1827. (Alexandre, too, found 'Lady Louisianne très jolie, et encore plus agréable'.) In 1796, when she was married, Young found her manner 'not the most agreeable: she has ease and elegance'.

She lives three miles from Bury in an unpleasing, but large, house: its park is immensely large, nine thousand acres, which are larger than our *arpents*. An *arpent* varies between 1/2 and 5/6 of an acre. The whole park consists of a lawn of superb turf, scattered with very fine trees. In the park there are many deer, solely for ornament: a few are killed, in the winter, for the table: there are also plenty of cows and bullocks and sheep for fattening.

Another of our acquaintances, one of the most intimate we have, is Sir Thomas Gage.[5] He lives six miles out of Bury, where we often visited him (Pl. 13). He is extremely agreeable, altogether friendly towards us. If they didn't live quite so far from Bury, we would see them more often. His wife, Lady Gage, is one of the most disarming women I've ever met. The family is Catholic, so they are excluded from public life. They are rich, for their family is a very old one.

Monsieur Gage's son by his first wife also lives in the country, but on the other side of Bury. All of them are very well disposed towards us. As they are practising economies, they do not entertain many people: they have been restoring an ·old-fashioned house, which is costing them a great deal and obliges them to economise.[6]

Mr Young was also one of our first acquaintances.[7] He has a great reputation in the world of agriculture, and has written much on the subject. He is a man of character and of wide acquaintance, and what is still more agreeable from society's point of view, is that he is very affable, always cheerful and never in bad humour. He is the most good-natured person in the world in answering questions, and always seeks to satisfy you. In spite of all that, I don't like going to his home,

[5] Sir Thomas Gage, 5th baronet. A member of one of the old Catholic families of Suffolk, he succeeded an uncle. His own father, John Gage, had been a page of honour to Louis XIV, and married a Rookwood of Coldham Hall, Stanningfield, a remarkably unspoilt house of 1595, with a long gallery, and its ancient private chapel beside this long gallery. Coldham Hall, Sir Thomas's mother's old house, was where he lived. His own paternal inheritance, the grander, earlier 16th-century house, Hengrave Hall, was lived in by his son and heir by his first wife at the time of François' visit. Sir Thomas's 2nd wife, who made such a delightful impression on François, was Mary, daughter of Patrick Fergus, of the island of Mont-Serrat in the West Indies: John Gage, *The History and Antiquities of Hengrave*, 1822, pp. 247–251.

[6] Hengrave is a distinguished small quadrangular house of Henry VIII's reign, with an elaborate front-entrance: its chapel has window-lights by glaziers from King's College chapel.

[7] See Introduction.

first because he keeps an extremely poor table, utterly slovenly; and then, on account of his wife, who looks exactly like a devil: she is hideous, swarthy, and looks thoroughly bad-tempered. They say that she beats her husband and that he has the good-nature to put up with it. I don't know, but if that's so, then it's his fault; one should blame him rather than her. She is always tormenting her children and servants, and is, more often than not, bad-tempered with visitors (Pl. 14).

Those were our greatest friends in the countryside round Bury, those who didn't go off to London for the winter – for it is a general rule for English people who live anywhere in the provinces to spend three or four months in the capital.

In the town we made rather more friends. The two most intimate, whom we have visited most often, are Mr Leheup and Colonel Schutz,[8] a retired officer who loves good food and drink and provides it for his guests. We have been there very often. The only disadvantage is that he likes to get you to drink too much. You have to watch yourself when you are at home with him.

In all our acquaintance, I have said nothing of Mr Symonds, our best friend, whom we saw daily and who has introduced us to everyone we have since come to know. After dinner, we spent part of the evening with him, either in our own lodging in Bury when he came in, or at his house, a mile out, when he was not in town. He has always shown us the greatest kindness and is always anxious to do whatever suits us best. It is he who presented us to the duke of Grafton, at whose house we spent a few days with him.[9] (Pl. 15)

Mr Symonds' nephew was in Bury at that time, having come to see him on shore-leave: he is lieutenant on a ship, although only nineteen.[10] During the five months that we saw him, we spent the whole day with him: so that we soon became the best friends in the world. We passed the time very enjoyably, so that when he left we missed him. By means of these friends, our time passed very pleasantly in Bury. The pleasures were not exactly lively, but to me the days didn't seem very long.

[8] The Leheups were Huguenots, and owned the manor of Hessett, 5 miles east of Bury, in the 18th century. In Bury, they had a house in Westgate Street. Colonel Schutz seems to have lived in Chequer-and-Crown Street: 'toujours avec les hommes' (Alexandre).
[9] They also knew James Oakes, wool merchant, 'qui fait un grand bien dans le pays' (Alexandre).
[10] Jermyn Symonds.

13. *Coldham Hall, Stanningfield, home of the Gages.*

14. *Bradfield Hall in Arthur Young's time.*

THE CLIMATE

I think that for a very long time people will remember the winter of 1783–4. I have never been so cold. It lasted almost four months, without the ground once being uncovered: there were two feet of snow which the ice made as hard as the ground. I don't know to what point the thermometer dropped, but the cold was as piercing as it could be. Several kinds of evergreen trees were frozen through, and the snow piled on the branches of the pines, which are numerous, causing the trees to split, sometimes in half, and crippling a great many.

The cruel winter punished us till the beginning of May. That month was fine, and we had some heat, but succeeding months were as miserable as the earlier ones, so that I can only conclude, from my experience, that the climate of England is very rainy, colder than in France, and a great deal windier. However, this is against the view of a lot of people who, generally speaking, see little or no difference between the two.

THE CONSTRUCTION OF HOUSES AND THEIR LAY-OUT

There is a general lack of building stone in England.[1] It is found in so small a quantity, and in so few places, that it is the greatest luxury for public buildings to be constructed of stone. Houses are generally of brick or of plaster and timber, and are therefore low-built and without architectural effect. However, they are very attractively built. Those that make up the towns and villages are small, for they house only one unit of a family (*ménage*); the general custom being that, when the children marry they take another house, move away from their parents and set up on their own, so they don't marry so young as in France.

But, coming back to the town houses, the ground floor is always lived in, and there the best rooms are. Here, more or less, is the lay-out of an English house. You enter by a small door surmounted by a little

[1] This conclusion is natural to anyone spending a year in E. Anglia. He modified it during his travels through the rest of Britain in 1785.

15. *Mr Symonds. Engraved by T. Singleton from a portrait by G. Ralph.*

pediment. The door is never a large one, for they have no need. First comes the entrance-hall, always very clean and tidy, more like one of our rooms than our vestibules, which are usually in a mess. Then comes the dining-room, always large. Above the dining-room is the drawing-room, which is always of the same plan and to which you ascend by the most thoroughly cleaned staircase: the balustrade is always mahogany, in the best state imaginable, the stairs, like the floors, are made of long boards of fir or pine, joined as carefully as marquetry. Above the hall is a bedroom, and sometimes another room or two. The kitchen is always on the ground floor and at the back. A custom that would not be liked in France and which is common in England is to have the dining-room below and the drawing-room above. They find that easier for the servants, and for themselves, a staircase of twenty steps is no great matter. But what I do find ill-arranged is never to have either an ante-room, or something of that sort, for the door of the dining-room always gives on to the entrance-hall, and that of the drawing-room on to the staircase-landing, which serves admirably to cool the legs down when the doors are opened.

I very much like the doors, which are simple and shut properly: they are usually two inches thick, most often of mahogany, and the lock is morticed into the thickness of the wood and never seen. All that one sees is these morticed locks of brass, and the key – always wonderfully made. The tables and chairs are also of the finest mahogany, and gleaming with polish like the best-tempered steel.

The fireplaces are not designed like ours: they have neither mantel-pieces nor mantel-shelves above, and are always square: their kind of grate is always iron, highly polished and gleaming.

Three-quarters of the houses have a little projecting turret[2] at one or other end, into which the dining and drawing-rooms lead, and which gives them an agreeable shape and plenty of daylight; for, in the circumference of the bow, windows can be fitted at three angles instead of two.

The country houses, that we would call *châteaux*, are usually built of brick. They are enormous, but heavy and architecturally unattractive:

[2] This seems a curious exaggeration: but their friend Symonds' house has one. He is referring to window-bows, and himself uses 'the English word bow' for these *tourelles* when describing the farm-house near Mistley, p. 123 below.

32

there is seldom a fine elevation. Their lay-out corresponds a little to that I have attributed to town-houses, for the English take no trouble to obtain the satisfaction of a pleasing lay-out: their houses never have corridors, private rooms or closets.

ENGLISH CLEANLINESS

What always gives the most delight is the dominant impression of cleanliness: the houses are washed very often, inside and out, which is done, as a rule, on Saturdays. People go to great lengths to preserve all this spruceness, with mats and carpets down everywhere, and strips of moquette on the stairs: nowhere a speck of dust. All this amazed me when I first saw it, and I did what I could to see whether this cleanliness is natural to the English, and thus inherent in all they do, or whether it is just for show, merely superficial, and I came to see clearly that it is a matter of show: everything that is likely to be seen has this precious quality, but they manage to overlook what you are not supposed to see. To give an example, I will refer only to the kitchen, which when people have any instinct for cleanliness should naturally be spotless. The worst thing you could do would be to go into the kitchen before dinner: you can't imagine the squalor. This is usually the work of women; they are black as coal, their arms bare to the elbow or revoltingly filthy and, to save time, they actually handle the pieces of meat. You may go into the kitchen of the greatest nobleman and you will find perhaps ten women at work, but I wager you will not see two napkins or dish-cloths; and if you were to find one in use, you will not want to wipe your hands on it, for it is used for everything.

One thing that everyone observes is the way all the beer is drunk out of the same glass, even when there are twenty at table. When you ask for a drink, they top up the old dregs in the bottom of the glass, and you have to drink or let it pass. This custom, dirty and sometimes disgusting, is so time-honoured that it has become a matter of politeness, at a ball for instance, to drink either punch or another drink after the lady has drunk, from the same glass, to show that you are not averse to what she leaves. One can happily do it sometimes, but there are many ladies to whom I should not care to make this gesture of politeness.

COUNTRY HOUSES

All that one desires for a country house is a nice position, usually at the heart of a fine garden, near a river or a lake, amid lawns and bordered by woodland so arranged as to leave views through to the most pleasing prospects, and to hide the sadder sights. This art hardly ever reveals itself: one could attribute the arrangement of English parks to nature. All the *châteaux*[1] I have seen in England are vast masses of brick, pierced with innumerable windows: outwardly extremely melancholy, and most of them very old. One sees no sign of development, or of the hands of able architects: they are impressive but nothing more. The interior is always decorated in the classical taste, like other houses: it is the prevailing taste in England. As for the *jardins anglais*,[2] this is their composition, their common quality: they are immense, and entirely under turf: it is usually fine grass, and beautiful: above this verdure, which continues the existing slopes of the hills, stand mature trees distributed in masses; they are massed so as to reveal views, a view of a picturesque bell-tower, an attractive village, etc. The woods hide anything that could offend the eye, where the landscape is disagreeable. A bridge, or a pagoda, or a little temple, may be built in order to arrange a view; when the hills don't slope together smoothly enough, a junction is arranged entirely at whim: if necessary, the whole hill can be moved. Above all, one does not forget to bring all the streams to a confluence and turn them into a river, the course of which seems so natural that one could believe it had always been there; and one creates islands, pleasant places; in short, nothing is forgotten. In a well-tended garden there is sometimes not an ugly weed to be seen in the entire vista, which is immense. That is what the English mean by 'a park'.

Near the house, and usually all round it, is what *they* call a garden. It is a small, well-tended place for walking: there are little gravel paths, well-rolled, the grass is cut every week, the trees are of very rare species, all coming along naturally, but with care taken that they are not

[1] This word can mean both castle and large country house, which I think is the meaning here. Certainly none of the castles he saw in E. Anglia is of brick, however massy. Is he thinking of Euston? The former Culford? Hengrave? They were certainly of brick, and very old.
[2] 'This is what the English call *parc*', he says, later on.

covered with moss,[3] that the ivy doesn't get near them, and a thousand other precautions and refinements that are practised unseen, but which help to make these gardens enjoyable. Nor are flowerbeds forgotten, and always separated from the park by superbly well-made fencing.

The English do not eat half as many vegetables as we do, which is why their kitchen-gardens are so extremely small compared with ours: not more than four or five arpents,[4] even for the biggest houses. The vegetables are very well cultivated, mostly in heated glass-houses, which are common in England: I can't speak as to the noblemen, but certainly for the ordinary gentry; indeed, I've seen them in the majority of town gardens.

Kitchen-gardens are not as well-kept as ours: the gardeners are not so fully trained in their work. I've noticed that often their trees were not well-pruned. They seem to like long branches that decorate the whole wall with leaves, and which naturally bear nothing like so much fruit as ours do. They are not familiar with the use of wire, and attach each branch with a small piece of cloth and a nail. In general, all that they know about the cultivation of kitchen-gardens and the various kinds of fruit they have, comes from France.[5]

There you have everything that goes to make up 'the English garden'. It costs prodigious sums to maintain; and more still because of the losses in converting pasture to park: they reckon the land loses half its potential revenue if you count the horses, cows and sheep you could be grazing there for eight months in the year.

Usually they stock many deer, which are as tame as sheep.

Many people believe that the 'English gardens' are made without artistic skill or knowledge, that taste alone presides, and that, in consequence, they can do the job themselves, for everyone thinks he has 'taste', all because no one can properly define what 'taste' is. The proof that it is only by dint of artistic skill and of working at it that one can make a passable imitation of nature is that, since England came into

[3] *mousse*; he may have meant lichen?
[4] See note, p. 27.
[5] François may not have known (or he would have mentioned it) that the greengage was introduced to England from France by Sir William Gage (1657–1727), 2nd baronet. An ancient greengage-tree at Hengrave is presumably related to the one named after him. Its French ancestors were Reine-Claudes.

existence, only one man has been reckoned capable of 'landscape gardening'. He died three years ago, and was called Mr Brown.[6] He is famous all over this kingdom. It is said that he had so sure and swift an eye for landscape, that after an hour on horseback he conceived the design for an entire park, and that after that, half-a-day was enough for him to mark it out on the ground. One must believe that it is impossible to draw up a plan for the English garden on paper – in the abstract: everything is determined by the particulars of the surrounding landscape, and the different view-points indicate what tree-screens will be necessary.

Gentlemen who are not wealthy enough to have parks have what they call lawns, a small area of land round their houses, with bordered walks, beautiful turf and a small clump of trees, all kept in extremely neat order. They themselves design these garden-walks. It's everything they need for the surroundings of the house, to give them an air of ownership and to walk in for half-an-hour after dinner.

Such are the habitations of the English. They give the impression of being very happy in them. In the country, they live a very retired life. All of them have various talents, with which they occupy themselves. Their wives and children take up their leisure hours. They don't appear to know the meaning of boredom, although I'm persuaded, from certain examples, that they are concealing it. But what is remarkable, in this connection, is that there is no word in English which expresses the reflexive verb *je m'ennuie*.[7]

HUSBANDS AND WIVES

Husband and wife are always together, and are content with the same society. It is the rarest thing to see them one without the other. The richest people have only four or six carriage-horses, and have no need of more, since they do all their visiting together. It would be more ridicu-

---

[6] Lancelot 'Capability' Brown died in February 1783. François saw, and commented on, some of his work.

[7] Ironically, the earliest recorded use of the English form of *je m'ennuie* is this, in 1768: 'my Newmarket friends who are bound to be *bored by* these Frenchmen.'

lous in England to do otherwise than it would be in Paris to go out always with your wife. They always give the impression of the most perfect harmony, and the wife, above all, has an air of contentment that always pleases me. I don't know what will become of me in France, but at present my preference would be to have an English wife. I don't know if it is one outcome of having to live constantly with one's wife that one marries later, but I suppose so. To have a wife who is disagreeable must, in England, make your life a misery. One tries therefore to get to know her before marrying her: she has the same instinct, and I believe that is the reason why it is rare here to marry before one is twenty-five, or twenty-eight. This arises also perhaps from the custom of setting up house as soon as one is married. One never stays on in the parental house, and must therefore have acquired some judgement to avoid follies, whether of extravagance or of conduct. I find this custom of marrying late much better, and more in nature.

Furthermore, here one has much more opportunity of getting to know one another before marriage, for the young people mix in society from childhood, always accompanying their parents. Young women are part of the company, and talk and amuse themselves with as much liberty as if they were married. Three marriages in four are based on inclination, and one sees by experience that the majority of them are perfectly successful. I think I can observe, in passing, that families are much larger, in England, than in France: nearly all the couples have eight, ten, twelve children – it's very common. So this union of husbands and wives has a political advantage, as well.

MARRIAGES IN SCOTLAND

The English government, always mindful of the public good, has felt this advantage, and found it so valuable that it has authorised marriages to take place in Scotland without the consent of either parent. It was formerly the same in England, but the facility was removed fourteen or fifteen years ago.[1] Today the whole of Scotland has that same privilege:

[1] Lord Hardwicke's Marriage Act (26 George II, c. 33, 1753) put an end to the Fleet marriages performed by bogus parsons, and made clandestine marriages impossible in

no need for the consent of either father or mother. The English often take advantage of this resource against their parents' wishes. The young man and the girl set off in a post-chaise – paying extra to travel fast – arrive at the Scottish border and are married at once. But if the father or mother of one of them sends after them, even if it's only a servant, if the servant catches up with them the Act of Parliament gives him the same authority over the youngsters as the parents themselves would have: small compensation that the law offers the parents for the authorised disobedience of their children. There is nothing much they can do other than disinherit them; but that happens rarely, the love for the children soon re-asserts itself, unless there are other reasons to the contrary.[2]

English husbands have an advantage over us that they sometimes take, that of divorce. It is true that there must be considerable grievances to obtain it, and if such grievances are there, the suit before the ecclesiastical court, and then before the High Court, can only be very expensive. So it is a remedy little used by people who are not wealthy. After the divorce, the two parties may remarry and resume the rights of ordinary citizens.

This seems to me very good. You can find a remedy against something that blights, as it must, all your days, and you are not deprived of the chance of living happily with another woman whom you love. England in that way has care of its population, which is a point of great importance for a country: in that way everyone is the winner.[3]

THE CLERGY ARE MARRIED

All the clergy are married, as well – which surprised me the first time I became aware of it. The bishops, too, have to set an example to the

---

England. But the Act did not apply in Scotland, and François' explanations reflect his youth and, presumably, the comments of his friends and acquaintances in Bury.
[2] On these runaway marriages, see below.
[3] This is slightly over-enthusiastic: between 1551 and 1857, only thirty-seven such Acts were passed. The 'care of England's population' is not necessarily at stake. François' host, the duke of Grafton, was one of the thirty-seven beneficiaries, and may unwittingly have given a cheerful view of the matter.

others. This is something that should be established in France, as it was, I think, before the Council of Trent, when it was decided to disallow it. Why should they be deprived of one of the pleasures of mankind? Why make them uncivilised, excluded from society? A married man has more reason to hold to his country: the interest of his family compels him. The celibate is a mere stranger.[1]

HUNTING

One of the greatest pleasures of the English is that of the chase – they are all mad about it. They hunt either the fox or the hare. The first is much more expensive than the second, and is only within the means of rich people. You have to have many hounds, horses, etc. I have watched, and have hunted with, the duke of Grafton's pack. He has, I think, forty couples of superb hounds and three men to look after them – and three horses for those men when they're hunting, not to mention all those he needs for himself and those he needs to provide for. This need of hounds is expensive, costing about ten or twelve guineas the pair: they are large and so beautiful, and very fast, and don't bay overmuch. It is an excellent pack, keeping together: you never see them split up. You often have to cover a lot of ground in pursuit of the fox, which always runs along the line of the hedgerows at a tremendous pace. The huntsmen think nothing of fifty or sixty miles, often going so far afield that their horses, exhausted, cannot get them home, and they have to sleep at the first inn they come to. That's what they call a *partie amusante* (good run for your money?).[1]

They rarely kill more than one fox:[2] when he is caught, they fling him to the hounds to give them the taste for another. This form of hunting is as tiring as it is dangerous: you have to be ready in an instant

---

[1] So it would seem to an intelligent but very inexperienced young man.

[1] A famous run (2 December 1745) was from Euston across 28 parishes to Finborough, south of Stowmarket (*Victoria County History: Suffolk*, II, 1907, pp. 357 and 375.)
[2] Hitcham Wood was noted for a fox 'who gave the hounds many a good run: they were never able to catch him, though in 1853 he had his closest run at Woolpit'. *Ibid.*, p. 358.

to leap hedges, fences, barriers, because the fields of England are mostly enclosed. They are so used to this activity that they seldom fall from their horses; but, when they do fall, they hurt themselves badly.

The English all have a passion for fox-hunting: many women, even, hunt assiduously. It is not without risk, and I don't like to see it: they jump like the men, indeed are always the first. Even the farmers take part in this national pastime, and when they are rich (as many of them are), they keep two or three hunters solely for riding to hounds. They are always the best mounted. I've seen two of them out regularly with the duke of Grafton's pack.

The upkeep of a pack of harriers is much less expensive: the hounds are smaller, cheaper to buy, and need only one huntsman and one other man with him to look after them. The hare does not cover such distances, ten miles is exceptional, which is why hacks can be ridden by the harriers without being over-tired. Nearly all the gentry ride with the harriers once or twice a week, and a good many have packs of their own.

SHOOTING

Shooting is not a general sport. They shoot only partridge, pheasant and rabbits – never hares, which are reserved for the harriers. Game shooting starts on 1st September; there is a considerable fine to be paid for shooting before that.

The English shoot with single-barrelled guns: very few people in England have the double-barrelled guns. Game is not enormously plentiful, even here, though Suffolk has more than the other counties.[1]

A man must have at least £100 a year in land to be licensed either to shoot or to have his own shoot: an Act of Parliament expressly forbids it to those who don't own such property: they are obliged to shoot with others.[2] No one has the right to shoot except on his own land; but

[1] In fact Suffolk and Norfolk were 'first-equal' above the other counties.
[2] As a rule, no tenant farmer shot, but many yeoman-farmers with 200–300 acres were within the law. Blackstone's *Commentaries*, which François obviously read with enjoyment, say (IV, p. 175): 'It is in general sufficient to observe that the qualifications for killing game, as they are usually called . . . are 1. the having a freehold estate of £100 *per annum*; there being fifty times the property required to enable a man to shoot a partridge

general custom – better, or more acceptable than the law – has established a mutual understanding between all those entitled to shoot that a man leaving his own property can go right ahead and shoot anywhere without getting into trouble with the owner provided he doesn't enter the owner's parkland. The rules of polite behaviour forbid this positively. It is also forbidden to walk over sown fields: if you are seen there, you can be taken to law and pay a fine heavy in proportion to the amount of damage. If you break down fences, you have to pay for them in full. The method of shooting with gun-dogs is curiously different from ours. They have six, ten, perhaps twelve, pointers: together they advance in separate lines: as soon as one halts and points, the master who sees him stops, gives a certain call, and they all stop, moving not a step further while the master goes to the side of his dog,[3] who would remain stationary for two days. When a bird is shot, this dog will never retrieve, and I imagine they are not trained to retrieve as there are many dogs and they would tear the game to pieces. A good dog costs, much as in France, 6, 8 or 10 guineas.[4] They are generally very handsome, with long tails, like hounds.

Women quite commonly in England take part in the shoot, and many of them are very good shots.

The names of those with the right to shoot are enrolled, and each pays a licence-fee of a guinea for the sport. I forgot to say that it is forbidden by Act of Parliament, and severely enforced, to sell game in any public place. The penalty is very considerable. I don't know whether this isn't harmful to the rights of property.

The King is the only person who hunts the stag:[5] I don't know whether this is because he alone has the right – various people have told me so – or because it would be too expensive a sport for others. The stag-hounds in his kennels are very tall and superb.

---

as to vote for a knight of the shire', and so on. In his *History of the Criminal Law of England*, 1883, a century too late for François, Sir James FitzJames Stephen wrote (III, p. 279): 'It was theoretically doubtful whether from 1604 to 1832 anyone could lawfully shoot a pheasant, partridge or hare whatever qualification he possessed.'
[3] To leave a bird unaccounted for – shot down but possibly still alive – was deemed unsportsmanlike. So there was no advance until the bird was recovered.
[4] Lazowski's MS. *Voyage en Suffolk* equated the guinea approximately with the *louis d'or*.
[5] François was curiously misinformed on this. Packs of stag-hounds were not all that uncommon in the 18th century.

DANCING

Dancing plays the smallest part in the pleasures of the English – in general, they have no taste for this amusement. Bury, for example, which is surrounded by a great number of houses of rich young gentlemen should have superb and frequent balls; and all those I have seen have been neither one nor the other, attended by scarcely fifty or sixty people.   .

PUBLIC BALLS

All balls are public events in England. (I say nothing of London, where private people do give balls sometimes.) They are given to celebrate some public occasion, or during the Assizes – when the prisoners come to trial – or for the King's birthday, or the Elections, etc. When there is a lull in these public occasions, a subscription ball is arranged. Twenty or so people promise to come, and thereby defray the costs of the ball: posters appear, it is advertised, and almost always one finds there more people than at the other kinds of ball.

For both kinds, it is the proprietor of an hotel who undertakes the expense. Every town has an Assembly Room which is let for the occasion to the owner of a coffee-house or an inn-keeper. He takes the money and pays the bills, and so much the better if he makes a profit. The charge is generally £4.10s per head for the public balls and a half-*louis* per man for the subscription balls: admission for women only 48 shillings,[1] the high price for men being fixed to avoid bad company; and as at subscription balls it is only those ladies who have subscribed who are allowed in, there is no fear of that same inconvenience. The expenses to the entrepreneur consist of six or seven musicians and tea for the whole company, as much as they can drink, at the public balls. At the subscription balls, he provides a cold supper with wine for all who want it. There are sometimes men who, for their half-*louis*, will drink wine, and punch, all night.

The ladies are always dressed up for the occasion, but with simplicity: their charm lies in combining those apparent opposites. They

[1] S. C. Roberts translated these figures as 4 shillings and 6 pence (instead of £4.10s) and as '10 shillings' which is the equivalent of a ½-*louis*, ladies paying only 2 shillings.

have no use for rouge, which is banished absolutely from England: it would be as rare for an Englishwoman to resort to it as it is in France for men to put putty over their faces.

The men wear very little finery: black breeches and silk stockings are the correct dress on such occasions. To make an extraordinary impression a man might go in a cravat, with his hair waxed *en queue*, and wearing his everyday coat. Elegant men have a new coat every time, but a plain coat of cloth, no splendour.

The two sexes dance equally badly, without the least grace, no steps, and no rhythm: they don't make a study of it, as we do. The women hold themselves badly, the head hanging forward, the arms dangling, the eyes lowered, etc: the men with their knees bent; they suddenly change direction with their legs; in short their appearance is most disagreeable as they dance. All English dances seem to be the same: all the ladies are ranged on one side, and the men on the other, each facing the chosen partner, doing their figure together, which consists of some jumps in the middle of the two rows, then holding hands and threading in and out between the second and third person to the right: thus one gets as far as the last person in the room and then has to rest while all the others do the same thing, one after another: so one dances for five or six minutes, then stands idle for half-an-hour watching the others dance and acting as pillars for them. It is reckoned impolite to go and sit down after one has finished one's task, as those who follow would have less of a dance.

Another, worse, custom of these balls is that you cannot change your partner; once you have engaged one, you must stay with her all evening, follow her about everywhere, fetch her tea, etc. You may leave her only very briefly to talk to someone else. When you have the bad luck to fall in with a disagreeable partner, you spend the most boring evening imaginable.

I hear that in towns where dances are more frequent, there is always a Master of Ceremonies, someone who is in charge of the ballroom, calls for the quadrilles, the minuets, etc., who knows your place in the first dance, so that he can find it for you in the others. He is a most useful man in a place of public assembly, for he prevents disputes.[2]

---

[2] François was able to confirm this when he visited Bath in 1785.

Minuets are danced in England almost like quadrilles; there is scarcely any more regularity in the steps, and no more grace: in general, a sad business.

These balls were for me very enjoyable because I found a large number of people there and was able to talk to people I was able to see only rarely, and partly also because my vanity was tickled. Accustomed to the character in France of being one of the worst dancers, I felt flattered to hear myself spoken of as a good dancer, in England, and to see a hundred people dancing worse than me. One likes everything one succeeds in: in France I didn't like dances, but in England I look forward to them with the greatest impatience.

GAMING

For the most part, gaming in England is very moderate. The most ordinary game, that everyone plays, is whist, which is played for stakes of [24 sols] a shilling, sometimes [a small écu] half-a-crown: that is quite general. *Crebidge*, loo, and quadrille are not so widely known and do not involve higher stakes. Billiards is played only to cover the rent of the table. *Tric-trac* is unknown. They have a sort of game played with counters which they call *begamate* (backgammon), which is only a child's game, and isn't played for money. Anyone who is in England and who wants to play only for the fun of it can play for very small stakes as – or even better than – in France. But if he wants a reputation as gambler, then he must pay dearly. In every town there is an informal club of men who gamble very high stakes on one card and who very often have the pleasure of ruining themselves. Their favourite games are whist, vingt-et-un and hazard. They play all night and perforce interest their wives and children in the outcome.

THE LIFE OF THOSE WHO ARE RUINED

When they have lost considerable sums, they borrow to pay their immediate debts, and as afterwards they must pay off the loan and for that purpose make economies, they set out with their wives in a 2-horse phaeton, a servant following on horse-back, and travel the provinces of their island, living in inns at great expense, for they are always extravagant. They go for a year or two, and when their economy has paid their debts, they can begin to gamble again, as they nearly always do. At least their courage in taking suddenly to this kind of life, very different from their former ways, means that their children are rarely ruined. Sometimes they grow so used to going on to inn after inn that they come to do it for pleasure, when their affairs no longer oblige them to. Those who want to make even more economy, and who are not discouraged by the difficulties of languages, cross the sea and go to France, Italy, etc., and although they pass in all those places as liberal spenders, their expenses are not half what they would be leading exactly the same sort of life in England.

COCK-FIGHTING

One of the games I think of as a game of chance, and which the English play losing a lot of money, is cock-fighting. It is a game of cruelty, a relic of barbarity, unforgivable in a nation like theirs. This is how it is done. They set up on a large round table covered with a carpet two cocks of a particular breed which has a disposition to fight. Their wings and tail-feathers are clipped, their beaks are filed down a little and each of their feet has a long steel spur firmly fixed. This is their combat-weapon. The spectators, as I say, place enormous bets, and each has a terrific interest in one of the cocks. After several rounds and jabs with the spurs it usually happens that the two cocks gradually grow as weak as one another, both covered in blood, until one seizes the advantage and overcomes and kills the other. It often lasts three or four hours.

All fighting-cocks have names well-known throughout England. Their lineage is carefully preserved. They are fed and trained so as to make them as vigorous as possible. They fight with incredible ferocity, and never give up until one of them is dead. Sometimes the victor dies shortly after the vanquished.

Another sport, more expensive, less cruel and much more entertaining, is horse-racing. Everyone has heard of the celebrated Newmarket races; they are known, I imagine, all over the world. However, I shall talk about them: but before that I want to explain what racehorses are. I was instructed in all this by the duke of Grafton, who has had the kindness to talk to me at length about it: he himself has eleven race-horses and I wrote down at once what he kindly told me.

The breed of original English horses is that of the cart-horses, strong, rotund, and – despite that – very agile.[1] All the others that we now see, even in large numbers, are of foreign breed. They came originally from Arabia and North Africa, but at a time long forgotten, and are no longer imported. Those destined for racing have been chosen, since that time, from among the most renowned Arab and Barbary breeds. Those people have, at all times, taken great pains in the breeding of their horses, and hold those genealogies more precious than their own. They never cross-breed. Their horses have always been recognised as the best on earth.

Since these rare and choice breeds have been brought to England, their purity has always been preserved, and they have always been mated among themselves, with no misalliances. Accordingly, the horse you see can be traced direct back to Solomon's mare and is its worthy heir in courage and speed. It remains to be discovered if Solomon liked fast travel and kept race-horses.

The breeds, then, are carefully preserved, on the side of both stallion and mare. That by itself means that racehorses are extraordinarily dear. From their tender infancy they are extremely cosseted. They are weaned in a meadow of luscious grass, in which is a little shelter they can enter as they please: there the mangers are always replenished with oats and they eat as much as they like and go back into the meadow when they are tired of oats. They are groomed every day with particular

---

[1] Robert Ryece wrote of them in 1602 in his *Suffolk Breviary* as 'many horses here bred of good shape and quick sperit' (ed. Lord F. Hervey, 1902, p. 43). Kenneth Clark (Lord Clark), whose father owned a prize-winning herd of Suffolk horses, wrote of them authoritatively as 'solid and heavy, but as perfect in proportion as the horses of the Sforzas and the Gonzagas' (*Another Part of the Wood*, 1974, p. 11).

care: at three years they are put into a stable intended for them alone, and a start is made on purging them of what humours the grass may have given them. They are covered by two or three woollen coverlets which are wrapped round their head, neck and their whole body. Each horse has a little groom with no other job to do than look after him. They are groomed twice a day; they eat nothing but oats and a very little hay – perhaps not even two handfuls a day. The same lads who groom them mount and ride them for between an hour and a half and two hours a day, and gallop them as hard as they can on a ride chosen for the purpose, where usually all the racehorses are together so as to incite one another to speed. Usually they exercise between eleven and midday in winter, and at eight in summer. On their return they are groomed again and well wrapped, and all doors and windows are shut to allow them to rest for two or three hours. Then they are fed again.

Every fortnight they are given a purge to evacuate every kind of humour and stop them growing fat, and indeed they are all as lean as they can be. The owner has to know what medicine suits each of them. All the time they are being given medicine they don't go out, which lasts for a day or two.

In every racing stable there is a time-honoured groom, in whom the owner has great confidence. He has the responsibility of watching over the young grooms who are called *jockeys*.

All these horses race as often as they can and as the owner judges them fit for it. They are shod in a particular way: their shoes are extremely light and serve only for the exact length of the race. On arriving, they have a bucket of water thrown over their heads to enable them to breathe more easily, and avoid being stifled, in air they can take in more easily than during the race. The horses race as three- to six-year-olds: it is rare for them to race after that. Then, when they are from a stud of great reputation and acknowledged beauty, when they have always shown themselves to be likewise, when, finally, they have very often won or run with some handicap such as an additional weight in the saddle, etc., they are sent to a distant county, where they are fed like the other horses: the sole employment of these stallions is to serve the mares of interested owners. There are stallions who serve at prices ranging from five guineas to fifty. All the neighbouring gentry send in their mares for five, six or ten guineas and are sure of a nice-looking and sound horse. As mare and foal will never become race-horses, but

47

hunters, hacks, carriage-horses, etc., according to the quality of the mare and the size of the stallion, it is from this, above all, that owners of racehorses recoup their enormous maintenance costs, and that England is supplied with such fine horses.

When at last the horse is too old to serve the mares, he is good for nothing. He is sold for between ten and fifteen pounds. He is fit only for the roads and is more liable than not to become lame on them: his feet accustomed to a particular terrain are cut open by stones, and he is not capable of prolonged work.

A horse that has almost always won and acquired by his own merit a great reputation, and whose pedigree is in good order, is kept most carefully for the racing mares, in order to have a new generation of race-horses: so one pays up to fifty pounds for the covering of a mare: the stallion is attended to with the utmost care for a period of two or three years, after which he is mated with ordinary mares, and joins the class I have already described.

Race-horses are generally stallions: the mares race also, but that is rarer. It is always when the two sexes have raced that the new race-horses are produced. The upkeep of these horses is something extra-ordinary. They cost, from birth until they are fit only to serve the ordinary mares, about sixty pounds a year – as much for the horse as for his valet-de-chambre, for, as I've said, each horse has a jockey to groom him.[2] The losses on the horses themselves are also very considerable. It often happens that a 3-year-old from a very good stud, and therefore very expensive, is found not be capable of enough speed; he is sold off at a very low price – fifteen or twenty guineas – the manner of his upbringing not fitting him even to be a good hunter, only a hack. No one would want him for breeding, either, for he never raced.

Another risk the owner has to run is that of a horse taking a fall during racing and, through the impetus of his terrific speed, fracturing a leg and becoming useless for racing any more. He is useful only to mares, but not to racing mares, only the others. Still, he must have raced, so that his form is known, and his plight attributed only to an accident.

---

[2] François is confused between jockeys and grooms, but it may be an 18th-century confusion.

48

Race-horse owners cover their immense costs only by the considerable bets they make at Newmarket and at other race-meetings, and the money they receive on account of the mares served by their stallions. But you can see from that how they can lose prodigiously and win only modestly – even with the greatest good luck, which is not a probability to count on. So I think it can't be greed for winnings that impels the English to own race-horses: it is custom, taste and fashion that bring them to it. With good judgement they are almost sure of being able to recover their expenses, and they all believe they have that judgement. The Government, which has an interest in the sport for the good breed of horses it spreads through the country, contributes a prize to winners at the Newmarket races. The races are run on six alternate weeks, each with a week's rest in between: so they last for three months. I was there for one of these weeks. The place where they run – the race-course – is turf, close-cut and fine, levelled and cleared. There are three or four different courses, one of four miles (one and a half leagues), one of two miles, another of a mile and a half, etc. The races take place on one of these courses after the bets have been laid, which are carefully organised before the beginning of each race.

The horses are started by a signal given by a public official: two others are at the finishing-post to decide the winner. If a horse's nose is only an inch in front of that of his rival, he has won, depending on the judgement of these two men.

I was astonished at the extraordinary speed at which they race: you can scarcely follow them with your eyes if you are near. They go faster than lightning. The jockeys have to keep their heads low in order to breathe: they cleave the air so rapidly that they would otherwise be stifled.

It happens very rarely that a horse falls, but when it does happen the jockey is hurled fifty feet beyond the horse, rarely escaping death, and the horse badly injured. But I'm told this is extremely infrequent.

As for betting, it's a real science, difficult to grasp, and I can't give you much idea. It is based on the age of the horses, their track-record, the weights they are carrying, the start they are given, etc. It is an expertise so difficult to acquire that those Englishmen who have it find it very extraordinary that Mr Fox was able to master it in five weeks of intensive study: they regard that as proof of his high degree of genius.

There, all bets are made by word of mouth, nothing in writing, yet it is rare for anyone to default. You are usually paid next morning at the coffee-house[3] where everyone gathers. However, just occasionally someone declines to pay up, or pretends not to have made the bet: this is the only circumstance in England where you may give yourself the pleasure of correcting a man with the aid of your cane, or a whip: you can also set your groom on to him, and gratify the groom on your behalf. Such blows are not actionable at law.

The races at Newmarket are more famous than those held elsewhere in England, partly because they last much longer and partly because the Government contributes prize-money. All the great noblemen attend, and the bets are considerably higher than at other courses. However, there are races in almost all the towns of England: their regular dates are fixed, and as they commonly attract a large number of betting people and others, a dance is held every evening at a public assembly-room. Some last longer than others.

There are in England some people called *black-legs*,[4] because they are always in top-boots, not having the means to buy stockings: they have their whole fortune in their pocket and have no other trade than going the rounds of successive race-meetings in order to bet on the horses. They wager immense sums, and for the most part pay up when they lose. They have a good basic understanding both of horses and of the betting odds so they very rarely lose. Almost all of them grow rich, although their fortune rests only on the flimsy foundation of such odds as their expertise can turn to advantage. It is noticeable that, as a rule, when they have made themselves a comfortable pile of money, they retire from gambling and live more like conventional people.

Finally, there is a great number of people who economise all through the year for the pleasure of risking the product of the year's privation on one five-minute fling.

The town of Newmarket is very small and has no specialist trade. All the market for goods is generated by the races. Several very rich people have houses there and train their horses all the year round, which makes for a very considerable consumption. At Newmarket you find the

[3] The Jockey Club rooms.
[4] The 18th-century definition was 'turf-swindler'. The modern strike-breaking connotation developed in the later 19th century.

best saddlers, farriers and other workmen connected with horses. People send their horses there to have their tails docked and ears clipped.

HUNTERS AND CART-HORSES

While I'm speaking of horses, I don't want to leave the subject without saying something of the other species.

Every possible kind of horse is found in England in its best form, and from the race-horses, which are at their best around here, to the cart-horses: all are such that you could not wish for anything else.

In proportion to the inhabitants, I think the number of horses in England must be double that of France. Every minor gentleman – they are very numerous, spread into every corner of every county – has two carriage-horses for his wife and himself, and another to ride: that is usual. He would have to be relatively poor not to keep these three horses because, if his fortune was a small one, he would keep some land in hand to employ these two horses.

If the gentleman is unmarried, or in holy orders, he will have a saddle-horse. All the farmers go about on horseback. The proliferation of horses is such that a very small farmer, going to market or to town, goes on horseback or in a kind of Tilbury[1] in which he and his wife travel very comfortably.

All these different types of horse are of the finest. As I've said, all the saddle-horses one sees belonging to a simple gentleman, or to a farmer visiting his field, would be as much as forty *louis*[2] in France. They are all well-made and groomed with the greatest care, which adds not a little to their appearance.

It is the farmers who are engaged, almost without exception, in raising the horses. They have for the purpose one or two saddle-mares and as many draught-mares which they keep in a meadow of rich grass during the summer, and in winter in one of their farmyards where they have deep litter to their bellies and where they are fed only chaff.

[1] A small two-wheeler very popular in the first half of the 19th century.
[2] Guineas, cf. p. 41 and fn. 4.

Obviously, this feed is not dear. However bad the weather, neither mother nor foal ever goes back into the stable, which keeps both of them healthy. The farm-hands who come and go make the young horses so tame that they come right up to you when you go to see them. The farmer keeps them in this way till they are three years old. Then, whether he has the horse's tail docked – which is usual – and sells afterwards, or whether he sells before, it makes no difference. They are commonly sold in their farmyard, but sometimes at fairs. These sales are always for ready-money, which means that the horses are sold cheaper. You can get a very nice saddle-horse for fifteen guineas, a fine carriage-horse for twenty or twenty-five, and cart-horses are in the range fifteen to twenty.

These are the qualities of the general run of horses, those most in demand; on top of that, everyone can find a horse to suit his special requirements. At many farms you will find other horses that are bred from a race-horse and a good mare and which have been carefully brought up. They will become fox-hunters (in great demand in England). Because they are finer, better horses than the rest, they will fetch up to fifty guineas, sometimes even more, but in France they would fetch a price – perhaps a good third as much again. That, I think, is approximately the relation between the prices: the same quality costs about a third more in France than in England.

I must say that there are excellent long-living horses, thanks, it's true, to the care that is taken with looking after them. The English in this important respect are admirable and have an extraordinary love for their horses: they all share it. England is perhaps the only country where you can travel with your own horses without a man to look after them: they will have the best attention in the world. The people at the inn will take such an interest in them that it can only be explained as part of the general feeling of the nation for these animals.

I don't want to overlook the cart-horses: they are the most necessary for trade and agriculture. So, although they may not be the finest horses, they deserve more than a little notice.

Each county has its own different breed of cart-horse, very distinct and recognisable, because in general they are developed without cross-breeding.[3] The Suffolk horse is reputed the best: stout, barrel-shaped,

---

[3] See Arthur Young, *Annals of Agriculture*, II, 1784.

strong head, the legs fine in contrast with the heavy frame. The farmers take very particular care to have a good type of cart-horse: they are a sound investment, for they remain strong even when old, and they are seldom ill.

Everywhere, in all countries, there is a tendency to ape one another: English farmers included. They go to see the races at Newmarket. Being unable to make their cart-horses race, the Suffolk farmers hold drawing matches.[4] The bets are sometimes very considerable. Times are set aside in the year when the farmers of a district bring their horses to a meeting: then one often sees the most marvellous teams. A purse is agreed for the horse that pulls best: then, one after another, the competitors try to haul a prodigious weight,[5] and the horse that moves it with the greatest ease and alacrity has won. Sometimes the wager is on a whole team: then, instead of one horse for each trial, a team of six is harnessed, and they move masses of a weight so prodigious that one scarcely imagines it. I have seen a single horse drag [blank: François' memory as well as his imagination boggled!]

Another kind of challenge for these same horses is to attach five or six of them separately to the same tree. The one who, at the voice of the horse-man, is brought to his knees first in the supreme effort to move the immoveable, wins the prize. It is easy to judge the real usefulness of such matches in maintaining the good breed of horses so necessary in the country.[6]

These good animals work every day from six in the morning till six in the evening, with only two and a half hours' rest.[7] They are given corn rarely – only when pushed to the limit. They eat chaff and hay, and at night are left in a meadow. They live to be very old, and are very vigorous.

Stallions are rarely put to work.

All the cart-horses have their tails docked at the first joint, so that one sees very little of their tail hair. Their manes are cut very close as well.

[4] To find the strongest-pulling draught-horse.
[5] Usually the trunk of an enormous oak.
[6] There is further description of Suffolk horses and drawing-matches in the section entitled 'A Journey in Suffolk' below, p. 137.
[7] These long hours were doubtless personally noted by François, but were not universal, and certainly not throughout the year: see G. E. Evans, *The Horse in the Furrow*, 1960, the first chapter of which gives a vivid picture of the horseman's day. ('Horseman' is the traditional Suffolk name for 'ploughman'.)

They are better harnessed than in France: all their bridles are leather, their collars small, not very heavy, there are traces[8] for pulling, and a broad[9] leather band along their backs to secure the two chains on the two flanks of the crupper (hindquarters). That is all their harness, and I don't think you could have anything lighter or sounder.

The cart-horses are looked after as carefully as the other horses. They always seem shining and clean, and never have sores such as one sees too often in France.

THE LABOURER'S DAY

Acts of Parliament are always marked by a depth of wisdom and justice that are easily recognised. They always come to the help of the unfortunate individual to shield him from the oppression of the rich. It is in this spirit of vigilance that the rules were made governing the labourer's day.

All working days are fixed between six a.m. and six p.m., summer and winter: from these twelve hours, one and a half are subtracted; half an hour for breakfast and an hour for dinner. This rule applies to everything called day-work.[1] I've already mentioned it in connection with domestic service. As for manual labourers, it is to their great advantage. In France, they work much longer hours, starting an hour earlier in summer and finishing nearly two hours later. Their wage is not fixed, but depends on the district they are in. In this part of Suffolk, they earn eighteen English (thirty-six French) *sous* in summer, and in winter thirty [presumably French] *sous*.[2]

---

[8] The traces were chains, weighing 16 or 20 lbs the pair.
[9] About 4 inches wide and often decorated with stitching.

[1] The Act of 1563 (5 Eliz. chap. IV), so much admired by François, in fact lays down for day-labourers that they shall be at work before 5 a.m. March-September and work till between 7 and 8 p.m. except for 'breakfast, dinner and drinking', not exceeding 2½ hours in the day. Between mid-September and mid-March, they shall be at work from dawn to dusk except for breakfast and dinner time. See also section on Husbandmen, Labourers, &c. under Servants, in Richard Burn, *The Justices of the Peace and the Parish Officer*.
[2] In 1767, A. Young recorded, in the Bury neighbourhood,

For this wage, which is enormous, they do not perform anything like as much work as our labourers. I've been near enough to go round behind some of them and watch them at work for a whole day, and I am sure that – despite the feeling of some English people who have travelled in France and don't agree – their workmen work very casually, resting often and conversing a lot.[3] I am certain that a French day-worker does almost a fifth more work in a day than an Englishman.

On the farms they hire their regular workmen by the year,[4] as in France. In the Bury neighbourhood they are paid between eight and nine guineas a year, and food, lodging etc. They have nothing to do but clothe themselves. The women are on the footing of three guineas, with the same extras.

At harvest-time, the arrangements are completely different: the farmers contract for all the hands they need, and make a bargain with them to complete the whole job. In the Bury neighbourhood, they give four and a half guineas to each man for cutting and harvesting all the wheat, oats and barley: the job lasts between three weeks and a month, because they take on enough men, in relation to the size of the farm, to complete the job over approximately that period. This part of Suffolk is the cheapest for this kind of work, so you must not see this price as one given throughout England for taking the harvest. There are counties where the farmers have to give six guineas and feed their men three times a day on meat and strong beer – these extras amounting to nearly two shillings a day from the amount that they eat. At this time, the

---

'In winter, 1s. and small beer.
In spring to harvest, 1s. 2d. and beer.
In harvest 1s. 8d and beer.'
For reaping, mowing, hoeing, threshing (task work), there were separate (substantial) tariffs. *A Six Weeks' Tour*, 1768, p. 52.
[3] Contrast William Marshall's observations just across the boundary in Norfolk: 'In respect of day-labourers, two remarkable circumstances are united: namely hard work and low wages! A Norfolk farm-labourer will do as much work for one shilling as some two men will do in many places for eighteen pence each. There is an honesty, I had almost said an honour, about them when working by the day, which I have not been able to discover among the day labourers of any other country [i.e. county].' *The Rural Economy of Norfolk*, I, 1787, pp. 40–41.
[4] These were properly known as servants, and lived in the house, or outhouses. See Blackstone, Burn (next footnote), and Ann Kussmaul's thorough summary in her book *Servants in Husbandry in early modern England*, 1981, pp. 4–6.

working day is not limited to twelve hours: it goes on as long as light lasts, and starts at dawn. In all these matters I can't speak of England in general: I'm in Suffolk, and am informed only about Suffolk. At least, everything I've written is true and known to me, either by personal observation, by asking the people involved, or by being told by people whose authority I should perhaps trust more than my own.

THE ENGLISH SUNDAY

Is there anything in the world so boring as a Sunday in England? If the week-days are dull, they are days of festival compared with Sunday.

I don't know precisely whether it is to some point of religion or in obedience to an Act of Parliament that we owe the afflictions of this day, which in every other country is noticeable for its happiness.[1] I'm inclined to think it is attributable to both, for as religion is all a matter of politics, anything connected with one is connected with the other. What is certain is that on Sunday you are forbidden to do anything enjoyable. You may neither sing nor play musical instruments; still less dance. All forms of card-games are banned. The people are not permitted ball-games, or skittles, or any game whatsoever. The strictest observers of these extravagant austerities will not even go where there is a congregation, but stay religiously, or rather dementedly, at home reading their mass-produced Bibles, of which they all have copies in

---

[1] The most recent Act of Parliament was passed in 1781: 21 George III, *c.* 49. It confined itself to the opening of places of amusement or entertainment on Sunday evenings, and of holding debates upon texts of Holy Scripture by incompetent persons. The opening of such places qualified them as 'disorderly houses', liable to a fine of £200 per Sunday. The rest of François' boredom must be attributable to 'religion'. The tone was set in Burn's *The Justices of the Peace and the Parish Officer* (innumerable editions, for every J.P. in the Kingdom certainly needed a set of these remarkable volumes). Under *Profanation of the Sabbath*, you read: 'Besides the notorious indecency and scandal of permitting any secular business to be publicly transacted on that day, in a country professing Christianity, and the corruption of morals which usually follows such profanation . . . [observance of the sabbath] humanizes, by the help of conversation and society, the manners of the lower classes which would otherwise degenerate into a sordid ferocity and savage selfishness of spirit.'

their houses. They will not even climb on to a horse, for all self-indulgence is frowned on.[2]

Don't think that I haven't seen all this: I see the evidence week after week, and dread Sunday more than anything. The Act of Parliament that regulates this behaviour has laid down considerable penalties for offenders and, what is more, offers a reward to informers.[3] Justices of the Peace, magistrates numerously scattered throughout the districts, in town and country, rigidly enforce payment by those who don't observe Sunday: the fine is too severe for any poorer person to be able to forget it.[4]

The smallest fine imposed is five shillings (six *francs*). If you prefer to go to prison for a day or two, you are free to choose.

The greatest noblemen, those with the highest standing in the country, are as subject to this law as the humblest peasant. The first person to see the custom being disregarded – even if it was only taking a gun and shooting a hare in one's own garden or taking out a pack of cards ready for a game, etc. – goes to make his complaint to the nearest Justice of the Peace, who is obliged to send the offender an *indictment*, or formal summary of the informer's report, with an order to pay a fine. This he pays at once, since a court hearing would cost more. As I say, a

---

[2] No drover, horse-courser, waggoner, butcher . . . or their servants shall travel . . . on the Lord's Day, etc.

[3] Between 5 Anne and 8 George III (1707–1768) several statutes authorised the rewarding of informers assisting the discovery and conviction of criminals.

[4] 'The solemn peal of the organ was superstitious . . . Half the fine paintings in England were idolatrous, the other half were indecent. The extreme Puritan was at once known from other men by his gait, his garb, his lank hair, the sour solemnity of his face, the upturned white of his eyes, the nasal twang with which he spoke, and, above all, by his peculiar dialect. He employed, on every occasion, the imagery and style of scripture. Hebraisms violently introduced into the English language, and metaphors borrowed from the boldest lyric poetry of a remote age and country, and applied to the common concerns of English life, were the most striking peculiarities of this cant, which moved, not without cause, the derision both of Prelatists and libertines.' That description of early 17th-century Puritans in the opening chapter of Macaulay's *History of England* fitted their descendants in the late 18th century. The poet Crabbe's study of it in 'The Frank Courtship' in his *Tales*, in 1812, is further evidence that in Suffolk its essentials had not changed. But the law had. 1688 and 1714 secured even the most Puritan nonconformists from persecution. They were not, however, empowered by Parliament to impose their Pharisaic Sabbaths on the rest of latitudinarian (and libertine) society, except over the opening of places of entertainment. For once, François' observations and his own 'informers' seem to have exaggerated the legal stringencies.

small portion of the fine is paid over to the informer. If the J.P., either out of consideration for someone to whom he may have obligations, or because he is nervous of that person's authority, refused to serve the fine, the informer, tempted by the thought of a more considerable reward, would prefer both his complaint against the offender and a charge against the Justice of the Peace. The offender, as man of substance, would pay the fine, and the J.P. would be ordered to pay two hundred guineas for having declined to administer justice impartially.

But what does one do on Sunday? All the men gather for the whole day in the tap-rooms, where they spend perhaps the whole week's earnings. The women meet after dinner, drink tea together, go walking along the main roads, and relax together in conversation after the week's work. In the evening, the whole family reassembles, and while they are waiting for supper, and later, for bed, the father or mother reads aloud from the *Bible* provided[5] according to the injunction of Henry VIII, and more often than not, after half an hour, everyone is asleep in his chair. All this is absolutely true: I have seen exactly this, many times, in the family in half of whose house we spent that white winter of our arrival in Bury, in '84. A gentleman of this county[6] made an admirable drawing which has been engraved and is to be seen everywhere. It represents a Sunday evening. The father is seen by a table lit by a candle, reading the Bible: he has a long pair of spectacles on his nose. The mother listens, eyes half-closed, and all the children are asleep, leaning against each other.[7] It makes a very delightful group (Pl. 16).

RELIGION

Everyone knows that England was Catholic up till the time of Henry VIII who, exploited by intolerable papal taxation and snubbed by an arrogant power which frustrated his government, itself often arbitrary, finally severed all connection with the Roman *curia*, and became king

---

[5] At first, in 1538, in every church.
[6] Sir Henry William Bunbury (1750–1811), born at Mildenhall.
[7] Bunbury may have done more than one version. Another shows father (without spectacles) asleep, mother half-asleep, young son reading from the Bible but nodding off, and daughter wide awake and smirking.

16. A Sunday Evening. *J. Brotherton, after H. W. Bunbury.*

and pope in one. England was at that time more heavily burdened by the popes than any other Catholic country; and the clergy, rich and numerous, made up a redoubtable party in the state. Perhaps, too, the desire to appropriate the immense possessions of the monks entered into the calculations of the plans of a King who was short of money, whose country was in debt, and who liked spending as he pleased. But although Henry VIII had broken with the pope, although he had suppressed all the convents of the monks and nuns, he had kept his country completely Catholic: he was the head of a Catholic religion in England. Soon after, the Bible was printed, based very largely on the Holy Scriptures, from which they merely suppressed what they wished to withdraw and added what was lacking.

This Bible was put into the hands of everybody, so that it could be read daily:[1] it remains there today. From that time, a change came over the Catholic religion.

---

[1] One copy was ordered to be in each church. Later in the Reformation, the copies

Queen Mary, who succeeded Henry VIII, was brought up in the Catholic religion. She brought it back as it was in her country, but the rigour with which she had it observed, the Spaniards who brought to it their bigotry, and the persecutions to which they subjected those who had already accepted the religious principles of Henry VIII, made Catholicism detested; and this ill-judged zeal did more harm than the persecutions of the imperious Henry. The long reign of Queen Elizabeth dealt the last blow to the Catholic religion; and if we must date the Reformation to the time of Henry VIII, we must date to that of Queen Elizabeth the establishment of the religion that is today general in England, and that we call Protestant.

I don't pretend to be able to explain the nature of this religion. Such pretension would be ridiculous at my age, and not being more fully instructed than I am. I want to speak here simply about some aspects of the Anglican religion that have come within range, and especially about the way I have seen it practised by the English.

They differ very little from us in belief. They believe neither in the transubstantiation of the body and blood of Christ in the Eucharist, nor in the authority that God has given the pope as visible head of the Church, nor in the intercession of saints, nor in the power of a priest to remit sins. Those are the main points in our religion that they do not adopt in theirs. The rest we have in common. Their religion charges them with the practice of the virtues, as ours does. So a decent man anywhere will be of a good and well-tried religion.

As to the way the English practise their religion, it is much easier than ours. They don't go to confession, they very rarely approach the Holy Table, and when they do, it is not with the same purpose as us: they do not believe they are eating the body of Jesus Christ (as I've already said), but they go to the Holy Table as a commemorative enactment.

They are not bound to go to church every Sunday: rain, fog, heat – the least thing keeps them away. But they are obliged to read the Bible as often as possible. This is the book in which the children are taught to read and the grown-ups perfect their reading.

---

multiplied until there was one in every shop and farmhouse. François is right about the change this wrought.

I have twice attended a service. It lasts an hour and a half and consists of a prayer with all the people making responses to the minister, then a reading from the Bible, then a sermon. There are always two ministers, one in a pulpit and the other below him.[2] The sermon has for its text either some point of morality, or a passage of scripture, or has the object of encouraging the observance of the laws, etc. Evening service is shorter. Everything that is read, or spoken, or preached, is in English, to be within reach of everyone. There are days appointed for the celebration of the Eucharist, when the minister takes the service at an altar which is always at the far end of the choir, and with no ornament. I suppose that this service differs little from the one I have seen.

The whole religion is based on the principle of political equality. Parliament alone is supreme: all others are equal.

Turning to another point – for one must say a little about things that touch everyone – I must mention the sacraments. English baptism is like ours, performed with the same idea; except that the child is not committed to the protection of the saints, whose intercession they believe to be powerless. The child is given a Christian name only to be distinguished from other members of the family: without the addition of this Christian name, the family name by itself would lead to confusion.

Confession is quite unnecessary. An Anglican may if he likes make his confession: he will receive absolution from a priest, but he will be absolved only in his own eyes: it will be no help towards his salvation. Whatever is the point of that? However, some people do confess in order to expiate, by their humiliation, the faults they have committed; it is very rare. Perhaps not one Englishman in ten thousand will make his confession.

Confirmation is thought a much more necessary sacrament: according to Protestantism it is practically indispensable. Their thinking is that a baptised infant has made no positive personal contribution: so, when he reaches the age of reason he must assume the character of a good Christian and complete in himself, by confirmation, the goodness of Baptism (that is the reasoning given me by all those with whom I've spoken about it). They don't believe this Sacrament makes a permanent

---

[2] He is thinking of the minister and parish clerk, who sat at the desk below the minister in 18th-century double-decker pulpits.

impression, for some have themselves confirmed more than once. I was told yesterday that there are three or four old women at Bury who have themselves confirmed every time the bishop comes to the town. Their explanation is that you can't have too much of a good thing.

Of the Eucharist I spoke earlier.

Marriage is something altogether peculiar: it is so different from our way of celebrating this Sacrament that I had to get someone with the patience to explain it to me two or three times before I felt I understood it.

Parish churches and certain chapels are the two places in which you may be married, though with special licence from the archbishop of Canterbury, obtained by means of his fee, you may be married in a private house and in an ordinary room, without recourse to any chapel. The ceremony has to be performed by a priest. It consists in both parties being asked whether they freely give their consent and whether their parents give theirs, then a ring is placed on the bride's finger, and the thing's done. A contract is drawn up, signed by all the interested parties, and this document is deposited with the parish priest.

Thirty years ago,[3] not only was there no need of a priest to perform this ceremony, but there was not even any mention of parental consent. The first available man could marry two people: the contract was deposited with the parson and was often signed only by the three indispensable signatories.

This is still the position today in Scotland.[4] There, the presence of a priest is as unnecessary as the presence of parents; which every year attracts a large number of young people (whose parents do not want them to marry in response to inclination) to go and get married in Scotland, where all parental power is null and void.

In the little town of Gretna Green, just across the Scottish border from England, a blacksmith makes a considerable income by the marriages he performs. There is a large house in which he receives all those who want to marry, and as they are in a great hurry to do it, for fear of the arrival of a courier who may be following them armed with the authority of their parents, they have to pay heavily and he makes a

[3] Before Lord Hardwick's Marriage Act, 1753.
[4] Cf. p. 37 above.

fortune. What are the parents' options? To disinherit their children – not very common; they will not let them starve for a supposed act of folly, which may turn out not to be one. There's a fuss for a year, and then they all adjust.

Not, however, that I approve this disregard of an authority established by nature. Whom should we respect if not our parents? Whom should we dread to hurt? The remorse that one must feel afterwards must poison the happiness of living with a woman one loves. The truth is that the English experience the effects of such a marriage less than we should. The moment a young man marries, he takes a house in which he and his wife live together alone: he avoids living even in the same town as his father (I know twenty examples of this). If the father lives in the country, the son will live in the town, and each lives rather withdrawn, in his own household, father and son seeing little of each other during the year. And so they prefer to have wives they love than be loved by their parents. It is in their tradition as it will not be in ours, and it seems to me somehow contrary to nature.

The Government's benefit is a large population. The number of couples who go off to Scotland every year is very considerable, and probably without that possibility they wouldn't marry, or at least not so soon. This is probably why the country tolerates this custom – peculiar to itself and against the law of nature. However, there must have been a sense of shame at this tolerance, because thirty years ago the same system prevailed in England and was abolished only this short time ago. The Englishman thinks perhaps that in driving back this custom – which clings to ancient barbarism – to the far north, or at least to the farthest north of England, it will be unnoticed, he will feel less disgrace, and the population will continue to benefit. But the truth will out, bad news precedes good, and everyone here knows that if the father wishes to prevent a marriage, the couple has only to hire a post-chaise and run away to win independence. Perhaps, some time in the future, the custom will be abolished in Scotland as it is in England.

The admission to Holy Orders is conducted, very much as it is with us, by the bishops.

Extreme Unction has no validity in the Protestant faith, in effect as in theory. They have no confidence in the mediation of men, and simply recommend themselves to God; they die on their own, either in confidence or self-reproach. It is my chief grounds for not liking this

63

religion. At least when a Catholic dies, he has a priest with him, reassuring him if he is frightened, and letting him see only a pleasing prospect. If he has done wrong to God, he confesses, receives absolution, and, as I am persuaded, dies in the belief that he is going to Paradise. That hope for the best, which never leaves us, coupled with his illness, ought, as I see it, to dispel all his fears and let him close his eyes without dread. It is a big advantage of our religion. But the English die exactly like dogs. If they are ill, the doctor comes; they die, and often one hears nothing until long afterwards, for they are accustomed to isolate themselves all the while they are ill. All the while they are left to their own reflections on the future. What consolations can a sick man, inclined to see black rather than white, offer himself? He may have serious matters to reproach himself with, and may be weighed down by thoughts that another person would help to dispel. I believe that one of the principal attributes of a religion, whichever it may be, is consolation, and I do not believe that Protestantism does much to supply it.

I have just spoken about the administration of the Sacraments in comparing the English religion with our own, but I must not forget to say that they really count only two Sacraments: Baptism and Eucharist – the three others are mere ceremonies and two don't exist.

It is obvious, from this short study, how easy it is for the English to practise their religion: nothing could be more convenient. They have no fasts, no meatless-days, no Lent: their Sunday service is not obligatory. What is it that they have to do? The answer is that it is not church-going, or eating fish instead of meat, etc., that makes for a religious man; and that it is solely belief that ranges him under the standard of religion; and that when the church is true, the practice of what it prescribes is what makes a good Christian. Now you will read me a sermon in which all the advantages of religion will be laid out, but it will be our religion that receives the panegyric: I do not believe that such satisfying reasons can be given in support of the English religion, for, according to the small amount I know about it, it seems neither consoling nor edifying.

As for the beliefs of the English, what are they? I have heard much talk on the subject since I have been here. Many have argued and I have not perceived any conclusion. The only thing on which the majority are agreed is that almost all English people hold different beliefs, all believe things peculiar to themselves: some of them, and nearly all the women, decline to believe in the Trinity and shut their books when it is mentioned during their service. From which I conclude that the bulk of all these particular believers believes in nothing whatever.

In general, there are few *dévots*, devout men or women. Even the old women rarely catch this malady. But the few who are are much more devout than ours in France. Their days are spent in reading pious works in retreat, and in penance if they raise their eyes from the ground.

The ministers of this religion are not so hard-worked as ours, whose most demanding duties are hearing confessions, carrying the Blessed Sacrament into the country night and day, etc. The parishes are much larger than in France,[5] and are served by a rector who fills the place occupied by the *curés* in France. He is paid out of tithe, has a house, a garden, and some acres of land. These livings are bestowed according to ancient custom or by virtue of charters, or by the lord of the manor, or by the bishop, or by the Crown. In general, rectories are well worth having and rectors are worthy men.

Besides the rectors, a large number of clergy live in the country round about the parishes: the majority have very considerable revenues from the Church, either a deanery or a canonry, etc., derived from the ancient endowments of the Catholic church. They help the parishioners both by alms and by sermons, for they usually take their turn at preaching.

These ecclesiastical benefices are generally in the gift either of the Crown, or the diocesan bishop, or the Lord Chancellor.[6]

I am left only with the subject of burial. This is the occasion, sometimes, of more pomp in the Anglican church.

It is customary to keep the corpse in the house as long as possible, as long as the living are not in danger of being infected: apoplexies and prolonged lethargies[7] are common in England and it is said that at one time many people stricken in this way were presumed dead and buried alive: so, to avoid the horror of such mistakes they prefer to keep the dead for a longer period – sometimes for as long as a week.

---

[5] One would have thought this would mean the English ministers were 'more hard-worked'.

[6] The statement two paragraphs earlier about bestowal of livings was more accurate.

[7] Apoplexy is what we call a stroke. In 1732, Arbuthnot, *Lighter rules of Diet*, defined lethargy as a lighter form of apoplexy. It may also have described a coma.

In the case of a gentleman or a man [? word missing], which is much the same thing in England, his funeral is splendid. He is brought to the parish or to the place where he is to be buried in a carriage made expressly for the purpose: it is a sort of coffer with four-wheeled suspension, adorned with fringes, pompons, etc., all in black. Six black horses, without the least patch of white, draw this first carriage, followed by two or three others according to the expense intended: each is harnessed to six black horses. The dead man's relatives, his people, travel inside. All these are escorted by thirty or forty men riding black horses and wearing long crêpe bands, their hair unpowdered, in the deepest mourning. Once the church is reached, the coffin is lowered, and the rector inters it without ceremony.

As the funeral of rich persons is magnificent, that of the poor is miserable. Three or four men carry the bier, which is draped in a black cloth: they are not in black themselves: if they feel tired, they put down their load on the ground, or on a convenient wall, then continue their trudge when they are rested. On arriving, they lay the dead person in his grave, and after a short prayer he is covered with earth; it is finished.

When the death occurs deep in the countryside, the body is brought in a cart, but without other arrangements.

TOLERATION OF OTHER RELIGIONS

All religions are tolerated in England – in fact, though not in law. In writing about London I mentioned the chapels of all the different religions, and the number of them: they are in the same way tolerated in the rest of the kingdom. At Bury, for example, there are six different religions, all of which have their tabernacles or chapels, and each practises its own religion in peace: however, it is forbidden to practise them in public, or to be summoned by bells.[1] Only the [established] Protestant religion has the right to make itself heard.

All except the Catholics have the right to have chapels belonging to the whole membership of the sect, as distinct from individuals. But for

---

[1] Not a likely occurrence with the Protestant nonconformists, to whom bells represented the Anglican 'steeple-house'. The Catholics would not have been at all averse.

the Catholics to be allowed to have a chapel, it must belong to one of them. In that way, the civil liberty, so generally respected in England, which makes everyone absolute master of his own actions in his own house, prevents outside interference with any cult.

However, an Act of Parliament which forbids the practice of the Catholic religion in England forbids also assemblies of more than eleven persons (it is an Act passed in Cromwell's time), so that if anyone were to go to a Justice of the Peace and report that he had been inside a Catholic chapel, that he saw a certain priest saying Mass, and described the activities in detail, naming those present, or some of them, and saying how many, the J.P. would have no option, in accordance with the penalties imposed under the Act, but to condemn the priest to life imprisonment. However, the Justice of the Peace always evades the rigour of the law: never is it put into force, for he looks for a flaw in the way the evidence has been brought.[2] For example, he will ask the informer if he is absolutely certain the prayers he heard were Catholic prayers? Is he sure, or was it merely an imitation of the ritual? Perhaps he was just drinking wine and eating bread? etc. And he will ask so many questions requiring so much detail that the informer can scarcely answer, and is dismissed without satisfaction. As all the Justices of the Peace are agreed on this procedure, the Catholics feel completely at ease: despite the severity of the laws relating to them, they practise their religion with no concealment, and everyone knows without demurring.

The chapel at Bury belongs to the priest himself and all the Catholics attend on Sundays and Feast Days without the least trouble. There is a Catholic bishop at Norwich who has jurisdiction over the individual priests, sends them his instructions, visits them occasionally, etc. The government, which tolerates the Catholic form of worship, excludes

---

[2] Sir William Holdsworth summarised the general position: 'In England the worst of the penal laws against the Roman Catholics had been allowed to fall into desuetude, and their enforcement was discouraged by the judges. But it was always possible to revive them from motives of avarice and revenge.' (*A History of English Law*, X, 1938, p. 114.) In 1778, a Catholic Relief Act passed easily to allow Catholic recruits merely to take an oath of allegiance to the Crown. But it led to the Gordon Riots in London in 1780, with 458 people killed and injured. For one reason or another (and of course reason was by no means always relevant in 'the Age of Reason'), Catholic Emancipation was not Enacted until 1828. François' evidence is valuable: among his English friends were leading magistrates, like John Ord, and Catholics, like Sir Thomas Gage.

those who practise it from all public life – whether in offices of state, the army or the navy: the magistracy is similarly forbidden to them, so that they are absolutely separated from the body politic of the English; nor can they vote in the elections for members of Parliament, even though they may otherwise have the necessary qualifications. To attain all these offices you have to take a test on oath, swearing you do not believe in transubstantiation – an oath no Catholic can take. (You have also to swear that you renounce the Pope and recognise Parliament as head of the Church.)

I find the Catholics much more zealous in England than in France: they are more scrupulous in their religious observance: it is because they are discriminated against. It is the disposition of all men in all countries to like doing what is forbidden.

FRAGMENT ON GOVERNMENT

Here's an amusing passage, you are bound to say! What! You! On the government of England! You are very brave and very brilliant, for all the English say that no Frenchman has understood their constitution; that Montesquieu and all those who pretend to know something about it know not a word about it. Show us, young Montesquieu; start, so that we can have a laugh!

All these gibes that, I know, people will make, disconcert me a little, I confess; they don't discourage me. I want to write what I know about. Perhaps it isn't very important, but even so, in writing it down I shall know it better and understand some things for the first time: I shall be instructing myself at least. So to the gibes I reply that I do what I can, that I know I do it badly, and so if anything good is there, it is more than one should expect and more than I myself hope for. However, I shall resume the serious tone of a writer and speak just as if I believe every word I say.

I don't wish to enter into great detail and pretend to explain the most perfect machine ever made by a collection of men: I want only to notice the chief features, those observable by any one, even me. Older and more experienced men scarcely get all the details right. I don't wish even to try what they alone could attempt, if not accomplish.

The present form of government has been in existence only since the last revolution, about a hundred years ago.[1] The people, sick of the sight of over-mighty kings, conceived the idea of diminishing their authority, and it was in the course of the cruellest convulsions[2] that this masterpiece of government was fashioned.

You will excuse me from giving a recapitulation of History, from following the thread of events marking the chronology of the English kings and the political state of government as it is today. What does it matter to me what it was and how it arrived at its present point of perfection?

All power is concentrated in the hands of Parliament and those of the King, but both must agree for authority to be effective; otherwise it is null. So I want to divide what I call *tout pouvoir*, all power, into two parts, legislative power and executive power.

The King and the two houses of Parliament – one composed of peers of the realm, the other of the representatives of the people – constitute the legislative power of Great Britain. This mixed government assures the crown of its pre-eminence and its prerogatives, but it confines the King's power within proper limits and protects the nation from any dangerous excess of his power. It preserves for the great their titles and positions, but deflects any usurping ambitions. It keeps immune the rights and liberties of the people, but by making them take a part it does not give them so much power that one might fear democracy. What one has to admire is that the present constitution has not only made it impossible for the legislator to take up bad causes, contrary to the prosperity and good of the state, but it even makes it necessary for him always to want and to seek the general good, because everything converges on that.

To attain such an end, what is necessary is that the three powers with an equal share of authority advance side by side, all three in agreement, and one may well take for granted the good outcome of their accord. If one of them disagrees, one may conclude that the exercise of power in this instance would have a harmful result. As their general consent

---

[1] 1688.
[2] This might be a Jacobite view of the events of 1688, but François is pitching it high. (He may be confusing the 1680s with the 1640s.)

69

gives sanction to the laws, it follows that all those that are passed are acceptable to the King, to the nobility and to the people, furthering their mutual interests and thus the good of the nation. If it happened that ignorant or corrupt men, or the enemies of their country, proposed in the House of Commons to overtax the people or restrict their liberties, can one imagine that a majority of votes in the Commons would ever support the party subscribing to that, or would take a stand against the call of duty, of honour and of their own interest? So it is proven, once and for all, that the House of Commons, which has the greater authority of the two, serves as shield and defence to the rights of the people, and that in defending them it has no thought of weakening its two partners in power.

The lords will sign nothing at all that is contrary to their interests, and will deplore every Act that weakens their power and reduces them to the level of the Commons. The King, for his part, will not let his prerogative shrink in his hands. So each of the three powers that, together, form the Legislature of England, will separately take the greatest care to preserve itself intact, and will always be ready to assail in moderation the other two. From these political contests, continuously sustained, is born the surest guarantee of English liberties, since two of the powers would combine against the one which tried to usurp power.

The House of Commons alone has the right to initiate new laws it thinks necessary, and it is done in the following way: one admires the wisdom of it.

A member of the House makes his proposal verbally and presents his case on the day he thinks most favourable. If he is eloquent, he may impress them and win their votes, but they are not in a position to make an immediate decision. The motion is proposed, the debates follow, the House delegates a committee to examine the subject of the proposal and report back by a given time. The members of the committee examine it with care, add to it, cut it, modify, etc., and they conclude by writing it in the form of a law such as they wanted. It is now what is called a *Bill*.

The Bill is given three readings at three separate meetings of the House, and if the majority still vote in its favour, the Bill passes to the Upper House, where the same procedure is followed. If the peers decide to make certain changes or corrections to the Bill, it goes back to the Commons to revise it again, exactly as before. Last of all there is the King. He examines, or has his ministers examine, the Bill. If he ratifies it, the Bill becomes an Act, and joins all the other laws.

If it is possible to make mistakes with such exact procedures, at least it is very difficult.

But how are these two Houses of Parliament formed? Who are the members? I have reserved that to deal with now. The Upper Chamber is composed of the lords, the peers of the realm, created by the King with no other consideration than his own wishes. Numbers and merit don't count. These are those who represent the true nobility; England recognises no others. This title, *Lord*, once conferred, remains hereditary in the family and always passes to the eldest son. Apart from the lords temporal created by the King, the spiritual peers, that is to say bishops and archbishops, also have seats in the Upper House. Judges are also admitted to it, not as voices in debate but as part of the legislature to be consulted when necessary.

All the members of this house have the privilege, truly a great one, to be judged only by the other members, whether on a civil or criminal charge. The bishops withdraw, because it is felt that their ministry is likely to make them too tolerant to do justice in all its rigour.

The Commons are composed of the representatives of the people, elected by the people. They change at each Parliament. I was fortunate enough to observe one of these elections, and am in a better position to describe what happens.

The King alone has the right to dissolve Parliament. When the House of Commons is too openly opposed to the King's views, he exercises this right in the hope that the new representatives will be less opposed to his will. When Parliament has been dissolved, the King issues an order to the sheriffs in each county to prepare for the elections. If it happens that the Members of Parliament are agreeable to the King, and he doesn't want to change them, and that the constitution might be in danger through the Members' desire to please, the constitution has provided against this, and ordains that Parliament must dissolve itself at the end of seven years. So every seven years, or when the King wishes, the members of the House of Commons are changed.

The King is also master of the recalling of a new Parliament only when he decides to, up to a period of three years; as public business is at a standstill, the constitution allows no longer period of delay. But what use to the King is a large part of his prerogatives which he cannot exercise? This power, which looks so absolute, is worthless, although the State has given him a fixed revenue for life, known as the Civil List, which makes him independent, as the chief member of the legislative power should be. Nevertheless, since the Revolution,[3] he cannot govern without Parliament, for if he tried to, the whole administration would be in a state of slumber, annihilation. Apart from any more powerful reason, there is that of the taxes which have to be renewed to pay government debts, other taxes that have to be maintained for the support of government, whether for the upkeep of the Army, which is never kept in being for more than a year; and without the renewing of the Act authorising the standing Army, the Army would be authorised in fact but without pay. So, whether Parliament is dissolved by the King or by the law at the end of seven years, the King himself, whose right is to convene Parliament, gives orders for the election of new members, and this election cannot be completed until forty days after the dissolution of the old parliament.

The Lord Chancellor issues the orders, called *writs*, for the sheriffs of the kingdom to proceed to the elections. Three days after the receipt of the orders the sheriffs send the borough officials an order, sealed with their own seals, to proceed in the course of a week and return the names of the candidates.

The county elections have to be organised by the sheriff himself, and must take place within the space of not more than sixteen and not less than ten days. There are two different kinds of elections; those for the boroughs and those for the counties.

Not every town has the right to nominate representatives: those who enjoy the right do so by virtue of charters granted before the Revolution.[4] Since that event, the Royal Prerogative no longer extends to granting towns the right to send members to Parliament. It is therefore only those which flourished, and were considerable, under Henry VIII, Queen Mary and Queen Elizabeth that have that right today. But since those times, many towns have developed, and by their trade, wealth and population are infinitely superior to the ancient towns that are represented: Birmingham, Liverpool, etc., do not send members to Parliament. On the other hand, certain towns have declined so much

[3] 1688.
[4] 1688.

72

that several of them are uninhabited, the houses or their sites belong to one or more proprietors, of whom one, usually the lord of the manor, has gained control of the greater part and so himself nominates the members of Parliament for these boroughs.

I must distinguish between two kinds of borough elections – one in those towns where there is a corporation, the other where the burgesses elect by the majority of votes.

The candidates for towns – those who offer themselves as representatives of boroughs – must be English (foreigners, even if naturalised, are excluded); they must be twenty-one years old, the age when an Englishman reaches his majority; they must have three hundred pounds sterling in land, exempt from all charges and liabilities; they must not have jobs in customs, salt-tax offices, etc. Before presenting themselves, they take an oath before the sheriff that they have all these necessary qualifications.

When the nomination is in the hands of a corporation, the Alderman (the leader of the corporation)[5] reads aloud the names of the candidates, and the other members of the corporation make their choice by writing the names on a register: the Alderman sees those names which have the majority of votes and declares them elected. The next minute, they are grabbed, placed on a sort of raised stretcher and carried on the shoulders of the people all round the town.

In the towns where there is no corporation, it is the freemen, those who have the right as burgesses, who elect: the under-sheriff presides.

The number of representatives returned by each borough is two.

The county elections take place in the county town. As I said, they must be conducted by the sheriff himself.

The candidates are gentlemen of high reputation in the county who have at least £500 sterling in lands, free of all charges and obligations, etc., that come down from the period when England was subjected to the feudal system, that infected all states in those rude times; they present themselves to the sheriff, who writes their names on a register and, on the appointed day, proclaims them publicly in a loud voice to the election crowd. I said that the elections were held in the county town, but when that town is on one of the borders of the county,[6] a town

---

[5] In Bury, the Alderman was equivalent to Mayor.
[6] See the next paragraph.

73

nearer the centre was chosen for the election, whereby the electors have less expense in getting there. If any difficulty arises, either over the candidates or over their rights, the election is always taken back to the county town.

Suffolk supplied me with an example of this. Ipswich, the capital, is not in the centre, the sheriff announced that the election would take place at Stowmarket, a little town almost at the centre of the county; but there were three candidates as a result of disputes, and so the election was moved back to Ipswich.

The electors, called *freeholders*, have to have forty shillings in property held under the same conditions as the £500 of the candidates: that is to say, free of all feudal dues; but those who are worth much more still never have more than one vote. This, together with the fact that every man who holds property from someone else, and so is incapable of voting to buy himself out of his obligations and become a freeholder, ensures that the government of England is truly democratic, under a monarchical form. Freehold properties, redeemed from all charges, are so much divided and multiplied daily that almost everyone has a vote at elections.

The form of the county elections in Suffolk, the manner in which they were conducted, very much surprised me. I saw four carts lined up in a field: the sheriff climbs up into one, the candidates and leading men of the county in the others. The sheriff begins by naming the candidates, then each candidate gives a very specific account of his political con-duct, motives and principles, and the applause or silence of the crowd demonstrates what they think of him. The attention and the respect that prevail in these meetings is as remarkable as it is admirable. Hat in hand, they all listen in silence, and once the speech is over the supporters raise their hats in the air, shouting '*M . . . for ever!*' Those with opposite sentiments are content to keep quiet. I have already said that, when there are only two candidates,[7] the election is soon over. After their speeches, the sheriff proclaims their names and that they are now Members of Parliament. When there are three or four candidates, the thing takes longer.

If it happened that after the speeches the applause of the crowd clearly picked out two of the candidates, and that the number of hats

---

[7] For two seats.

74

raised was very much larger for them than for the other two, so that there was no chance of being mistaken, the sheriff would immediately proclaim them Members of Parliament, provided that the others didn't insist on a *poll*, as they have a right to do. The poll involves registering every freeholder in order to be sure that all those who elect have a right to do so. The poll is always conducted in the county town, and means new expenses for the electors. The friends of the candidates, in this case, at once spread out through the county and bring back as quickly as they can all the supporters they can find. The candidates pay for the travel of all their supporters. The poll is announced for a certain date, and on that day the county town is full of people. England was divided a long time ago (that of Alfred the Great) into a hundred parts, which to this day are called Hundreds.[8] For each of the Hundreds of the county, a little wooden booth is built, in each of which is a returning officer who collects in a register the votes of everyone in the Hundred and after the polling is over, delivers the register to the sheriff. Each freeholder votes for two candidates. The sheriff counts the number of votes for each candidate, and publicly declares the two with the majority of votes Members of Parliament.

That is all done in admirable order, and one cannot suspect any partiality; even less suspect any corruption. How could even the richest man buy enough votes to gain a majority? What about paying for their travel? It is a recognised practice, and as it is followed by all candidates is no corruption. Formerly, candidates were allowed to provide their supporters with open tables of food: perhaps the differences of hospitality, quantity of wine, etc., affected the decision, harmed their interests. At present, all that is reformed: everyone pays for himself. I think, from everything I have seen, bribery and intrigue may do their utmost, they will be found to have very slight effect on the elections.

When I say 'what I have seen', I speak of something very astonishing to anyone believing there may be corruption in the elections. Sir Charles Bunbury is one of the leading Suffolk gentry, through his family which has always been in Parliament, and through his very considerable wealth: he himself has been a Member of Parliament for the county for

---

[8] These ancient local government districts were called Hundreds for a different reason, and cannot quite be traced back to Alfred the Great, but François may easily be excused for not knowing!

thirty years. He was supported by all the gentry of the county and consequently by the more enlightened part of it. Yet I myself saw him rejected by the farmers and *freeholders*, who barely have the qualifications to vote, and who rejected him because he was in favour of the coalition of Lord North and Mr Fox; these lower orders, ill-informed by bad newspapers, attribute to Lord North, the author of the American War, all the misfortunes that have befallen them; they take no account of his talents, nor of the fact that he had no alternative. The same thing happened to Mr Coke, the richest and best-loved man in England, and to a thousand others: as partisans of the coalition, their political principles were not generally approved.[9] With these examples before my own eyes, I wonder at people who talk of corruption!

The county members are those you address to secure improvements in the county – a canal, a new road, etc. They produce a memorial on the subject and present it to the House of Commons.

The members of the Lower House assemble six weeks after the date when the election was ordered. This gives time for everyone to assemble; then they proceed to business.

*   *   *

The third branch of the legislative power is the King. His title of King puts him first, but I put him third, for I find that, if the King of England holds the third place in the kingdom in terms of authority, that is as much as can be said.[10]

The privileges of the Kings of England, compared with their actual power, demonstrate the vanity which, content with titles without substance, enables men to believe they are 'somebody', that they command others, when in reality those they command obey only if it suits them; and they can do nothing except on those terms.

[9] François began this long political section rather diffidently, but he has perfectly grasped the main point about the great 'popular' General Election of 1784: the majority of ordinary voters were shocked at the cynicism of this coalition between two arch-opponents. A leading Whig and supporter of Fox, 'Mr Coke' withdrew his candidature two days before the election. 'Mr Coke' was also the celebrated farmer on his estates in north Norfolk, and so comes into François' story later. That the electoral defeat happened to 'a thousand others' was an exaggeration, but 160 of Mr Fox's friends failed to re-appear at Westminster. François failed to see that this verdict was a resounding vote of confidence in George III; indeed he could not see how George was a King at all.

[10] It is significant that the son of Louis XVI's Grand Master of the Wardrobe should detect little authority in George III.

I have already mentioned the power of the King of England to dissolve Parliament when he wishes, his power not to re-convene it till after seven years, his power to make war, peace, military appointments, etc., and much else that it would take too long to recite. But really are all these privileges? Does he want to make war? – Parliament withholds the money for it. Does he want to dissolve Parliament? All business stops; the army disbands itself for want of pay; the King having only a Civil List too small to meet his expenses is short of cash; the interruption of affairs creates much disaffection, there is rebellion and perhaps the King abdicates without shedding a drop of blood. He is privileged to choose his ministers: Parliament doesn't like them, and presents an address to the King on their lack of confidence in his ministers. The King persists: another address. Then the two Houses decline to have any more to do with him. The King is stubborn, the Parliament is dissolved, another must soon be summoned: it is against the minister! The King must always give way and royalty is in fact, in England, a will-of-the-wisp who ascends a throne of his own in a democratic state. The real power, that of making the laws and raising the taxes, belongs to the two Houses of Parliament and the King. It is these three together who are what a Frenchman calls King, but the King of England is no king in a Frenchman's eyes.

Although the King shares so unequally in the legislative power, he holds intact in his hands the executive power. He names the judges, Justices of the Peace, sheriffs, officers in the armed forces, and ambassadors, treating with foreign powers in his own name.

The division of legislative and executive power proves obviously that the English government is democratic, without any fear of the disadvantages of a democracy, *coups*, rebellions, etc.; and monarchic, without any fear, in the faintest hearts, of the abuse of power. The rights of King and Parliament are so balanced, so well mixed, that a tendency arises in each to extend its rights, and that, precisely, is the surest guarantee of liberty.[11]

---

[11] Here François is echoing the well-known views of his countryman, the baron de Montesquieu (1689–1755) whose book *l'Esprit des lois* propagated the theory that liberty depended on the complete separation of the legislative, executive and judicial powers in the state: it was based on a somewhat theoretical study of the working of the English constitution. Blackstone, too, said: 'Herein indeed consists the true excellence of the English government, that all the parts of it form a mutual check upon each other.' In

It seems to me well proven that the English government is the most perfect of all: we try to find fault with it, but in vain. The worst seems to be an excess of liberty, but what a pleasant handicap for a people to be too free, above all when all the other parts of the machine are so combined that, although the people may be too free in fact, no part of the machine can cross the boundaries assigned it by the legislature. Those who don't believe that that government is best under which people live most happily should travel in England. If they find ten Englishmen discontented with their form of government, indeed ten who do not believe that it is the most perfect that men have yet created, I will readily agree that it is the worst of all. But if you compare it with that of France, how many thousands of Frenchmen would find their own imperfect, and no one would be enthusiastic in the way the English are for theirs!

Is not one of the proofs of good government the wealth, the opulence, which is demonstrated everywhere, even though individuals are weighed down by taxation? But these taxes, although excessive, are fairly apportioned: no one complains of the taxes, only, sometimes, of their apportionment.

The French province that, to the eye of a traveller, makes the richest impression is Flanders: it is nothing, compared with England. And why is it richer than any other? Because it is not France proper, but alone is treated like a foreign province.

Commerce flourishes everywhere here. Agriculture is held in the highest regard: the labourer is not oppressed, is even treated with consideration by the upper class; the simple peasant, more comfortably off than ours, is well clothed and eats meat every day. Is not all this influenced by government?

One excellent thing is that each individual may help with his own ideas to suggest improvements to government. If he finds something to put right, he produces a memorandum, gives it to a member of the Lower House, who raises the issue. If it is a good idea, genuinely useful,

---

1865, Bagehot's famous work on *The English Constitution* showed that times, and the relative powers, were changed and changing. But even in Blackstone's day it ought to have been perceived what strong administrative functions the Justices of the Peace combined with their judicial ones.

it is adopted, and the humblest person can contribute to the good of his country.

The right of people not to be arrested except for a felony is peculiar to England.[12] If it is found that you were unjustly arrested, you may always take action against the magistrate who has used his power unjustly, and the considerable fine he will be liable to pay will make him cautious about repeating the mistake.

The method of bringing cases to law, and the respect for justice that permeates this country, these are things that have pleased me enormously: being totally new to me, they have struck me the more.

THE ADMINISTRATION OF JUSTICE

The administration of justice in England deserves the utmost praise. I have twice witnessed the equitable manner in which the English proceed, whether in criminal or civil cases, and I can assure you that, almost despite myself, I was full of feelings of respect and admiration.

I have already said that all executive power was in the hands of the King: the law gives him it. Parliament legislates, the King executes the laws. This power does not lie idle in his hands; but as he cannot exercise it himself, he transfers it entirely to six judges whom he appoints annually to administer justice throughout England.[1] These six judges are chosen from among twelve persons steeped in the study of the laws, who form a judiciary body and who have entrance to the Upper House of Parliament not as debaters but to give advice when it is called for. The six annually appointed by the King have each of them a district which they are obliged to visit twice a year. They have £2,500 sterling, which is about 60,000 francs of our money. The government treats them thus well to give them a sort of extra standing, to put them beyond the

---

[12] Blackstone's *Commentaries* first appeared in 1765, but the 4th edition, published in 1770, took full account of the changes in the law following the Wilkes case. Here François had probably been reading Lord Camden's justly famous judgement in *Entick v. Carrington* (1765), establishing the limitation of a Secretary of State to arrest 'from state necessity'. This, and *Habeas Corpus*'s security against wrongful arrest, must have seemed very impressive to an intelligent Frenchman. At p. 89 below, he refers to Blackstone by name.

[1] He seems to be referring to the judicial committee of the Privy Council.

influence of the King who appointed them, and to shelter them against the corruption that might subvert them in the cause of some rich person. They cannot be removed from their commission unless Parliament obtains an order from the King.

The English constitution does not allow a standing army, not even a small number of troops to deal with malefactors, like the Marshal's cavalry (*maréchaussée*) with us. These troops would necessarily be under the King's command and might be used in a *coup* against the Constitution. The troops can no more be maintained, they would become too greatly detested by the citizens; they are already barely tolerated by the people: such a thing would destroy the liberty of the individual, something the English watch jealously. Such troops would never be able to arrest a criminal unless he was caught red-handed: otherwise, a respectable man would run the risk of being deprived unjustly of his liberty; the violence that would sometimes be necessary would prevent the English from believing that no-one can touch them, something of which they are so proud, particularly in front of foreigners.

So they cannot have troops to rid society of the number of scoundrels implicit in it, but they have another, perhaps better, means. The government offers a good sum of money to the person or persons who bring in a wrongdoer together with proofs of his delinquency. The sum is proportionate to the crime or to the means employed in catching the criminal. In this way, a man who would have no desire other than to defend himself is prompted by self-interest to cleanse society. He must have sound proof of the crime of the man he has arrested; for if it turns out that he has neither proof nor legal probability, and no authentication, the accused may, in his turn, bring an action, and exact compensation, for his unjust treatment: the compensation would be money, perhaps a large sum. Proofs of 'legal probability' are a witness and several convincing circumstances; 'authentication' is two or more witnesses.

*   *   *

The accused is brought before a Justice of the Peace. If he finds on the evidence that the accused is guilty, he gives judgement at once: either, if the offence is slight, naming the penalty, or, if it is serious, issuing a warrant, or order, to commit the offender to jail. All these cases are precisely anticipated in Acts of Parliament. The penalties Justices of the

Peace are allowed to impose are light ones: inconsiderable fines, or a few days in jail. If the J.P. issues a warrant, he explains in it the information put before him and the motives that decided him. This will be the foundation of further proceedings against the offender.

Prisons are very healthy in England. Generally, the principle is that they should serve only to secure the persons detained, and not provide their first stage of punishment. So the prisoners there do well, may read and write, work to provide some amelioration of the austerity of their régime, and see their relatives and friends. Most of them live together, with a fire in winter, and are as happy as one can be after losing one's freedom. They cannot remain here very long before their trial; as the judge returns every six months, the longest they may be here is five and a half months. I say 'before their trial' because sometimes the penalty the judge imposes is to remain in prison for one or two years.

The times when the judges come to administer justice in their districts are called Assizes. The time is announced long in advance, by the High Sheriff and by the public newspapers.

The Assizes are held in the towns which have held them from time immemorial; ordinarily in the county town, but not always. Bury for example is an exception to this fairly general rule. The Assizes of Suffolk are held there because from the time when there was an abbey there, before Henry VIII, justice was administered in the abbey.[2]

On the first day of the Assizes, the judge begins by reading his commission, which is a letter from the King, sealed with the Great Seal of England; then he gives a brief address, either on the undesirables he believes to be slipping into the county, or on the administration of justice in general.

It is only on the second day, early in the morning, that the trials begin. The first thing is the reading aloud of the names of all the Justices of the Peace in the county, so that everyone may know them. It is a very old and curious custom that everyone present pays a shilling. Next, the oath is administered to the Grand Jury. The oath they take is

---

[2] In fact, it was administered outside the abbey, on the hill to the east of Bury where François stayed with Professor Symonds. In fact, too, Bury in the Middle Ages lay at the heart of the equivalent of a county within a county: it was called the Liberty of St Edmund.

to be faithful to their religion, their King and country, to act according to their conscience, and to take no account of their private interest.

The Grand Juries are made up of gentry of the county, the more comfortable off and best thought of; they must have an annual rental of at least ten pounds sterling, in lands or property in the county; they are chosen by the High Sheriff and change at each Assize. Care is taken that all the gentry in the county have a turn. There are 120 for each county and at least thirteen must be present at each session; their job is to decide, on examining the warrant of the Jusice of the Peace, whether or not the penalty awarded the accused was justified. They give what is called a *verdict*, which is their decision, written on a small sheet of paper.

In order to concentrate on the proceedings, the Grand Juries have a small room near the Assize court-room, and there they examine all the warrants with full consideration. To return a verdict they must all be of the same opinion: the essential quality of the verdict is that it is signed by all the Grand Jurors present, which sometimes takes a very long time. They are shut up in their room and stay there until the arguments of some bring the others round to their opinion, so that in the end their verdict is unanimous. It has happened that they have taken thirty-six hours. They are allowed nothing to eat and drink but bread and water.

If the Grand Jury, by their verdict, think it would not be just to proceed with a case against an accused person who had been thought guilty, the prisoner is at once set free. If they think the case should proceed, it is begun at once. It is a public court and the whole process takes place in front of everyone. The court is made up of two advocates, the clerk of the court, the Solicitor-General's clerk, and petty juries. The accused stands facing the judge; his fetters are removed so that he may have the air at least of being at liberty; he swears that he will speak the truth.

The judge's bench is always set high up so that he may be seen by everyone: the place for the petty jury is beside him, so that he may speak to them, as I am about to explain.

The petty juries are made up from the farmers, the peasants of the county; they must have land worth ten shillings a year. The High Sheriff chooses them to the number of 110, their names are written on cards and at the beginning of each case twelve are chosen in a kind of lottery; these twelve take an oath before the case is opened, to judge according to their conviction and not to let themselves be seduced by any personal interest; they swear by their religion. They take their seats near the judge, in the customary place, and always listen with the greatest attention. It is they who have to judge the accused.

One cannot believe that there is ever the slightest collusion between petty jurymen and either the accused or the accuser; since their names are drawn by lottery, it happens most often that they do not know each other at all, neither on one side nor the other. One might well believe, also, that as these gentlemen are uneducated and are guided only by a very rough good sense, they are bound to make bad judgements. But careful observations made over a great many years prove that, in a hundred cases, they return ninety-five verdicts according to strict justice; besides, they are directed by the judge, who always gives them his advice before they pronounce. The witnesses and the accuser all take an oath, before the trial, to tell the truth and not be swayed by any personal interest. Oaths quite useless: would they get through a single trial if they were religiously observed?[3]

*   *   *

I have already said that all trials are held in public. The judge interrogates the witnesses and the accused, one after another; he writes down the abridgement of their replies, in order to have a precise summary of the facts. The accused can always have an advocate; when he has one, the advocate speaks in his defence as much as he likes; when the accused cannot afford an advocate, the judge himself serves as one; the accepted understanding is that he must be intent on disclosing the man's innocence, and he never puts the kind of leading questions that are used in France and Italy to trap him and make him contradict himself in his replies.

The accused is able to speak as much as he wishes and to defend himself as best he can; the judge never interrupts him. I actually saw, in one case, the prisoner interrupt the judge three times, and all three times the judge stopped to let him explain himself[4] – a truly touching

---

[3] 'False reflection', François has added here.
[4] Who was this paragon of a judge? At the March Assizes (24–25 March), the judge was Sir George Nares, D.C.L., M.P. (1716–1786), justice of the common pleas from 1771. A number of his judgements were included in Sir William Blackstone's *Reports*, Vol. II. He is said to have been parodied as Sergeant Circuit in Foote's farce, *The Lame Lover*. My guess is that it was he who submitted to the Bury interrupter. At the Assizes

83

compassion, proving how much it is hoped to find the accused innocent!

Those stolen goods that have been recovered and the tools and weapons of thieves and murderers, etc., are always produced in court.

When the judge finds that the evidence is sufficient, or that he has extracted everything that the witnesses and the accused can say, he rises[5] and reads aloud to the petty jurymen his notes on the trial, expounds the law, indicates the most serious points, and gives the reasons for his opinion; he always recommends the jurymen to acquit rather than condemn when there is doubt.

The petty jurymen deliberate among themselves for long or briefly, according to the ease of deciding the case, even arguing it out until they reach agreement: then they can reply *'Guilty'* or *'Not Guilty'*. If the verdict is *Not*, the accused is released at the end of the sitting. If the verdict is *Guilty*, the judge himself pronounces the sentence. The petty jury has judged the accused guilty, and the judge pronounces the penalty the law imposes for the crime. I must remark in passing that, in order to pronounce a sentence of death, the judge must place on his head a small flat four- or five-cornered hat.

The judge has no power to set aside the punishment imposed by the law and already pronounced. Only the King can do that, and he must do it by himself. But the judge may commute the sentence, and change it to something so small that it is like granting a sort of pardon. It is usual for him to pronounce at first the sentence prescribed by law, and to reduce it later: it is very rare for him to enforce it in its full rigour.

THE GOVERNMENT PAYS FOR
THE ARREST OF CRIMINALS

It is the judge who decides on the sum given by the Government to those who arrested the criminal. The sum is always a considerable one.

---

on 31 July, the judge was a very ambitious Scot, Alexander Wedderburn, Lord Loughborough, chief justice of the court of common pleas in 1780, and a famous turncoat. In 1793 he achieved the Woolsack. I don't quite see the Bury prisoner interrupting him three times: I could be wrong. He was once very helpful to Arthur Young (Young's *Autobiography*, pp. 207–8).

[5] One wonders? Surely the court, too, would have to rise? Perhaps they did.

I was present at a trial at the end of which the judge awarded eighty guineas: forty to the person who was robbed, and who called for help, and twenty to each of the two men who seized the two criminals; for there were two robbers, which increased the difficulty of making the arrest, and also increased the reward.

There is always a lapse of time allowed between the sentence of death and the execution. It is a necessary formality because the King may grant a pardon; he is not, however, made to sign death-warrants, except for the London criminals; but his right (to pardon) must be maintained. If he wished, he could always exercise it. What is frightful for the condemned criminals is that they know their sentence and the date of their execution at least a fortnight in advance, except in the case of certain crimes when they are despatched next day.[1] A few days' grace is regarded as merciful. If I were in their shoes, I should think it compassionate to end my life as soon as possible. The judge settles only the approximate date of execution. The day and the hour depend on the sheriff, who is obliged to be present (or, failing him, his under-sheriff).

In civil cases, the procedure is absolutely the same: Grand Jury returning verdicts, petty jury deciding on guilt or innocence. They are directed, perhaps more, by the judge's opinion: at least that is a more circumstantial one. In the summing-up that he reads to them, he is careful to disentangle main facts from all the subordinate ones that could confuse them, even mislead them. Invariably, these civil trials are held in public.

THE JUSTICES OF THE PEACE

I have referred to Justices of the Peace and to Sheriffs, but without explaining what they are. I think this is the time to speak of them: perhaps I should even have begun with them.[1]

[1] In fact, a law passed in 1752 (25 George II, c. 37) ordered that persons convicted of wilful murder be executed on the next day but one after sentence, and the body to be anatomised or hung in chains.

[1] 'The justices of the peace were the most important and the most ubiquitous organ of local government' (Holdsworth, *A History of English Law*, X, p. 128). It seems likely that

The Justices of the Peace are magistrates appointed every year by the King, on the nomination of the Lord Lieutenant of the county. They are chosen from among the gentry, the middle class, and even tradesmen; they take an oath on their religion to exercise their functions with integrity and love of justice. Their number is not fixed and is entirely at the discretion of the Lord Lieutenant.

There are two kinds of Justices of the Peace: those whose jurisdiction extends no further than their towns or villages, and those who exercise their powers throughout the county. The first sort are changed every year, the second are for life. There are a great many of them and they are spread everywhere. They are responsible for seeing that the laws are observed and for fining the transgressors. In all proceedings their evidence is enough, their statements are always sure proof of a mis-demeanour since they were made on oath.

Four times a year, they hold a tribunal known as [Quarter] Sessions, where one of them chosen by themselves presides. There they judge in public the petty criminals: these procedures are similar to those I have described above, petty juries deciding whether the person is innocent. These sessions may not try the higher range of criminals – those whose wrong-doing is finable by more than eight shillings, though sometimes subsidiary misdeeds amount to more. The Justices of the Peace produce at these sessions the warrants they have issued, and usually it is at the sessions that delinquents pay their fines. Those who have broken the laws are required to present themselves to pay what they owe, other-wise the sum, however modest, becomes considerable, and they end up by having their goods seized; or by imprisonment if the goods don't amount to the value of the fine. Such imprisonment is commonly brief, perhaps for a week, and is not in an ordinary prison but in what are called Houses of Correction: there the prisoners are made to work and whipped and chastised as ordered by the judge or Justice of the Peace. I

---

a source of first-hand information to François on this and similar subjects was the first of his acquaintances on arriving in Bury, the Rev. John Ord, D.D., squire of Fornham St Martin, who was for many years one of the four chairmen at Quarter Sessions for Suffolk (and died in 1816). His younger brother, Craven Ord, was a distinguished antiquary, whose visit to Hutchison Mure we notice later (p. 102). Mure and the Ord brothers had uncles, William Mure and Robert Ord, who were barons of the Scottish Exchequer.

shall probably have a chance to see these Houses of Correction in the tour I propose to make through England.[2] I shall describe them then. I cannot do it now on mere hearsay, knowing nothing for sure about them.

The Justices of the Peace are always persons of the best reputation in the county: if they were to hold other public offices and, through misconduct, be obliged to retire from them, the Lord Lieutenant would immediately deprive them of their commissions as Justice of the Peace, even if they were magistrates for the whole county. The object of this wise strictness is certainly to inspire greater respect for these magistrates, who are granted this commission as public proof of their good reputation.

As I said, no Justice of the Peace can refuse to discharge justice, even against his own friends. I referred to it in my description of Sunday and the question of shooting on that day: it is the same in all cases. Any J.P. who refuses either to try a case or to listen to an informer, someone who comes to file a complaint, would be fined £200 sterling. It is not necessary to have much knowledge or education to be a Justice of the Peace, nor even to have made any study of law. They each have a very detailed book, arranged as a sort of index of all the misdeeds known to the law, and their punishment. With that, the only requirement is to be able to read to dispense the law.

THE CONSTABLES

As it is often necessary to inform a man that his misdeed has been observed, that a charge has been laid against him, or that he has been awarded a fine of so much; or it is necessary sometimes to conduct convicts to Houses of Correction; and as the Justices of the Peace cannot perform all that by themselves, they have under them, in all the towns and some of the villages, constables, men appointed from among the small shopkeepers and the people, and paid by the Government. Their job is to carry out the orders of the J.P.s. One is obliged to assist

[2] I hope to edit the journals of this tour and publish them, over the next year or two: N.S.

them in carrying out their duty: anyone refusing may be fined. Their office is in general a disagreeable one, but they are not looked on by the people as tyrants: on the contrary, they are well regarded, and it is rare for the people, even when disaffected, to attack the constables.

These officers have very wide powers; they can imprison and arrest and force one, in suspicious circumstances, to say what one was doing; they keep order in public houses. In a word, their duty is to maintain the peace wherever there is any disturbance.

There are two kinds of constable: the High Constable and the Petty Constable. The first has authority throughout the county, the second in the town or village where they live: they have to watch the safety of the main roads.

They are appointed by the King, usually for life, unless they misconduct themselves.

THE SHERIFF

The Sheriff[1] is the highest officer in the county, representing the King's authority and is in fact his steward. There have been sheriffs from the time of the Saxons: even in their day they exercised a wide authority. The only difference lies in the way they were elected. They were elected by the people of each shire, and it was necessary only that the people's choice was approved by the King; but as these election-assemblies were very uproarious and anyway the kings were very anxious to choose for themselves the officers who managed their affairs, in order to appoint people who would be devoted to them, they ended up by making the choice, not by themselves, but with the concurrence of other well-disposed people. Originally, some counties had hereditary sheriffs. Their powers were so extensive that its inheritance was dangerous to both King and people, and was abolished.

Since the time of Henry VI, the election of Sheriffs has kept the same form as it has today.

[1] The High Sheriff of Suffolk in 1784 was John Wenyeve of Brettenham. Apart from Blackstone's *Commentaries*, it is likely that François consulted Sir Charles Kent, Bart., of Fornham St Genevieve, on the duties of the sheriff. Kent had served as sheriff in 1781, the year before he was created baronet. See p. 25 above.

There is a Sheriff for each county. He holds office for only one year. He is chosen from among those leading gentry of the county who are not Members of Parliament. The same man cannot be Sheriff twice. Every year, on the day after St Martin's Day, the Lord Chancellor, the Chancellor of the Exchequer, the President of the Privy Council and the Earl Marshal choose three gentlemen for each county and take their names to the King who, with a pin, pricks for each county the name of the one he wants. The commission, sealed with the Great Seal, is despatched to him forthwith, he takes the oath and goes to his county. It is generally held, and Blackstone,[2] one of the most celebrated lawyers England has ever had, supports this view, that the King, by virtue of his prerogative, is empowered to choose whichever Sheriff he likes without consulting those persons I have mentioned, who form a council for the purpose. History furnishes only one example where the royal power has exercised its own authority, and that is in Queen Elizabeth's day: by herself she named the Sheriffs for the whole kingdom one year when the plague prevented the usual assemblies at Westminster.

The powers of the Sheriffs are so great that the legality of their election is very important; so it is always done with the concurrence of those four officials as well as three judges. It would perhaps be dangerous for the King nowadays to attempt to appoint the Sheriffs by himself, and not all rulers are sure of being obeyed so strictly as Queen Elizabeth: the enthusiasm she inspired in all England and the despotism she disguised by her extreme popularity may well have allowed her to go further than she was strictly entitled to by prerogative, and a right disputed throughout England would be unlikely to remain one.

The Sheriff judges all causes above a forty-shilling limit. He still has jurisdiction in many other civil matters. It is up to him to decide the qualifications of candidates seeking election in boroughs or counties, as well as those of the electors: he sets the date of the election and presides over it. Holding his office from the King, and in line with the law and the findings of a special commission, he is the chief man in the county while his period of office lasts. He may order the arrest or imprisonment of anyone who disturbs the peace or attempts to do so. He is responsible for tracking down and apprehending all traitors, assassins and other malefactors, and having them jailed: he is responsible for all the

[2] François made good use of Blackstone, but this is his only explicit reference to him.

prisoners and has to be able to produce them. If they happened to escape, he would be heavily fined, for the law puts them in his keeping.

He also has to see to the carrying-out of all the sentences of the courts. For both civil and criminal cases, he chooses the Grand and Petty Juries. To enable him to fulfil all these different duties, the Sheriff has several officers under him: an under-Sheriff, bailiffs and jailers. He has an allowance of £500 a year to pay their various charges. He chooses the under-Sheriff from among the attorneys. This under-Sheriff has to fulfil the Sheriff's functions in almost all cases, for there are very few in which the presence of the High Sheriff is necessary. But so long as he is under-Sheriff, he cannot at the same time practise as attorney; for a year he has to abandon that profession, so as not to betray the interests of the King, the Sheriff or the county.

The bailiffs are in the same position. Their responsibility is to tour the county and gather up the juries at the time of the Assizes, to be present at the sessions to keep order, to accompany the judge and the Justices of the Peace at the Assizes and keep order at all places of assembly. The Sheriff usually employs them to make close enquiry into the whereabouts of vagabonds and deserters, and to arrest them and conduct them to prison. They are very clever at this business: rough characters, the lowest of the government officials, and for that reason armed with a commission from the Sheriff, who is responsible for all their actions.

He is similarly responsible for the conduct of the jailers. They have to keep the prisons in a state of high cleanliness and look after the prisoners, committing to prison only those against whom the warrants of the J.P.s are in order, and legally executed. They have to provide a fire for the prisoners and to protect them against anything dangerous to their health. All these instructions are precisely set out by law, and if the Sheriff neglected them he would face a severe penalty. The fine is ordinarily £200 or £300. That is why care is taken to choose for Sheriff gentlemen of enough means to pay the King and the county any fines he might incur.

It is his duty, when the judge arrives in the Assize town, to go ahead of him at four or five miles distance,[3] with a carriage drawn by four or

---

[3] This must be a mistake – something like 400 or 500 metres was presumably intended, or perhaps 4 or 5 minutes. The word *milles* is plainly written.

six horses, escorted by thirty or forty men in his livery, mounted and surrounding his carriage. The judge climbs into his own carriage and travels at the rear while the Sheriff goes on in front. For the duration of the Assizes, he has to pay all these men, and his carriage is at the disposal of the judge to bring him from his house to the Court and back again. The Sheriff accompanies him all this time in person, and keeps virtually open house, receiving for dinner and supper all the gentry of the county.

Nearly all the leading gentlemen in each county are Sheriffs in their turn; they undertake it with repugnance. It is an honour to have been Sheriff, but being it is very troublesome: nearly all of them suffer some vexation, either because some prisoners get away, or because the people he has responsibility for do something stupid for which he has to pay, etc. For the rest, it is very costly. Generally you reckon that a Sheriff has to spend, on being Sheriff alone, £400 or £500 in the year.

CAMBRIDGE

On 29 May we went to Cambridge, just for three days. Mr Symonds, our friend, who is Professor of Modern History, was still there and was due to return soon after;[1] we wanted to profit by his last few days in residence to see what was to be seen with the advantage of his guidance.

Cambridge is only twenty-seven miles from Bury; one goes through Newmarket,[2] which is about half-way. Cambridge is too famous for its university for foreign visitors to dispense with seeing it. It is extraordinary that only two towns in England should have universities, and that all the young men who have studied in the other parts of the kingdom, should have to come for some time there to take their degrees, whether in medicine or law or in preparation for the church: the two are Oxford and Cambridge. I think there are many advantages: the brightest minds, and, above all, those types of intellect necessary for

[1] Presumably to Bury, after a brief summer term. See p. 16 above. He was a Fellow of Peterhouse.
[2] See p. 50 above.

scholarship, are concentrated in these two places. The young men have less means of getting into mischief[3] and every means of instruction and greater endeavour.

The University of Cambridge is made up of sixteen colleges, all forming one body and having one set of rules for study. But as for the finance and administration of the college, each has its own system; which is natural, because they are all differently endowed. All these colleges were founded by the gifts of kings or of private individuals: their goods are mostly landed estates and very considerable; each has its officials to manage its affairs, and they are numerous.

The college buildings are prodigiously grand and some are really remarkable for architectural nobility. Trinity College is the finest of all, and has two beautiful courts surrounded by buildings, and a great garden. Each college has a library, more or less grand according to its wealth. That of Trinity College is prodigiously large, containing at least thirty thousand volumes, the majority of them scholarly works duplicated in most of the other libraries. This library is built of very beautiful stone, and its ground floor is a very large colonnade which in winter serves as promenade for the whole college.

King's College and Clare Hall are the two colleges that, for magnificence of buildings, rank next to Trinity. They, too, are built of stone, the first in the classical style and a little heavy,[4] the architecture of the second is lighter, but less magnificent.

These three colleges and some others are built on the same side of the town, on the same alignment: they have very beautiful gardens, through which runs the river, which is quite wide. The stone bridges, which face each college, have a very beautiful effect – especially when seen one above the other along the river. Each of the gardens has eight or nine acres planted with great avenues of trees, some of chestnut, some of elm. I saw in the garden of St John's College two sycamores that captured my admiration: perhaps sixty or eighty feet high, and the trunk, three feet above the ground, could be nine or ten feet thick: the branches, spreading out a great distance, give a wide area of shade. Some of the

---

[3] François appears to have been himself quite disinclined to misconduct.
[4] James Gibbs' building, 1723–9, is certainly large and its central portico perhaps a shade heavy, but it needed monumental qualities to stand alongside the chapel.

trees in these gardens would make superb timbers for the Royal Navy, but the colleges who own them would, I imagine, sooner have the shade they give than the entire navy.

Several colleges are very badly built and in general not much to look at: I saw nothing remarkable except at those I have mentioned. I saw the one at which Cromwell was educated,[5] including his room and a pastel portrait of him:[6] there is an expression of sternness, but also rather fine features, and the stern qualities do not obscure the lines of genius and eyes full of fire.

Each college has a chapel. That of King's College is utterly beautiful; vast and raised to a prodigious height, the vault is borne aloft solely by the two side-walls and without the aid of a single pillar, which is perhaps unique for this type of building, and a most difficult feat of construction: it was built in the time of Henry VI (or of our Charles VII).[7] The woodwork of the choir is very fine, the style of its carving remarkable.[8] I climbed right up to the top of the chapel, on to the roof – all of lead – in order to see from there the town and all the colleges: they make a delightful picture. The timber-work of this building[9] is prodigiously light and admired by the experts who come to see it from afar.

As well as the individual college libraries, there is one for all the university teachers, who can come and take out books merely by giving their names: it is extremely large, containing nearly 80,000 volumes, among which various manuscripts are valuable for their antiquity. This library building is of stone, fine architecture in the classical taste.[10] You see another building in this court, also of stone, and of a lighter design though equally noble: it is the Senate House where the young men who wish to take their degrees sustain their theses. The building is large, about eighty feet by thirty, I should think, and the elevation appro-

[5] Sidney Sussex College.

[6] This must be the portrait given to the college in 1766 and now pronounced by J. W. Goodison to be 'probably after Sir Peter Lely': number 155 in 'The Catalogue of Portraits in Christ's, Clare and Sidney Sussex Colleges', *Camb. Antiquarian Records Society*, 1985.

[7] In fact it was begun under Henry VI, in 1448, and completed a century later, in 1547, after three main bouts of activity.

[8] Renaissance work, 1533–6, having the initials of Henry VIII and Anne Boleyn.

[9] He means the roof-timbers.

[10] This is now known as the East Range of the Old Schools: it was designed in the Palladian way, 1754–8, by Stephen Wright.

priate: it is adorned with several marble statues by a Frenchman named Roubiliac, one of them representing the duke of Somerset.[11]

The same sculptor has done still more superb statues which one sees in various Cambridge colleges. The most remarkable is that of Newton, in Trinity College chapel. The most inexpert cannot help admiring so fine a statue; the face and, above everything, a superb flowing robe, fastened at the neck and descending the whole length of the back to the ground, are features of a work that is beyond all description.[12]

But we return to the Senate House. There is a gallery right round the cornice[13] for the public to listen to the dissertation of theses: it is of wood and very well carved. It is in this hall that the elections of members of Parliament for the university of Cambridge are held, for each college has a certain number of votes according to its importance: each college chooses delegates to vote for its candidates.

Cambridge has produced England's greatest men. All of them have studied in its colleges except [blank],[14] who was at Oxford. It would take a long time to recite their names, and you will readily excuse me. But I do find it odd that, of two universities conducted more or less the same way and recognised in the same way by the Government, the smaller has produced the greatest men that England can name, and the larger can name only one who does England honour. Oxford University is very much larger, being made up of twenty-four colleges.[15] As to the syllabus of studies of the young men I have seen there, I can say nothing. It is a particular arrangement and extremely hard to understand; I confess I found it impossible to follow a word of it; I have a vague idea but am unable to express it coherently. I put a great many questions to Mr Symonds about it. M. de Lazowski himself set down

---

[11] François' guess is not far out: the interior measurements of James Gibbs' Senate House, 1722–30, are 99 × 42 feet. He is rightly proud of Roubiliac, but this statue of Somerset was carved by Rysbrack, 1756, who came from Antwerp.

[12] It is widely known through Wordsworth's description of it in *The Prelude*. Roubiliac's ten other works in Cambridge are all to be found in Trinity College.

[13] Of the (ground-floor) first storey.

[14] In his manuscript of his travels through England the following year, François named Locke as Oxford's contribution. It may be that he was slightly prejudiced by his East Anglian friends, like Professor Symonds!

[15] In fact twenty-one in 1784, but that still leaves Cambridge with only two-thirds of Oxford's number of colleges. This is a well-worn subject for argument between the two.

several questions for him in writing on the subject, to which he should have replied, but he has so far not done so. Although he is a professor in one of the colleges, he does not understand the regulations and is obliged to have recourse to old books, read up the origins of the university, etc., so that we cannot have any answers to our questions for three or four months, by which time we shall not be here.[16] That is what decided me to describe my trip to Cambridge without details of the syllabus of studies, the most interesting subject! Perhaps when we go to Oxford we shall find someone there better informed on that matter than Mr Symonds, who at least will put me in the way of speaking of it.[17]

The colleges and especially their garden walks make up the chief ornament of Cambridge. Otherwise, the town is very depressing, poorly built, and the streets narrow; only one little square for the market gives any relief. The provisioning of the colleges and the money they expend makes a livelihood for the whole countryside around: there is no [other omitted] trade in the town.

For this little journey we made use of the post-chaises I have already described (p. 5 above), carriages gentlemen normally use for travel. They are extremely convenient and go very fast, but they are very dear: for in addition to the charge of 11 [old] pence [*sols anglais*] a mile, which are 22 French sols, you have to give the postilion one and a half shillings every twelve or fifteen miles when you change postilions; and you have to pay the *tournepeaks*, barriers where you pay a toll for the use of the

[16] Mr Symonds had met his match. The last few words give some clue to the time when François was writing this passage. They originally planned to leave Bury, to tour England, after Bury Fair in October, but were delayed by illness. So I think these Cambridge notes were written immediately, in May–June, and copied out word for word the following January before their big tour.

[17] It is curious that François makes no reference here to their introduction by Symonds to Richard Watson, bishop of Llandaff, who was Regius Professor of Divinity. He had also been a lively professor of chemistry, and one would have thought his intelligence and varied talents would have interested the young Frenchmen and their tutor. The story comes in Arthur Young's *Autobiography* (1898 edn, pp. 123–4). Lazowski, 'an infidel', according to Young, 'never lost himself so completely as when he entered into an argument upon the truth of Christianity with the bishop of Llandaff, for though civilly done, the bishop ground him to powder!' Speaking French with difficulty, the bishop began by addressing them in Latin. 'The Frenchmen of course replied with plenty of bows and grimaces . . . and he was compelled to address them in his broken French . . . relaxing his episcopal dignity, he conversed with them at ease, and quieted their ruffled spirits.' Perhaps one sees why the episode was not reported home.

road, sometimes a very heavy toll. Between Bury and Cambridge, only twenty-seven miles, there are four of these toll-houses. At three of them you pay 6 [old] pence, and at the fourth 9 [old pence], making a total of 27 [old] English pence, or 54 French sols, merely for the use of the road. That is excessive.

THE NUMBER OF TRAVELLERS ON ALL THE ROADS

You cannot imagine the quantity of travellers who are always on the road in England. You cannot go from one post to another without meeting two or three post-chaises, to say nothing of the regular diligences.

POST-HORSES AND HORSES FOR HIRE IN BURY

I can give some idea of this great wheel-traffic only by giving the list of post-horses of Bury alone. Bury is on the road from London to Norwich, but this is the only main road that goes through it.[1] There are 125 horses, for the post and the diligences, at the service of the town. I had the count made for me by one of my friends, who has certainly done it accurately: if he has erred, it can only be on the low side, for there is a duty on horses, and innkeepers have an interest in saying they have fewer than they actually have. Above this great number of horses, you can reckon at least fifty more hacks to let, either as saddle-horses or for cabriolets.[2] Saddle-horses cost two shillings for an occasional hire, and three when you take them for the day to go on a trip for two or three days. Cabriolet-horses, with the cabriolet, cost four shillings the occasional hire and five for the day when you are going on a journey. The saddle-horses are passably good, their saddles and bridles smart enough. The cabriolets are much more so, the harness always good and the

[1] In fact the main London–Norwich turnpike ran through Newmarket and Thetford, missing Bury by a dozen miles; but it says much for Bury's liveliness and prosperity that its road-links with London and Norwich gave François the impression that this was the main London–Norwich road.
[2] Cabriolets were gigs with hoods.

horse passable. You have, by these three ways of travelling, the utmost convenience in going from one place to another, and above all in going comfortably. I don't even find the prices very exorbitant. When you take a post-chaise to go out to dinner or see someone in the country, five or six, even ten miles away, you pay from five to eight shillings, according to the distance. These post-chaises are more reliable, and one makes more use of them, than the other carriages: you can use them even for paying visits in the town. Certainly, we have nothing in France so convenient in a small provincial town.[3]

OUR ESTABLISHMENT AT BURY

I explained (p. 17) that at Bury we had half a house where we did our own cooking and where, in a word, we set up our small household. The house cost us two *louis* and three *livres*[1] a week and was extremely convenient. Three rooms and a kitchen on the ground floor and three on the first, with two servants' rooms, made up our apartment; they were well, or rather very neatly, furnished. One of our servants did our cooking and a woman helped him, washing the dishes, etc.: it was more for the sake of appearance and because Mr Symonds practically forced us to take her that we had this woman: she was not much use to us except for going to market – for our Frenchmen would never have been able to make themselves understood. This was a much better arrange-

---

[3] This is the best place to recall an anecdote in Young's *Autobiography* (1898, pp. 121–2) describing the duc's visit to his sons during the late spring: 'Soon after his arrival in England, hearing that there were such carriages at Bury as were called buggies, and desiring to make use of all sorts, he ordered one to be hired to convey him and Lazowski to Bradfield. On its coming to the door, Lazowski perceiving that it was drawn by one horse only, it ran upon the quarter [a part of the horse's foot]: he would have persuaded the Duke not to attempt driving, as it would be 20 to 1 that he would overthrow it; but the Duke, full of presumption, held such prudential advice in contempt, and, whipping away, had not gone half a mile in a cross road before he overturned the carriage and the fall dislocated his shoulder. The Duke was conveyed to Symonds . . . and expressed no more desire to drive carriages he had never seen.'

[1] If the *louis* was approximately a guinea (cf. p. 41, fn. 4), their rent was a little over £5 a week.

ment than if we had been boarding with an English family, and we had the pleasure of inviting our friends to dine with us from time to time.

I must not forget to mention here how kind to us the owners of the house were, who lived in the other half of it: this meant that we had company all the more agreeable because we could go there when we pleased, and I think it contributed not a little both to my progress in speaking English and to our spending very agreeably time that might have been irksome.

In very little time we found that we knew all the people of Bury and, as we made progress in the language, so we became more familiar with them. We could, at the end of four months, be regarded as inhabitants of Bury; but with our own way of close-speaking, which showed everyone that we were not even inhabitants of England.

THE CLIMATE

The winter has been as hard in Suffolk as in other parts of Europe. The severity of the season was general and the winter of [the early months of] 1784 will long be remembered. The ground was covered with snow for so long and the snow fell so often that we could not go out for walks.

OUR PLEASURES DURING THE FIRST WINTER

Our greatest pleasure, all this time, was to play billiards, and we often repeated it. The billiard room at Bury is very good.[1] It was set up by subscription, the chief persons of the town have each given two guineas towards the billiard table which cost sixty. It is made entirely of mahogany.[2] It is farmed out to a man who charges a few pence for each game and pays for the upkeep of the table and the lease of the room. The subscribers have forbidden him to let in anyone but themselves

[1] Was it one of the assembly-rooms? Efforts to locate it from contemporary newspapers have so far failed.
[2] And, presumably, slate?

and reliable visitors, so that it was courteous of them to let us play. I have gone on so fully about the way the billiards room was set up to give you an example of the interest that individuals in England have in promoting the good, or the pleasure, of the public; for the subscribers pay like the rest and have no privileges.

We went daily to see Mr Symonds, who lives a mile from the town, up on a hill to the east. Even when he was at Cambridge[3] we continued our regular walks in this direction, because we would go to collect his nephew either for a walk when the weather permitted, or just to see him at home, or to bring him back to town. How many times we visited that house walking in snow half-way up our legs!

Generally, we would go out to dinner in the town once or twice a week: it was our sole treat, and not very lively, for, as a rule, the dinners were rather solemn and we seldom found any young people there.

AT HOME WITH MR SYMONDS

When we got back from Cambridge, we left our house in Bury in order to move in with Mr Symonds, who took us *en pension*; it was not without regret. We had been very free, going to see anyone we liked, or who came to see us; and in giving up that manner of life we accepted the limitations of seeing only members of the circle of Mr Symonds, who lives almost always on his own and whose conversation is sometimes on the heavy side. Despite these considerations, we abandoned our initial liberty, persuaded that living habitually with an Englishman and speaking with the members of his household would force us to speak English even among ourselves – which we had not been doing – and make more rapid progress. Our manner of living in this house was very joyless as we had well imagined. Committed to being very often with our host, we were obliged to listen daily, and sometimes twice a day, to narratives of a long journey he had made in Italy, and that he was writing down and sending to the printer daily.[1] One may imagine the

---

[3] In term-time.

[1] They were observations on Italian agriculture that he had made back in the 1760s, and was re-modelling for Vols I and III of Arthur Young's great new monthly series, *Annals of Agriculture*, of which 46 volumes appeared down to 1806. Young himself wrote

vanity of a man who falls half-asleep after dinner and has everyone yawning with sitting so long at table . . .

We each had at his house a very pleasant room, but to reach it had to climb sixty-four stairs, four or five times a day. The hours of our meals were strictly fixed: at nine, breakfast; at three, dinner; at nine in the evening, supper. But what vexed me most was that the rule of the house prevented me from going out for a walk after nine in the evening, and that the doors were shut and locked at that hour (Pl. 17).

The distance from the town – which was not very great, for I could usually walk it in ten minutes – was enough to stop me going there often, and little by little led to our neglecting our friends. One thinks twice about going to a town, and for every three times we would have gone out visiting if we had been actually living in town, we stayed at home at least once because we were in the country.

OUR ACQUAINTANCES

Springtime brought a great many people back to the country, and our acquaintance increased accordingly. Mr Mure[1] was the first of them. He is a prodigiously rich old man; his family is Scottish; but although the elder branch is fairly affluent, he himself was so poor that for some years he was a carpenter or joiner; all the wealth he has acquired is due to his successful speculations and his commercial talents. He is at

---

of 'the admirable essays of my valuable friend Mr Professor Symonds upon Italian agriculture, the most perfect specimens' (C. Maxwell ed., *Travels in France*, Cambridge, 1929, p. 1), and the great musicologist Dr Burney, a connection of Young's by marriage, wrote to him: 'Mr. Symonds' Essays on Italian Husbandry are extremely curious, and furnish a species of information totally different from what can be acquired from any other author.' (*Autobiography*, ed. Betham-Edwards, p. 144.)

[1] François excusably spelt him More, and hitherto his editors have followed this spelling, so failing to identify him. François' description makes it clear beyond question that this is Hutchison Mure, the rebuilder of Great Saxham Hall. Furthermore, François' description explains the curious plan of the Hall, which had hitherto baffled interpretation. Great Saxham lies 4 miles west of Bury.

17. St Edmund's Hill, Bury, home of Mr Symonds. Notice the window-bow.

18. Culford Hall, before its rebuilding in 1796. Home of Lord Cornwallis.

present so rich that no-one knows what he has. One believes him . . .
[*sic*] but as the principal part of his wealth is in plantations in the West
Indies, the income from it increases and diminishes all the time according to good or bad management. For some years he has taken in hand a
lot of his land and farmed it himself: he is said to be an excellent farmer.
His crops have been superb. This year, he wants to introduce a new
species of cabbage into this neighbourhood as good winter-keep for his
animals.[2]

Mr Mure's house is a curious building in the middle of a big, ill-kept
park: a year ago it was the stable of a house that had been burnt down,
he added two wings to it, and so created a building that is bizarre
without being disagreeable; except for the middle section, all the rest
has no first floor. The ground floor, which is very large, furnishes all the
rooms, the English needing a great many; for the one used for breakfast
is not used for dinner, and the reception-rooms are scattered about
informally.[3] The garden is agreeable enough, without being very well

[2] The elder branch, Mure's uncle William, was indeed affluent, as a baron of the
Scottish Exchequer. Uncle William's political involvement with Bute and Argyll,
among the earliest patrons of Robert Adam, explains, perhaps, Hutchison Mure's
obtaining plans from the great architect in March and April 1779, before going ahead
with his own design. In April 1783, when Mure was starting work, the Earl Bishop
wrote from Londonderry to Arthur Young: 'Mure I knew always to be a prince in his
ideas: I am glad to hear he is able to be so in his works.' (*Autobiography of Arthur Young*,
1898, p. 114.) In a letter to *Country Life*, 1 January 1987, Mrs Diana Phillips, working on
a biography of a Jamaican sugar-planter who was familiar with the business of Mure,
Son & Atkinson, says he attributed Mure's failure to 'the keeping of four expensive
Houses, each more extravagant than the other, at the same time that they had thrown
away their business!'
[3] In 1774, Mure had castellated the 5-gabled Elizabethan house, possibly in emulation
of his uncle's house in Ayrshire. When it burnt down in 1779, a new house was begun
'from a plan of Mr. Adam but was not proceeded with. Mr. Hutchison Mure now
resides in a very good house built from a plan of his own.' This was recorded in 1788 by
Craven Ord (B.L. Add MSS. 7101 fol. II), an admirable antiquary and younger
brother of François' first visitor, Rev. John Ord, on their arrival in Bury. But without
François, we should not know that the site of the stables of the old (south-facing) house
provided the platform of the present house. This perfectly explains the long, lateral
entrance-hall running north–south, leading into the principal rooms which all face east,
except the main drawing-room, properly at the south end of the house. He had not
practised house-carpentry for nothing. (For the building, see John Gage, *Hist. and
Antiquities of Suffolk: Thingoe Hundred*, 1838, pp. 107–110; N. Scarfe, *Proc. Suffolk Inst. of
Archaeology*, 1955, pp. 230–231; and Julia Abel Smith, *Country Life*, 27 November 1986,
pp. 1698–1702, a delightful article, concluding that Mure designed his own house 'with
a little inspiration from Adam's plans.')

kept; there is a lake and a river which create a good effect.

Mr Mure is a great amateur of the arts and of new inventions. In this field, he showed us several extremely curious instruments: one is for drawing reliably a long perspective from nature; another is a little box, about as big as a snuff-box, which he puts in his carriage and connects to one of the wheels, and so measures with the greatest accuracy the distance of all the places he goes to; and he showed us a sort of inch measure marked off in perfectly accurate divisions, and very useful for astronomy and navigation. The artist who made it has a machine by which he can make these divisions in a moment.

This house is not really very cheerful, although there are young people. Mr Mure's daughter and sons didn't seem to me to be very fond of laughing.[4] The worst drawback there in going to dinner with Mr Mure is the great length of time he stays at table, generally three and a half hours. I once sat there five hours, without leaving the table, just eating and drinking. As the ladies leave, he forgets himself and keeps us there no end of a time.

Lord Cornwallis spent the summer at his house three miles from Bury. The house is just like a great square lantern, for the four fronts are so similar that the first time we were there we didn't know which side contained the entrance. The number of windows is immense. The house was built in the time of Queen Elizabeth, altogether in the Gothic taste (Pls. 18 and 19).[5]

[4] The young people's seriousness may have been a response to living with 'a prince in his ideas': their ingenious and speculative father was declared bankrupt at the end of 1793, and at 83 the shock proved too much for him. The estate was sold to the Rev. Thomas Mills, who raised the single storeys to double ones and added, in the centre at the rear, a three-storeyed music-room, octagonal, the ceiling delicately painted with medallions containing the muses. I have found no illustration of Mure's house as it was during the brief period 1784–1793, as the French knew it.

[5] Culford Hall – François rightly thought of it as a *château*, not necessarily a castle – had been built c. 1586–91, by Sir Nicholas Bacon of Redgrave, rich and powerful eldest son of Elizabeth's Lord Keeper, presumably to be better able to keep a political eye on Bury. He left it to his seventh son, Sir Nathaniel, the painter and naturalist. Through his widow, beautifully commemorated in Culford church, it passed to the family of her first husband, Sir William Cornwallis of Brome. Unluckily François' friend, the noble old Marquess Cornwallis, pulled down the Elizabethan house c. 1796, and replaced it by the rather dull white-brick block designed by the Bury mason Robert de Carle the younger: this was used to illustrate the earlier editions of this book. The tall, spectacular redbrick building François used to visit was probably the best-designed Elizabethan house in Suffolk.

CHARLES EARL CORNWALLIS. 1783.

19. *Charles, Earl Cornwallis, 1783. Thomas Gainsborough.*

Lord Cornwallis is generally regarded as a most excellent man and the best of neighbours; the best of husbands and fathers; the respect people feel for him in this neighbourhood is general. Nor do people deny his great talent in the military field: his most temperate supporters regard him as third among England's generals; his keenest supporters rank him with the other two. What is certain is that if England had sent to India a man with vice-regal powers, it would have been Cornwallis.[6] In the late war he was taken prisoner by the French and the Americans, and he says he was so well-treated by the French officers that that is one more reason to show his gratitude to all Frenchmen: to us he has shown extraordinary kindness. In early spring he gave orders to his gardener to bring us the produce of his garden until the time when, as he said, we should come and eat it with him at his home; and we had the benefit of this for a long time.

He is straightforward in his manner, and is not at all formidable. We have always been extremely well treated by him, whenever we have been to see him.

Sir Charles Davers is Lady Bristol's brother. He is a member of Parliament for Bury, and very much liked in the town because people see that his conduct is always guided by respectability, and that they can rely on his always acting in accordance with his principles. He is a very kind man, but one who pays no compliments and doesn't like having them paid to him. He lives a mile and a half from Bury, in a great house which he maintains rather badly, without caring. His park is also neglected: if the grass didn't grow naturally there, there wouldn't be any (Pl. 20).[7]

We kept all our old friends, and the new ones did not distract us from them. There were a great many of them, and although I name only a few, you are not to believe that we had no others. But to give the names of everyone we got to know and to describe the characters of them all would be a long business and of very little general interest.[8]

---

[6] This happened to the old man in 1805, and he died there, doing his duty.

[7] Rushbrook Hall was a great moated 3-sided Elizabethan house of the late 1570s, with the north range doubled in width *c.* 1735, soon after this primitive painting, Pl. 20.

[8] Alas, no: two centuries later, *we* want to know everything about his wide acquaintance in Bury. He may be equating his father with 'general interest'.

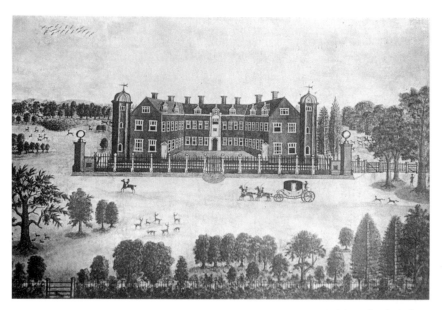

20. Rushbrook Hall, home of Sir Charles Davers. Provincial, primitive, shortly before c. 1735. (From Rushbrook Parish Registers, Woodbridge, 1903)

I have spoken of the inconveniences I experienced in living under Mr Symonds' roof, and the boredom of his long disquisitions, but I haven't yet said anything of the advantages we enjoyed there. First, and very considerable, was living with a very kind man. All he seemed to desire all the time was to give us pleasure and all possible attention. A large garden, and the country around, were constant inducements to go for walks, from which living in the town would have discouraged us; books in English and French in a well-chosen library were there for us to choose from, and our host had the goodness to correct our translations and compositions that we brought to him daily after breakfast. Some of the acquaintances we made through him can be reckoned among the benefits. One of the greatest pleasures he liked to offer us, and which became one of the greatest bores, was to be at home every Tuesday to anyone who wished to come and take tea and play cards. But these assemblies were laced with a certain dignity, the master receiving his visitors in rather too stiff a manner, so that everyone deserted after the second or third Tuesday. The old ladies came, but after that not a single young person. All those who could have made these after-dinner parties amusing never came, and the best I could hope for was a game of whist. What was to be done among a set of wrinkled and serious faces, licensed by age to think themselves very superior to me, and who – whether by a sort of natural disdain or by habit and a distaste for conversation – said nothing worth saying? Such were our pleasures for eight months.[9]

THE CLIMATE

The weather has been invariably unpleasant except for the one month of May: we could never count on having two fine days running: rain came regularly every alternate day in great abundance, and the intervening days were cold, with winds or fog making them worse than the wet days. What a frightful climate! This is said to be the driest part of England. A series of observations made by I don't know whom should persuade us, say Mr Symonds and several other English, that it doesn't rain more here than in France and that in France the climate is more or less the same. I protested in vain that I had never seen more frightful

---

[9] There is an awkward conflict of evidence here. Addressing all this to his father, he perhaps naturally makes no reference to his father's visit to them in the late spring. Arthur Young recorded in his *Autobiography* (ed. Betham-Edwards, 1898, pp. 154, 121) a delightful visit they all paid to his friends the Plampins, a family long settled at Chadacre, three miles from his home at Bradfield and in 1988, appropriately, a successful farm-training centre and institute: 'At Chadacre, six miles from Bury, resided John Plampin, Esq., who had three daughters, all at this time unmarried and at home. [There was also a son, 22, already well advanced on an enterprising naval career: see *DNB*.] I was intimately acquainted with them. Two of these ladies were much distinguished by their beauty . . . I introduced my friend Lazowski to them, and he was much at Chadacre, admiring not a little the youngest of them. They persuaded their father to give a ball, at which the duc de Liancourt, his two sons, Lazowski and myself were present, and the evening passed with uncommon hilarity till the rising sun sent us home.' Then Young continues: 'Mr. Symonds afterwards gave a weekly ball when the Frenchmen were with him, and these parties were uncommonly agreeable.' If Young was not mistaken, and it seems unlikely that he was, then one can only wonder why François painted so unconvivial a picture of his host. During this visit, the duc came a cropper in a buggy (p. 97 above). The saloon at Symonds' house, designed for him by Robert Adam in 1773, with twin-columned screens at either end, and a large bow overlooking Bury, would have been ideal for a small ball. It survives in what is now a private Catholic school, very much rebuilt (see Pl. 17, and end papers).

weather repeated day after day, and that it was sometimes warm in France . . . They replied that summer had never before been like this over here and that we should have a better autumn. A lovely consolation! Meanwhile we have had a fire nearly all summer, and the month of August has consumed as much coal in England as October consumed wood in France.

As this district is sandy country, the farmers are happy with the wet weather, the crops are very fine. But what does that matter to me? I have no interest, direct or indirect, and shall not make a sou by them. If wheat is abundant, a tax will be put on something else, it will all even out in the end; on the other hand, I would gain immeasurably more by having some fine weather.

A GARDEN-WALK OF MY DESIGN

The bad summer weather often prevented us from taking any exercise. In a moment of stress and boredom occasioned by having to stay indoors, day in, day out, I proposed in jest to Mr Symonds that we should make him a new garden-walk. He took me at my word, and next day I started to trace it out. Some days later, experts in the design of garden-walks came to see us and made a few corrections (but very few) to my plan; in a short time, our work started. Our two servants and my brother and myself worked three hours a day, from six to nine, before breakfast, and we put all our strength into it: thus the need for movement and exercise turned us into manual labourers in England. The path is half a mile long and 4 feet wide, we had to dig it through pretty thick turf made very compact by the foul weather. We worked on it for fifteen mornings and to our honour and glory it was finished. I myself could not have a hand in the completion, as I became quite seriously ill. But that was how, combining the practical work with the theory developed in conversations on the subject, I contrived to learn the art of the English garden and to prepare myself in case, one day, I feel like creating one in France.

A TOUR IN SUFFOLK[1]

Mr Young, of whom I have spoken, becoming one of our best friends, suggested joining us for a 5 or 6-day tour that we ought to make in the county where we were living. The suggestion was so agreeable that it was accepted with one voice and many thanks, and we prepared to leave in two days' time, on 21 July.

M. de Lazowski and Mr Young hired a cabriolet, and my brother and I went on horseback: no servants, for we travelled as farmers and people wanting to learn. We went first to Sudbury, on the road[2] to London. As far as this town, the road is agreeable, especially at the approaches: the road passes through a very beautiful and very long village called Melford. So far, the soil is clay, the fields are not well enclosed, and in general the farming has a slight air of neglect, although this is the time of year when the earth presents its finest fruits: I saw none of those crops that, in response to the efforts of a hard-working farmer, give pleasure even to the ignorant traveller.[3]

After Melford, the agriculture improved. The entire village of Melford is built along the main road, which makes it seem even bigger than it is: its houses are all well built, and the air of prosperity is obvious: the landscape composed of patches of verdure and varying groups of trees and of houses is very cheerful, and everything, down to

---

[1] 21–26 July, 1784. Arthur Young published his own description of it, 'A 5-days tour to Woodbridge, &c.' in his *Annals of Agriculture*, Vol. II, 1785; it was republished in Vol. XIV of the French edition of his works ordered by the Directory in 1801 – *Le Cultivateur Anglois*.

[2] One of the roads from Bury to London.

[3] Lazowski's commentary, addressed to 'mon ami', almost certainly the duc de Liancourt himself, was transcribed by M. Jean Marchand from the original belonging to the late M. Ferdinand-Dreyfus and which I have been unable to trace. I owe the transcript to the kindness of Mlle. Françoise Marchand. Where Lazowski's notes amplify François' description usefully, I have translated them as footnotes, often at some length. Here he adds: 'The farms are small-holdings of from 20 to 60 acres. These are labourers who, having acquired a little capital, set up as farmers, and who are not in a position to make the large improvements demanded by good farming. The methods are bad – those of France – the land is idle and one sees wastelands . . . Round here, the land looks very different from what our eyes are used to: farmhouses show no sign of prosperity, and 'les cottages' are neither numerous nor clean: but I don't want to amuse myself with reasons – it's up to you to draw your conclusions, and to me to give you the material by furnishing you with facts.'

the smallest wooden huts, is painted up and carefully maintained: fences and palings painted white surround the house and small garden which always has some flowers. In a word; always a marked superiority in the houses of the English lower classes over those of the poor French peasants, which it has so often been painful to observe.[4] On reaching Sudbury, we had breakfast and sent out to look for a manufacturer who instructed us a little in the town's trade and its population.

It is a very singular thing, and one which the best informed people would be hard put to it to explain: how it is that the population of towns varies so in the quality of its inhabitants: and why is it that all the classes of citizens are not spread through every town and why some are inhabited only by the dregs of the people and sharks? One remembers, I am in England where the nobility and gentry who live for two or three months in the year in the capital spread themselves evenly through the provinces and around all the towns.

The countryside round Sudbury is agreeable enough, the hills and vales offer agreeable prospects, and yet the town and its neighbourhood are inhabited only by people with no fortune, by smugglers and bankrupts, etc.; it is a misfortune I cannot explain, but it is certain that there isn't a respectable man in the place![5]

There is a considerable trade here in woollens and silk stuffs. The latter are all for the London market, being funded by merchants from the capital who get the work done here at the lowest rates: there are about a hundred looms at work.

There is a much greater number of woollen looms – I'm not sure how many: the manufacturer was not able to tell us. The cloths are coarse and thin, a kind of double serge, good for clothes for working women: they come in lengths of between 27 and 40 yards (the yard is three feet).

The trade of the town is as considerable as it can be: that is to say all hands are employed in it. Even new hands would find work here. In the time of the American War it languished and was reduced almost to

---

[4] Lazowski's comment was: 'It is impossible to give you an idea of any comparable village in France, unless it is in the province of Flandres, and there they are not so beautiful.' Lazowski merely mentioned Long Melford Hall, 'built in the reign of Elizabeth judging by its style': a good guess though it was mostly built in Mary's reign, in the 1550s.

[5] This judgement may be thought to be less than well-founded after so brief an acquaintance! Indeed it is partly contradicted by the following paragraphs.

nothing; but it has recovered its former vigour. They say, though, that as for camlets and calendered cloths, France is beginning to take their business.[6]

The workman is paid between 12 and 16 shillings a week: the shilling is 24 French *sous*.[7]

Round the outskirts of the town, land rents are 12 shillings an acre.

From Sudbury we were to get to Colchester for dinner. The road was even more agreeable, the countryside very varied and the soil becoming more and more sandy. I saw a lot of land that had not been cleared and was covered with a kind of pale green bracken, which suggested a very poor soil.[8] However, nearby there are other poor lands producing good crops and proving the advantages of enclosures, which are generally recognised: as much to enable animals to be put in to enrich the land as to conserve moisture in it.

Here the farms are large, bringing in two or three hundred pounds sterling a year, and there are few small ones. They have a four-year rotation of crops: 1st year, turnips (a kind of root-crop); 2nd, barley; 3rd, clover which was sown with the barley;[9] 4th, wheat; and the land

[6] Lazowski adds important details. The serges go for working-women's clothes in some parts of England, but 'this demand is nothing compared to the quantity exported to Spain, which takes all the produce of this factory.' He explains that it was the Spanish entry into the American War (in 1778) that caused much unemployment here: until then, the American War had not affected it. He also explained that the serges were made with a kind of long-haired wool not found in France, that was not carded but combed for spinning. He groaned about restrictive practices at Lyons, confining the silk factories to the town and forbidding the work in the countryside around: 'for it is impossible to conceal from oneself that, in silk-making, the advantages are all on our side.' Then he adds this: 'Despite their busy woollen manufacture and the new silk draperies, they complain at Sudbury that France has prodigiously increased its woollen manufacture and smuggled over the English wool. We owed this expression of grievance to the silence we had kept until then, while Mr Young put the questions: they hadn't yet tumbled to the fact that we were French, and so gave rein to their indignation. This is well-founded: it is impossible to deny that there is considerable smuggling of wool in Suffolk: yet their resentment is the result of a prejudiced misunderstanding.'
[7] Lazowski's note here: 'Like our pound, the pound sterling is made up of 20 shillings, each worth only 23 to 23½ sous.' Young adds that the say weaver got 10–12 shillings a week if good, many got less, and that silk was made here through dearness of labour at Spitalfields: no baize, but calamancoes at Lavenham.
[8] Dinner, remember, was an afternoon meal. There are patches of glacial sand: he was probably noticing Leavenheath, Boxted Heath, Horkesley Heath and Mile End Heath.
[9] Arthur Young reckoned this four-course, or Norfolk, system one of the best ever invented, 'but to sow clover with that second barley, and then wheat again on that

never lies fallow. The turnips are used for fattening the cattle and sheep, most of which are sent to London.

I saw near the road six very nice houses belonging to the gentry.[10]

The road does nothing but rise and dip, in some places it is shaded by very tall trees.[11] Our horses went very well, considering they are hired: only the cabriolet-horse, tired by going up-hill, began to need a touch of the whip.

We went through Nayland,[12] a large village situated on the same little river as Sudbury. It has been made very navigable, carrying great quantities of coal.[13] The houses in the little town are well built.[14]

---

clover: this is very bad for it fouls the land' (*General View of the Agriculture of Suffolk*, 1797, p. 36).

[10] Lazowski amplifies: 'From this road you see a number of cottages, neat, well-built, with little gardens enclosed by fences of differing designs but all painted grey-white. French eyes used to miserable labourers' cottages can hardly believe these are farm-workers' cottages. The effect of these houses is made that much more attractive by being interspersed with the more massive houses of the gentry. I counted six of these in a stretch of 3 of our leagues [4½ miles], and one of them merits description. It is near the road: to one side are fine out-buildings, and, in front of these and in line with the house, is a paddock for pasturing horses. At the far end of this paddock, someone saw the need of a horse-lodge, and built it in the form of a temple. An ordinary roof is supported in front by four columns bearing a pediment. The pediment and colonnade, of the simplest Order, are painted grey-white, and you have no idea of the charming effect this object creates.' I have so far failed to identify this temple for horses.

[11] There is a steep rise from 80 to about 200 feet above sea-level leaving Sudbury and a similar fall to the river and rise at Nayland: otherwise this is rather a flat road, though it may have seemed less so on horseback. Brunning's Farm, north of Nayland, was called High Trees in 1784.

[12] François has mistakenly written Newton. Thanks to Lazowski's notes, we know that they observed that 4-course rotation at Newton before coming to Nayland.

[13] Constable, a boy of eight, was already making these scenes 'Constable Country': 'I had often thought of pictures of them before I had ever touched a pencil.'

[14] Lazowski went further: 'Nayland is a superb village. You will have some idea of it when I tell you that, just riding through it, I saw three inns of the best appearance, each of them with post-chaises for hire. Nayland, on the same river as Sudbury and which carries barges to that town, is backed by hills that run westwards. The valley in which the river runs is scarcely three-quarters of a mile broad. All the crests of the slopes which enfold the valley are covered with clumps of trees (*bouquets de bois*) which form the backgrounds to several houses scattered over the hills in this way. You are half-way up the slopes to the east and have a charming view: it is of no great extent, but it is rich, joyful (*gai*) and it makes a picture.' John Constable was not the only one to notice. Lazowski seemed not to notice the pouring rain.

The weather was very bad, and the rain, which the wind blew into our faces, prevented us from seeing all this country with the same pleasure we might have had on a fine day.

Colchester is situated on top of a hill of considerable height, the houses built from the bottom to the summit on a very steep slope which our horses had a struggle to climb. We arrived by a very fine street, and soon after I noted a second quite as fine, which, running at right angles to the first, formed, so to say, the framework of the town.[15]

Here we are in Essex, but only since we entered the town: this is the one point in our tour where we had left Suffolk.[16] Three things in Colchester should excite the curiosity of strangers.

First, the castle, which is extremely ancient, is square built and very large, its position commands the town and surrounding country: one sees from the top all the land around for a great distance; it was famous in the time of Charles I for the sieges it withstood.[17] Inside, an old library is preserved: about a hundred books in an enormous room.[18]

Second, the Theatre[19] (*Salle de comédie*), which is one of the most pitiful I have seen in my life: you couldn't get 200 people in, and all the seats are simple wooden benches. The back of the stage is an old wall

[15] North Hill and High Street, and this was no figure of speech: the framework was supplied by the Romans.

[16] In fact they crossed the Suffolk–Essex border, the river Stour, at Nayland, and re-crossed only after visiting Mistley and Harwich. The great manor of Nayland did include the Horkesleys in the Middle Ages, but François is not likely to have been thinking of this.

[17] It was the whole town, within its Roman and medieval wall, that withstood a grim siege for twelve weeks in the summer of 1648: it was occupied by a Royalist force of 3,000. The Parliamentarian army under Fairfax was content to lay siege, drawing the surrounding lines steadily tighter and keeping up a damaging bombardment. Lazowski, a romantic, was deeply moved by the story of the shooting, after the town had surrendered, of the Royalist commanders Sir Charles Lucas and Sir George Lisle. He wanted to go and see their place of execution, 'but it isn't known'.

[18] The books were bequeathed to the town by Samuel Harsnett (1561–1631), a Colchester baker's son, who became Archbishop of York. They were kept with a learned library, the Castle Book Society, founded *c*. 1750 by Charles Gray, M.P., who lived in an adjacent beautiful house, the Hollytrees. He had put a roof on the south part of the castle and a cupola over the great stair, using the largest keep in England as his own garden ornament.

[19] Built behind the Moot Hall (Town Hall) as the New Theatre in 1764, and replaced on a different site in 1812, and by the delightful Mercury Theatre in the 1970s.

which represents, I suppose, now the palace of the Caesars, now the gardens of Semiramis, and the beautiful piazzas of Rome, etc. The *décor* matched the furnishings, and although no actors were present, we felt we could judge what the productions must be like.

Third, the assembly room (where the dances are held). There are public balls every fortnight. The room is large and well lighted, 74 feet by 34.[20]

Colchester's trade, like Sudbury's, is very flourishing for a small town. Always more work than workmen: 500 looms clattering. The cloths resemble Sudbury's, but are not so fine: they are intended for Spain and America.[21] They are first sent to London, in four waggons that leave regularly three times a week: each carries 250 pieces of cloth, worth 5 guineas apiece.

There is a small ribbon-factory, but I know no details.

The rain, which fell in great abundance, did not prevent us from leaving for Mistley as soon as we had eaten our dinner. No one can

[20] Lazowski's findings were 72 by 30 feet. Does anyone see them measuring it out, one foot in front of the other? Lazowski was more enthusiastic about Colchester than François: 'It is one of the great towns of England . . . well built . . . lively manufacture . . . assemblies with dances every fortnight in winter, every month in the summer: the assembly room is in the excellent inn at which we alighted . . . There are plays in some months: the playhouse unpleasant.'

[21] Lazowski is more illuminating: 'The cloths are all a kind of double serge, entirely exported to Spain for the Central American market; also a small quantity to Portugal, the American War had very little repercussion in this market, though that with France and Spain brought it entirely to a halt. (See Sudbury, p. 00.) It has recovered its entire business. To make these serges they comb, but do not card; however, they use only a small quantity of the long wool from Lincolnshire and every last ounce of short wool from Suffolk. The weavers earn 10 shillings a week, 14 including their wives' work. The combers get 3 shillings a day: this big wage produces idleness and drunkenness, so that they scarcely work four days a week.'

Lazowski continues: 'There are 500 looms at work in the town, but they do the work of a thousand by means of a mechanism that halves the amount of work and means that instead of two men on each loom you need only one . . . All the pieces of cloth are sent to London to be dyed, and shipped on. Formerly they went by water to Harwich but it has been found more expedient to send them by waggon and they leave every week with four loads of 250 pieces of cloth worth 5 pounds sterling. [François recorded three loads, worth 5 guineas: one learns not to treat one's sources *au pied de la lettre!*] There is certainly error in this information, which was not checked with the manufacturers', Lazowski added, showing meticulous concern for the truth.

reproach us for losing any time. It was half-past seven when we left, and we still had ten miles to go before reaching Mistley.[22]

Nightfall stopped me seeing the countryside, so I can give no account of it. Only I did notice that the soil got steadily sandier, and that there were many climbs and descents: apart from that, nothing new.

Mistley is a very small place, fifty houses at most, which are so well built and so spruce that you see at a glance that they all belong to the same owner. Mr Rigby owns the whole town and a superb house and fine park, of which I'll speak soon. All the houses except one belong to him, but the owner of this last one would never sell it to him; and, so that strangers don't compare it with the others, he has painted his red, since the others are white.

The inn belongs to Mr Rigby. It stands in the square, in a pleasant position, from which one surveys a great expanse of water – an estuary formed there by the sea, rather than the actual mouth of the river (the Stour, the same that runs past Sudbury). On the far bank you see a delightful water's edge, well planted and stretching for over a dozen miles (Pl. 21).

The inn is large, well-furnished, and the service all that you could wish. Immediately facing the inn is a circular fountain, the water-level three feet above the ground, in which you water your horses. The water spouts continually from a swan's mouth (Pl. 22).[23]

The quay is consolidated with a large brick wall to which the whalers[24] are moored; beyond is a warehouse of some size in which the

---

[22] Lazowski noted, on their way from Colchester to Mistley, a stop at John Brand's forge at Lawford. 'On the way, we saw the establishment of Mr Brand, a simple uncultivated blacksmith, who has become one of the leading English inventors. His forge is in a dip, as he needs water to work his machines: he has found a way of having in the bottom of the valley a triangular shaped piece of water: the effect very agreeable. He is the inventor of a plough, a drawing of which I have with me.' A drawing of Brand's Plough is reproduced on p. 154 below.

[23] The swan still dribbles perpetually into the fountain in front of a pedimented terrace of four cottages designed as such by Robert Adam (Pls. 22, 23). The Thorn Inn still faces these cottages and the swan across the little square. (The old name for this part of Mistley was Mistley Thorn.) The new 'model' part was shown in great detail in one of the beautiful drawn and coloured surveys of the Rigby estate by Bernard Scalé in 1778 (see his survey of part of the park in Pl. 25). The volume of Mistley surveys is the pride of the newly opened Colchester branch of the Essex Record Office.

[24] Mistley was evidently involved in the local attempt to revive the deep-sea fisheries and Greenland whaling trade.

21. *The Mistley Thorn Hotel.*

22. *The Swan fountain, Mistley Thorn. Compare Pl. 23.*

23. Robert Adam's design for four cottages, Mistley Thorn, 1779. (Sir John Soane's Museum)

merchants can store everything free of charge. At the end of the quay is a small ship-yard where I saw two frigates[25] being built (Pl. 24).

The trade here was created entirely by Mr Rigby. It consists of coal and corn imported from other parts of England, and can employ four or

---

[25] 'frégates de quarantes' is his description: forty-tonners' is S. C. Roberts' translation! '44 guns' is Lazowski's record, not far adrift. *Terpsichore* left the stocks at Mistley in 1785, 682 tons and 32 guns. (She may have been *intended* for a bigger armament. Lazowski recorded that they went down-river to be armed at Harwich.) In July 1797, she suffered casualties (including Captain and 1st Lieutenant killed) under Nelson at Santa Cruz, just thirteen years after they had seen her building at Mistley. She survived till 1830 (*V.C.H. Essex*, II, 1907, p. 310). I have found no trace of a second Mistley frigate at that date. Lazowski had a more businesslike approach to what was going on at Mistley: 'where the sea in all weathers draws away sloops, luggers, all the coaling and coasting vessels: a new place created by Mr Rigby, Paymaster General.' Richard Rigby (1722–88) succeeded to his father's estate in 1730. A swashbuckling politician, he fought a duel with Lord Cornwallis in 1764 and was Paymaster to the Forces from 1768–84, all through the American War. One sees how warships came to be built at Mistley. In those days, public money could be held in the minister's own account: when he died, it was said, not unjustly: 'he left near half a million of public money'. His nephew and heir Francis Hale Rigby was already in residence at Mistley in 1784, and is presumably the Mr Rigby who received Lazowski and the boys.

24. *Mistley from Brantham. Elias Martin, 1776. (National Museum, Stockholm)*

five vessels.[26] Some time ago this place, though small and in its infancy, got involved in smuggling, but the individual had no luck: he was caught, hanged, had his goods confiscated, etc. Alongside the port there is a lime-kiln, clad in brick and given the shape of a fort. It has a fine effect.[27]

The other end of the town is no less agreeable. There stands a new church built from the designs of Mr Adam, an excellent architect. I never saw anything more elegant than this building: there is some hint of Chinese and Turkish[28] in the construction, but with simplicity and delicacy. The interior is all one conception, with no ornament. The church serves as an eye-catcher from the house.[29]

Mr Rigby's house, of white brick, stands on an eminence. It is one of the most elegant brick buildings I have seen. To describe every part of this house seems to me not only difficult – since I saw it only in passing – but it would serve no useful purpose. That is why I shall abridge as much as I can.

The saloon and dining-room are two superb rooms, as much for grandeur and proportion as for the furniture. A discerning enjoyment has called forth everything that could be found, regardless of expense: here pictures, vases, bas-reliefs in marble, all require appreciative attention. These two rooms[30] are separated by several smaller rooms, all notable for their taste. The windows all along this side of the house, which is the main front, frame a delightful view: the estuary formed by the river-mouth is bordered on both banks by well-cultivated fields and

[26] Lazowski was more precise: 'Newcastle ships bring the coal which is either distributed by cart into Essex or Suffolk or carried on upriver by barge to Sudbury. The whole neighbourhood brings its corn here to be embarked or stored for the London markets and all the coastal ports. There are six ships at the quay – a fine sight.'
[27] Lazowski sniffed: 'une affectation trop recherchée ... un château de cartes'. One wonders if he would have been happier with the all-too-utilitarian aspect of the quays today.
[28] He perhaps saw a slight resemblance between the twin lantern-cupolas and minarets.
[29] As Lazowski put it, 'it was designed as an ornament to the park, an object of perspective'.
[30] Rigby added these two rooms to his father's house. Adam's designs for them c. 1780 survive: ceilings, carpet (1774), mirror frames ('glass-frames', 1778) every last detail, several in colour. The road along 'The Strand' passes a parapet he designed for an artificial bridge. The house was demolished in 1835, the year it appeared engraved in Thomas Wright', *History of the County of Essex*.

embellished with houses, farms and churches, and ends at the town of Harwich which one can make out in the distance: the little town lies at your feet, the church to the left of it and, if you lean out a little to see further to the left, the eye follows the river to a substantial village only two miles away. The whole water-surface of this valley, covered with shipping, is a marvellous sight at high tide; when the tide is out, the landscape loses some of its beauty, although it is still very interesting.

All the rest of the house lives up to the magnificence of the saloon and the dining-room. The furnishing of the bedrooms is simple but elegant and singularly neat and tidy. There are eleven guest-rooms; several with a little sitting-room and *cabinet de toilette*.

If the house is beautiful, the gardens are even more so, at least they made much more of an impression on me. The truth is, I had already seen fine houses, but I had not seen any English garden coming anywhere near this one.

We first went into the pleasure-garden, the closest to the house (Pl. 25). It is composed of groups of very rare trees, raised with care and disposed with art on a carpet of turf which is mown every week; this grass is admirably fine and smooth. The walk is a gravel path which takes in with a charming curve every part of the garden and is carefully arranged to pass the foot of every handsome tree: among the rarest I noticed two tulip-trees that could have been sixty or eighty feet high, and the trunks of which I reckoned to be about nine feet in girth three feet above ground; they had had their splendid flowers and all I saw was the faded remains.

Leaving the first garden, which is really a large grove enclosed by a wide ditch, we crossed a road and entered another garden, then another, and so on for more than two miles, then we made the tour of the last and returned along the far side of each of the gardens we had been through. I observed everywhere the same care and the same neatness. The walk is wide and sometimes grass, sometimes sand. Mr Rigby accompanied us all the way in his open carriage.

The abundance of evergreens is extraordinary, the rarer varieties in quantity, and the majority are tall and superb. The cause of the division of the pleasure-garden into groves like that is that, before Mr Rigby laid out his park in all this stretch of country, there were roads and paths that he couldn't close; and to prevent passers-by from crossing and spoiling his garden, he was obliged to divide it into groves and enclose

120

25. Mistley Hall, pleasure gardens, kitchen garden and town. Bernard Scalé, 1778.
(Essex R.O. Colchester)

them. All these groves occupy about three-quarters of the extent of an extremely large meadow in which I saw a great many fine cows belonging to the proprietor's farm. Nor is there a lack of game. I saw with pleasure, in this same meadowland, numbers of hares running about among the pheasants; it would have been a pleasure to have a gun, but I suppose there is never any shooting, and that this is the sanctuary for all the game of the neighbourhood. The deer are carefully preserved here: it is a luxury in English gardens that I like very much; they enliven the parks, in general very wild, and amuse any solitary walker with their agility.

The kitchen-garden stands behind this walk, and is the best I have ever seen. There are nine acres divided into five parts by brick walls eighteen feet high and covered with superb fruit trees of every variety, brought from France.

The hothouses are very large and well exposed to the sun. There is a double one arranged so that with very little imagination here, in July, you can imagine yourself under an arbour of beautifully ripe grapes.[31] The dwarf cherry-trees which adorn this hothouse were all red when I saw them, creating a charming effect; peaches and pineapples were of a quantity and size quite mouth-watering.

The park is very large, perhaps 1100 or 1200 acres; the land is everywhere very uneven, which in some places produces a charming effect: the valley bottoms seen from afar have a wild and sombre look that make one pensive and that provide an agreeable contrast with the view of the estuary[32] seen from other parts of the park.

Mr Rigby's farm is in the park. It presents a pleasant enough picture from several points on the other side of the valley.

The soil around Mistley is sand, on which, however, the good farming of the district has managed to raise fine crops. The fields are enclosed and much divided so as to conserve through the shade of the hedgerows the moisture needed by the sandy soil, naturally very dry.

---

[31] A Frenchman would associate the ripening of grapes with late September.

[32] He uses the word *mer*, which is perhaps understandable – the estuary here is a mile across. Elsewhere he uses *baie* and seems not to have known the meaning of *estuaire*. Admittedly we still use 'bay' where the shores of the estuaries curve appropriately! 'Jacques Bay', 'Holbrook Bay', etc. The total acreage of Rigby's park, gardens, plantations, meadows and fields surveyed by Scalé in 1778 was just over 940 acres. The deer were paled in the south-east corner.

We had risen early to visit Mistley and the weather was very favourable. Back from our walk, we breakfasted and left for Harwich, about a dozen miles from Mistley.

The road and the weather were agreeable. We saw one of Mr Rigby's farms.[33] It is remarkable: for its position overlooking the valley, where the river is a good three-quarters of a mile wide, and for its design as a building, which is very elegant for a farmhouse and more like the home of a gentleman of leisure than a farmer. It is built in brick with stone string-courses, two storeys, five window-bays on each front and, at one end, a little turret which the English call a 'bow', a feature of one of those sitting-rooms that are so common in England. In front of the house a very well-kept lawn, surrounded by evergreens, comes right up to the front door. It is all framed by a little fence, at elbow height, freshly painted white. Behind the house are the farm-buildings: barns, a stable, etc.; they are weather-boarded and stained brown and covered with thatch. This kind of building is very common and is, I suppose, the least expensive: it lasts a long time. The boards are generally fir or pine, preserved by their own resin and by the staining.

The lands of this farm are quite extensive, worth seven or eight hundred pounds sterling, and lying all along the estuary: transporting the crops is easy.

The rest of the journey was across a countryside interrupted by hills and woods, its variety preventing me from noticing its length.

Harwich is built right on the point of the right bank of the mouth of the Stour, forming a kind of triangle of which two sides are parallel to the edge of the sea. The town is badly built, the streets are narrow and without alignment, the gutters don't drain the water off the streets: it is full of mud, even in summer.[34]

This town's only branch of trade is the cod-fishery, supplying the London market. For that, she sends out about thirty boats a year. They are of a peculiar construction (I have seen one): very short, and the planking is twice as thick as that of an ordinary vessel and is lined with

[33] Presumably Nether Hall, Bradfield: until the railway was laid to Harwich, the road meandered close to Nether Hall.

[34] In fact, the streets form a sort of grid. The weather had been wet.

lead in order to hold water and bring in the cod alive.[35] Each can cost up to a thousand pounds to build. A great many packet-boats leave Harwich for Holland and the North.

The King has a Navy-yard for the building of men-of-war; the only one in England where anyone is allowed in. I walked in and saw two frigates building, to be named *Pollux* and *Hannibal*. Perhaps we shall capture them?[36] No other vessels were building.

Three years ago, a camp was established half a mile from Harwich on a large site:[37] from up there, the town, the countryside and a great expanse of the sea were under observation.

The port is nothing much. Our idea was to take a boat and go by water to Ipswich, so getting the benefit of the view of the whole shore-line of the estuary which is, they say, altogether delightful; but we couldn't carry out our plan, as the winds were contrary and strong: nor could we cross over to visit a fort built on a small island in the sea – very interesting, especially to Frenchmen.[38]

We were therefore obliged to return to Mistley for the night, after having a very bad dinner in a very bad inn.

---

[35] Lazowski's account of these special cod-smacks – he called them sloops – was more precise. 'In the middle of the hold are two tanks, the full capacity of the ship: the tanks 6 or 7 feet long, separated by large 9-inch oak planks, especially strong to stand up to the weight of two such tanks. The bottom of the boats, under the tanks, is pierced with holes an inch in diameter to admit the sea-water in which the cod swim until they reach London. They reckon these sloops make as good speed as any other, despite the sieve-like effect of the holes.'

[36] Lazowski recorded only one warship, of 74 guns, building in the yard, though 'no one was working'. '*Pollux*' must have been named '*Castor*' in the event, 32 guns. François guessed well: she *was* taken by a French squadron of the Brest fleet on 10 May 1794 but re-taken on 29th. In action in the West Indies 1809–11; and ended up a convict-ship at Portsmouth in 1818. In the West Indies, with Lazowski's 74 guns, *Hannibal* took *La Lentille*, 42 guns, in April 1795 after a 19-hours' chase: the French captain said *Hannibal* 'sails like a witch'. Grounded in action in Algeciras Bay, July 1801: 143 killed and wounded and obliged to surrender. (V.C.H. *Essex*, II, 1907, pp. 310–11.)

[37] 'In 1781, two regiments of militia were encamped here, the Suffolk and Bucks': W. H. Lindsey, *A Season at Harwich*, 1851, p. 65.

[38] Lazowski realised that Landguard Fort, controlling the mouth of the double estuary of Stour and Orwell at Harwich, was on the southern point of the Suffolk shore, a spit rather than 'a small island'; also that it was built from fear of a Dutch, rather than a French, landing. For the first time we see these Frenchmen not just as Anglophile, but as French patriots and potential enemies of England.

On the 24th [July 1784], we left early in the morning to go to Woolverstone, then on to dine in Ipswich and sleep in Woodbridge. But we mustn't go so fast. From Mistley we came to a long wooden bridge and crossed the river,[39] which, incidentally, leaves infamous mudbanks at low tide: they are covered only by the spring tides, so that reeds and tall grasses grow, and there is a scent of a sewer!

The other side of the estuary is even more agreeable than the Mistley side; the land better farmed and more peopled. All the little houses spread through the countryside are infinitely neat: we went inside one and watched a mother and her children engaged in spinning a fine wool while the father was out working the fields. I noticed that this house was of a cleanliness absolutely unknown in France.[40]

Soon after, we met a burly farmer mounted on a good horse and out looking at his crops. He had the air of a wealthy man, and though he was dressed like a farmer, something in his manner revealed a man of affluence![41]

Mr Young stopped him and asked several questions, most of which I remember though something may have slipped my memory, but this was the gist: nearly all the farmers round here own their farms, which they could do only after acquiring some wealth; the farms are not large, worth, as a rule, not more than three or four hundred pounds sterling;

[39] At Cattawade Bridge, the lowest crossing of the Stour where it becomes an estuary: here they crossed from Essex back into Suffolk; and here Thomas Tusser, Arthur Young's famous 16th-century precursor as agricultural propagandist, farmed at Braham Hall, Brantham.

[40] In his *General View of the Agriculture of Suffolk*, 1797, Arthur Young, as Secretary to the Board of Agriculture, characterised this peninsula between the Stour and Orwell estuaries on his frontispiece map of the soil of Suffolk as Rich Loam, the only district so distinguished. But his book, in the early years of the French wars that undid Suffolk agriculture by encouraging a total turnover from mixed farming to arable, already began to suggest the end of the golden age depicted by François. Of the cottages, Young wrote in 1797 that 'respectable individuals' had built 'neat and comfortable cottages for the poor; but such instances are not general . . . In Suffolk they are in general bad habitations . . .' Lazowski was every bit as impressed as François with the neatness of the cottages and the intelligent conversation of the farmer: unfortunately neither records whether they were in Brantham, Tattingstone or Holbrook when they made these observations. From the next sentence, it appears they were in Brantham.

[41] Arthur Young named him as Mr Palmer of Branton (i.e. Brantham).

125

they get their muck from London and a sort of chalk they mix with it from Kent; they arrange for the muck to come from London on the barges that take there the local produce and that otherwise might return empty, so the cost is low (it argues intelligence and imaginative calculation to enrich the soil with fertiliser that has been transported a hundred miles and make a profit on it). He added that the lands never lie fallow but are cropped in the four-year rotation: first, turnips; second, barley sown with clover; third, the same clover by itself; fourth, wheat.

What I found absolutely astonishing is the way in which not only the farmer but everyone Mr Young questioned on the way replied to his questions with – everyone – more intelligence than peasants are supposed to have.

I forgot to say that a mile or so back we passed this man's farm: a large house is surrounded and set off by a small, beautifully tended, flower-bed and there are trees he has planted solely to please himself.

The whole countryside is pleasantly divided by valleys. The fields are always enclosed and small; numerous houses and farms; everywhere the air of opulence and neatness.

The fields were full of cattle – an immense number of sheep as well as of bullocks, a kind of small oxen driven every year from the Scottish mountains to all parts of England to be fattened, then eaten;[42] they have no horns and are much preferred to other cattle as being tenderer and more easily fattened up. There are few cows; those I saw were all feeding calves, which shows that it is not for their milk that they are kept.

As we passed, we saw an estate which belonged to one of our Bury friends, and who has sold it. All it wants is a house to make it a very

---

[42] On Scotch cattle, Young wrote: 'In those parts of the county where the sheep and cows do not consume the turnips, the common practice is to buy black cattle, at fairs, from north country drovers for that purpose. . . . The greater part are Scotch: Galloways, Fifes and Highlanders.' He went on: 'The late Mr Mure, of Saxham, stall-fed on a very large scale upon cabbages and potatoes. This is a branch of the farmer's business in which *general* details are nearly useless: it is only by the recital of particular experiments that any accurate conclusions can be drawn (loc. cit. pp. 188–9). Young recorded (p. 179) that the Suffolk breed of cattle was 'universally *polled*, that is, without horns', and celebrated for its great yield of milk in the district between Woodbridge and Coddenham, Framlingham and Hoxne. We come there later.

delightful place; the stretch of water, which is immense, has the appearance of a natural river. This place is called Holbrook.[43]

A little further on is Woolverstone, which belongs to Mr Berners. He has built there, a short time ago, a fine enough house in the modern taste;[44] however, its position gives it all its merit; it is on top of a hill[45] in the middle of an immense park, very ill-kept. It consists merely of a large expanse of enclosed ground artlessly covered with turf and trees; the vistas are neglected. In a word, it is as nature wanted it.

The position of the house is very agreeable, providing, over the trees that cover the slope, a view of the Ipswich river, which is more than three-quarters of a mile wide and forms a perfect crescent round the park; and through the branches of these same trees you glimpse the water that bathes their feet; and in some places where the trees are taller you seem not to be separated from the far shore by water.[46] In the background of the picture, completing it to perfection, is the town of Ipswich, although at that distance you cannot make out the details.

The great number of small vessels with which this river is always covered brings to life this superb view, but what seems to me sad is that you can see everything at a single glance, and that the view is not truly fine till you go up to the first floor: from the ground floor one sees too little.

[43] Their Bury friend, Sir Charles Kent of Fornham St Genevieve, is named as the proprietor of both Fornham and Holbrook on Hodskinson's delightful map of 1783. The map shows very ambitious landscape and water-gardens both here and at Tattingstone. At Holbrook the serpentine water was crossed by two bridges at the narrow top end. Three smaller ponds with woodland walks and a glade lay to the east. Sir Charles Kent must have toyed with the idea of building there, but sold to Charles Berners (who succeeded his father at Woolverstone in 1783) to provide him with additional gardens a mile and a half from his house at Woolverstone. Two of Luigi Mayer's enchanting water-colours of Holbrook's water-gardens in 1799 illustrate D. E. Davy's *Journal*: S.R.S. 24, 1982, p. 53. The water survives, rather dwarfed by the recently established Alton Water Reservoir at Tattingstone.

[44] It was designed for William Berners in 1776 by the architect and surveyor John Johnson (1732–1814), who had worked for him over the previous ten years in the development of the Berners estate in Marylebone. Detailed decorations – urns and a medallion on the pediment, capitals under it, pairs of sphinxes over windows, are by Coade (Nancy Briggs, *Proceedings Suffolk Institute of Archaeology*, 34, 1977, pp. 59–64). William Berners had been succeeded by his son Charles in 1783. François is right: 'la position en fait tout le mérite'.

[45] In fact, on a low spur overlooking the Orwell estuary.

[46] Lazowski wrote of the 'superb tall forest trees . . . In all, this view is imposing and magnificent.'

As soon as we had seen the house and park we were on the road to Ipswich, continuing along the river, or rather estuary.[47] You pass another village and the road is agreeable all the way.

Ipswich is situated at the head of the estuary as it is near this place that the tide ceases to rise and fall.

The town is badly built, the streets narrow, without any alignment, and the road-surface as bad as could be. As England is short of stone, the towns that are paved are paved with cobbles tightly packed, which present the foot with a series of bumps, as disagreeable when you are riding in a carriage as when you are walking.

The town gives the impression of being empty: one sees hardly anyone in the streets, and this impression derives a little from the spread of the town which is much increased by the large number of gardens within its bounds. They boast that this makes the air very salubrious.[48] Ipswich is very well inhabited, many gentlefolk living there, and, besides that, tradespeople. All gather every evening in a coffee-house, where one can play cards and eat, which is very convenient for strangers (Pl. 26).[49]

As to trade, I was told it was considerable. It consists in exporting the produce of the neighbouring countryside both to London and to the North. In this last business the vessels bring back planks of deal, in

[47] He seems not to have known the word *estuaire* and here uses *baie*: at p. 126 above he uses *mer*. Lazowski likewise uses *baie*. (See footnote 32 above.)

[48] Rev. Richard Canning (1708–75), in his Account of Ipswich in the 1764 edition of *The Suffolk Traveller*, wrote 'One favourable circumstance is almost peculiar to this place, which is that most of the better houses, even in the Heart of the Town, have convenient Gardens adjoining to them, which makes them more airy and healthy, as well as more pleasant and delightful.'

[49] At the corner of Tavern Street and Tower Street, where Chaucer's forebears had once sold wine, it had been rebuilt at the beginning of the 17th century with flamboyant wood-carvings, including Faith, Hope and Charity at eye-level on the corner-post. In 1767 it had coffee, tea, card and dining rooms. It was then acquired by ten shareholders, including Richard Canning, and Daniel Bamford became landlord. An information was laid against him for allowing billiards to be played and the Justices found against him and revoked his licence. The conviction was quashed by the Court of King's Bench. The fine front was destroyed in 1817 in the interests of providing a few extra inches of paving, though the carved corner-post seems to have been inserted into the new front. (John Glyde, *Illustrations of Old Ipswich*, 1889, pp. 34–36). The Assembly Room adjoined until 1821, when a new one was built in Northgate Street. The site of the Old Coffee House is occupied at present by a glossy British Home Stores.

128

26. *The old Ipswich coffee-house, 1815. (John Glyde,* Illustrations of Old Ipswich, *1889)*

great demand for the staircases and floors of houses; they also bring back other products of the North.[50]

Mr Young had an acquaintance in the town whom we went to see. He is a gentleman farmer; that is to say he runs his farm himself. His farm is in the most agreeable position, on Stoke Hill, to the east of the town,[51] from which unfolds on one side the estuary I have already mentioned with Mr Berners' house in the distance; on the other side, the town, at your feet, and three valleys meeting, in each of them a little winding stream. It is a lovely position (Pl. 27).

The farm of this gentleman has nothing remarkable about it except two or three artificial meadows, a novelty for this country, which has none.[52] His clover and lucerne are good.

---

[50] This is the only point where Lazowski amplifies François' account: 'coastal shipping considerable, a large number of fishing boats, and direct trade with the Baltic. Vessels export from Ipswich cloth, beer, iron, lead, various goods made in England, and silver; and import pitch, tar, hemp, planks, masts and, sometimes, grain; sometimes the boats carry only silver and ballast.' These references to *l'argent* are perhaps to the circulation of silver coin, or coin in general, in the aftermath of the bullion crisis of 1783? Sterling reserves fell almost as low as half a million, to balance a note circulation of £7 millions. Confidence returned in 1784. One had thought of bullion being transferred in well-guarded coaches.

[51] Plate 27 shows the prominent brick farmhouse, drawn by R. B. Clamp in about 1820, with the towers of Stoke church and St Mary Quay almost in line just above its roof. Mr Savage's mill-house, on the extreme right, was the scene of a half-hearted bread riot in 1800. Stoke Hill stands immediately *south* of the town, and is now covered in streets of small houses. Samuel and Nathaniel Buck's *South-west prospect of the town of Ipswich*, 1741, showed Stoke Hall and church in the right foreground. We know from Arthur Young that his acquaintance here was Mr Turner. My grangerised copy of Richard Canning's edition of the *Suffolk Traveller*, p. 41, was annotated in 1777 by Samuel Pickering, Notary Public of Ipswich, and his hand avers that the modern house by Stoke church was 'rebuilt by Nathaniel Turner Esq.'. G. R. Clarke, *History of Ipswich*, 1830, p. 263, confused the matter by stating: 'Adjoining the churchyard is a handsome spacious brick mansion called Stoke Hall, built in the last century by Thomas Cartwright, esq., wine-merchant. There are very extensive vaults . . . calculated to contain altogether fifteen hundred pipes of wine . . . The family of Turner resided here many years . . . J. B. Smyth the present occupier has greatly improved the place.' There is no doubt of its pleasant position when Mr Turner showed it to Young and the Frenchmen in 1784. François and his earlier editors misnamed it Stock Hill. Young says he 'catched a hasty walk with Mr Turner and had the pleasure of finding that he fed his farm horses last winter with carrots and no corn whatever – in as good health and did work as well as when on corn alone'.

[52] An exception was at Babraham, where artificial meadows were created in 1653: V.C.H., *Cambridgeshire*, VI, 1978, p. 25, and A. Young, *Annals*, XVI, p. 177.

North west View of Ipswich taken near M.r Theverages House.

27. *Ipswich from Stoke Hill c. 1820. R. B. Clamp.*

Another prospect, even more agreeable, of the town and its environs, is from a priory.[53] A beautiful house and park belong in fact to an old clergyman, but he is not a prior.[54] From there you get a much better view of the town, although it is right under your feet: the park extends further out, and the countryside from here has a most happy appearance.

It is a very extraordinary thing that at Ipswich, which is a big town and the capital of a big county, there is not a single inn that is even barely passable; whereas usually one finds in the simplest villages superb inns, lacking nothing, not even cleanliness.

After a bad dinner we left for Woodbridge. Nothing in the world is as delightful as those nine miles; the soil sandy, sometimes dry on the tops of hills, but always productive; fine harvests down in the valleys where it gets moister and so more fertile; the farms are spread out on this side and that, and some churches and very pretty houses of the gentry. It all makes the most agreeable effect.[55]

Three miles from Ipswich is an enormous farm where a great number of bullocks are fattened. I heard that it belonged to a gentleman who lived there and farmed it himself. His estate must be considerable to require such extensive buildings.[56]

Woodbridge is in absolutely sandy country. The town is small and built along two streets that form a very obtuse angle on the slope of a

[53] Christchurch Mansion, or Withepole House, was built *c.* 1548 on the site of a priory of Augustinian canons founded in 1177, on rising ground just outside the north gate of the town. House and park are preserved, and few towns in Europe have so agreeable an asset at their door.

[54] Rev. Dr Claudius Fonnereau (1701–85) succeeded his brother Thomas, M.P., in 1779 (J. S. Corder, *Christchurch or Withepole House*, Ipswich, 1895, pp. 33–34).

[55] At Rushmere Heath they forked left along 'the back road' over Beacon Hill, 'not the high road', said Young, 'which is much inferior. A vale and landscape to the left as beautiful as I remember anywhere to have seen.' To the left, at Bealings, two charming little valleys converge to meet the Deben at Martlesham Creek.

[56] Hard to identify. Young described it as 'the farm of – Kirby, Esq. Besides a farm of his own within 2 miles of the town [Woodbridge] he hires another of 750 acres of General Phillipson.' Lt.-Col. Richard Phillipson owned Kesgrave Manor 1769–89, and I think Kirby's farm may have been what later took the name Pogson's and was associated with the Biddell's famous farm, Hill House in Playford. Arthur Young had 'no doubt that' Mr Kirby would find 'his common crop of ray grass disadvantageous' but was delighted to find he fed his horses on carrots in winter, 'and they never were in so good order'.

little hill, two hundred yards away from an estuary down which it carries on an extensive trade in coasting and smuggling.[57]

Although there are rather few houses, they are agreeably built, all very cheerful and neat; nearly all of them are shops, for all the inhabitants are either merchants or shopkeepers. The district round about is pleasing, and the view from the church[58] remarkable for the detail laid out before you.

On arriving, we went to see Lady Blois, who lives a mile away.[59] We had already been there in April, when my father came over to see us. I have not previously mentioned our earlier visit, because this more extensive journey includes everything I could have said about the other. Besides, on the first visit all we saw was the two nursery-gardens near the town – one of nine acres, the other of four or five: they were well stocked with small evergreens, some of the species very reasonably priced: the soil of the larger nursery is sandy, and very dry; in the other it is slightly moister.[60]

[57] Church Street and Seckford Street do bend back obtusely from the line of the Thoroughfare, and smuggling was a principal trade of the Suffolk coast, clandestine and very ill recorded!

[58] The church-tower is 108 feet tall, and does command long views.

[59] Lucretia Ottley (1755–1808), daughter of a planter on St Kitts in the Leeward Islands, married (as his second wife) Sir John Blois, 5th baronet, in 1772, when she was 17 and he was heavily in debt from card-playing. He had sold their estate at Grundisburgh to the Gurdons ten years earlier, and moved to Cockfield Hall, Yoxford. In 1772 he let Cockfield to Chaloner Arcedeckne for 21 years. In 1792 Chaloner Arcedeckne built himself Glevering Hall, Hacheston, and the Bloises seem to have re-possessed Cockfield. Otherwise it is hard to explain the heartfelt sighs for Cockfield and 'Lady Blo' committed to François' father's journal in October and November 1794 as he ploughed through a very stormy Atlantic en route to America: e.g. 'Ah, Cockfield, Cockfield, quand m'y retrouverai-je! comme j'y serais soigné.' (*Journal de Voyage en Amérique: Duc de Liancourt*) See Introduction p. xxxv above. François must have had the Bloises partly in mind when he wrote his section on 'The Life of Those who are Ruined', p. 44 above. An entry in Lady Blois's account-book (1778–93) suggests that her husband had not been cured of card-playing: '4 Sept 1781, rec'd of Sir John his winnings at cards, £52. 10. 0' (R. T. L. Parr, *Yoxford Yesterday*, typescript in S.R.O., Vol. II, p. 232). While Cockfield was let, the Bloises hired from Francis Brooke a house in Melton, precisely a mile from Woodbridge on the Yarmouth road. It had belonged to William Negus, father of (the illegitimate) Francis Light, founder of Penang. It owes its present name, Red Towers, to later redbrick additions, but the outlines of the original house are easily made out.

[60] Young says: 'Examined Mr Wood's nursery at Woodbridge.' Lazowski reported *three* fine nurseries at Woodbridge: they had not time to see them. Isaac Johnson's map of Woodbridge in 1827 (published by Loder of Woodbridge in 1828) shows nurseries on

The following day looked like being one of the most interesting of our tour for two reasons: we would see superb husbandry in very poor soil, and, in particular, the cultivation of carrots for feeding cattle.[61]

So, on the Saturday we left early in the morning, passing through Melton and crossing the river on a very good bridge to the other bank of the estuary. The further we went, the more we were advancing into a shifting sand that was very tiring for our horses and where the cabriolet could only with great difficulty get through, although Mr Young and Mr Lazowski went the whole way on foot.

This place pleased me. It is wild and inhabited only by a great number of rabbits. The slope of the hill is covered by fine enough trees, but the top is bare and scarcely green at all on account of a species of poor grass and gorse[62] that grow here.

After two miles we came to the first of the farms we toured.[63]

---

three sites and all belonging to Mr Wood, the Woodbridge panjandrum of that day (forebear of the Page-Woods, lords Hatherley): one below the Quaker Meeting in Turn Lane, the other two forming the headquarters of Charles Notcutt's Nurseries today, alongside Fen Walk, (then 'Nursery Lane') and opposite the Cherry Tree Inn.

[61] Arthur Young, much excited, wrote: 'The principal object of this little tour is now at hand, the husbandry of the *Sandlings*, as they are termed – the triangle formed by the three points of Woodbridge, Bawdsey Cliff and Orford. I had of late years been exceedingly solicitous to gain a thorough knowledge of the culture of carrots.' They all gained a very thorough knowledge indeed.

[62] *jonc marin* grows on saltmarsh: even *juncus quarrosus*, the heath rush, is not found here at Sutton. Francis Simpson agrees that François may have intended to write *ajonc*, gorse, because he certainly used *jonc marin* to describe gorse at South Creake, p. 177 below.

[63] First came to Sutton, on the farm of Mr Gerrard, wrote Young, *Annals*, II, 1785, full of detail on carrot-culture. Then Mr William Waller of Sutton, with 2700 acres, ploughing 1000 and with 1000 sheep. (The Wallers still live beside the Deben.) Advanced to Shottisham: Mr Curtis's field of carrots very fine. Then, at Ramsholt, Mr Weedon's carrots for horses and much lyrical description of the Suffolk horse. More true bred twenty years ago when they drew team against team, 'the best of twenty pull' (see François on 'Hunters and cart-horses', above, p. 53). Young deplored the dangerous modern tendency to breed the Suffolk punch for coach and chaise: 'improvements in objects of luxury are contemptible in comparison with those which take place, in the farmer's walk, of a strong, powerful and hardy race': Mr Weedon takes 'a bett' with Mr Lazowski that a horse would draw 30 comb up hill. At Alderton they found Mr Ablett with more carrots, and Mr Wimper with cattle and oxen, 'noble beasts'. At Hollesley, they were much struck to find the Lombardy poplar so generally introduced – scarcely a house without some: this is because a great number of landlords were the occupiers of their own lands. Alderton especially is full of them – gentlemen farmers from £200 to £500 a year: homily on 'the admirable effects which flow from a wealthy yeomanry'.

I cannot give a perfectly detailed account of this day, it would be too long. I shall not say how many farms I saw, but just what I observed.

It is in the past twenty years or so that all this countryside – perhaps twenty square miles – has been inhabited. The extreme depth of the shifting sand had until then defeated the reclaimers. I do not know what good angel brought me there fresh at about this time. What is certain is that I saw some very fine crops in land that – simply judged by someone who will not make a perfect connoisseur of soil – one would suppose could produce nothing. An acre is rented at five or six shillings a year. On it grows passably good wheat, very good carrots densely cropped, oats, barley and, above all, broad beans, as fine as any I ever saw – prodigiously tall and all in flower as we went past; peas do well enough, but the fields growing this crop were not numerous.

The land is not much enclosed in this district, except round the villages, where they are correspondingly more productive. There are a great many houses, and like all those I have noticed they are neat and brightened by a flower-garden. We went into several of them. The furniture was in good order and in each of them we saw a good clock – a luxury peasants now enjoy. The wife and children had pretty faces and worked together at wool-spinning.

But back to the carrots, the object of Mr Young's admiration! He assured us that their cultivation was peculiar to this corner of Suffolk. That was why they especially earned my attention. There are entire fields full of them; they take the finest and send them in large quantities[64] to London; the rest go to feed the horses and pigs. Everywhere they are

---

This country abounds in game especially pheasants. Not a pond or scarcely a large dyke at Alderton, Hollesley, Shottisham or Bawdsey that has not good carp and tench. At Capel St Andrew, Mr Gross's great farm, 2700 acres, determined to sow no more carrots, so eaten up by the innumerable hares which his landlord, Lord Archibald Hamilton, preserved. At Wantisden, Mr Curteen of the Hall has 4 acres of CARROTS FOR HIS OWN CONSUMPTION. He never sold to London. 'Here at last, after a research that has employed me from time to time for years, I have found what I wished.' The day was closing. We were obliged to reach Saxmundham at night. 'Here ends our carrot intelligence', but not without a review of the several particulars. That day, 24 July '84, was a red-letter day for Arthur Young. He repeated and amplified these details in his *General View of the Agriculture of Suffolk*, 1797, pp. 106–117. The others responded suitably well to Young's enthusiasm.

[64] François wrote *en petite quantité* which is clearly a slip.

given to pigs, even in some parts of France, but nowhere else are they fed to horses. I even believed that, on account of their strong scent, they were disliked by horses who would need to be starved before they ate them; but to my great astonishment, when I offered them to my horse I saw him eat them greedily – leaves and all.

As there are meadows all along the Woodbridge estuary which borders this district, they graze their cattle there in the summer; it is only in winter and spring that they feed them on carrots, and fatten their oxen and bullocks on them.

During all the time when these farmers cannot graze their horses on their meadow-grass, they give them carrots and chaff and very little hay (chaff is straw and cut hay, two-thirds straw and one of hay), but no oats at all; and this is enough to sustain them. At work and in good health, carriage and saddle horses would not do so well, because the carrot heats them slightly, or at least makes them liable to perspire, and a horse going fast could easily get a fever.

Carrots are sown on Lady Day[65] and at Whitsuntide they are first hoed: twice more during the summer. That costs between fifteen and eighteen shillings an acre. Each acre produces, on average, ten loads (of forty bushels) after they have been cleaned. I saw immense fields of them. Two loads a week are fed to six horses, with as much chaff as they want and very little hay between Christmas – or sometimes earlier – and Whitsun, and then they lift the remainder and pack them in cellars[66] to prevent their rotting.

In all these farms, the rotation of crops is first, carrots; second, barley (sown with clover and ray-grass); third, clover and ray-grass, two or three years; fourth, peas; fifth, rye.[67]

Sometimes, this arrangement is changed; it is up to the farmer. Often it goes: 1. turnips; 2. barley; 3. rye or peas; 4. carrots.

Through these various methods of cultivation they have a great many cattle and especially sheep, and in consequence a great deal of manure and profit.

[65] 25 March, the Annunciation of the B. V. Mary.
[66] *les serrent dans les caves* . . . Young says nothing of cellars: perhaps François meant 'hollows'.
[67] This was Mr Gerrard's rotation at Sutton.

I don't want to go into much more detail, although I easily could, on the subject of the cultivation of this whole district: I could lose myself in overdoing it and my account of it all would be no more interesting. It is enough for me to say that this immense tract of country, in which the soil is nothing but shifting sand, has not only been brought into cultivation, but even made very profitable: and all that by cultivating turnips and carrots, which – grown in very light land – serve to feed a great many animals and so produce a great deal of manure. The knowledge possessed by all these farmers is incredible: you have to see them to believe it possible that plain farmers will talk for an hour on the principles of their art, and the reasons behind their different methods, with a man like Mr Young, who is extremely well informed, particularly on everything to do with agriculture.

Nor should you think that it is a poor cattle they rear in this way. Their horses are the only good and dependable ones in this county; a breed of cart-horses altogether distinctive; with short legs, large heads, great girths, the legs strong and jointed low: so that they are not very grand creatures but they have extraordinary drawing-power: they are all sorrel-coloured (*alezans*).

These horses work ten hours a day and are always glossy-coated and healthy: their drawing-power is incredible: we saw one who often drags as much as 25 comb of wheat in a waggon, and the farmer offered to bet that he would pull 30 comb; whereas the ordinary load for a horse is 5 or 6.[68]

The farmers of this district generally all meet together every year to compete with their horses.[69] Usually they meet and each makes a certain contribution (over half-a-guinea) towards a dinner and a silver cup that they buy for the winner. Then, each competitor harnesses a team of six horses to an enormous tree or to a block of immovable stone: the team which, at the command of the waggoner, makes the greatest efforts without being shown the whip, wins the prize. I was assured that very often the horses strain so powerfully that all six of them fall on their

[68] A comb was 4 bushels and a waggon about 25 cwt, so with 30 comb, or sacks, the horse would be drawing a weight of nearly 5 tons. Apparently a team of four good horses could, without hurting themselves, draw such a load thirty miles: Young's *Farmer's Tour through the East of England*, 1771.
[69] For these drawing-matches, see section on 'Hunters and cart-horses,' above, p. 53.

knees. Occasionally, the prize is offered for the horse that drags the heaviest loads, in accordance with the rules. Such kinds of contest had much better be encouraged by Government than the Newmarket races: the breed of these horses is more useful. Nor should one condemn the dinners that follow such matches; nor rate the farmers fools for spending thus money they have amassed by the sweat of their brow. It is in such meetings of professionals that each one clarifies his ideas, learns a new method that his neighbour has tried out and proved; that discussions ensue; and it is partly, I think, a result of these frequent meetings that this country has the good agriculture that distinguishes it from other parts of the world.

We made much mileage that day in going over all the farms we knew to be the most considerable, and all that day was spent in the most satisfactory way. The end of the day put a stop to our investigations, and we relaxed at Saxmundham. It is a kind of village, but it is well lived in.

We had intended to return next day to Bury, as Mr Young had various things to see to on his farm. He had soon to deal with the harvest on his farm. Yet I badly wanted to see Sir Gerard Wanneck's house, which is superb, the only house in Suffolk really worth seeing. I proposed at supper that we should go to see it next day; I was enjoying the trip and not at all put out at the thought of prolonging it a little. My proposal was first considered and discussed, then approved; and so we decided to lengthen our tour by a day.

*   *   *

The day on the 15th was not fine: we had a little fine rain from time to time – although the English called it mist – and it allowed us to see nothing through it. But as it looked fair in the east, we hoped all morning for a sight of the sun by midday. And hope consoles.

I saw nothing notable on the way that day except that the land grew more fertile at every step, and the sand richer; the fields were enclosed and narrower; I saw no more carrots.

We arrived at Sir Gerard Wanneck's house[70] at nine in the morning and presented a letter from Mr Symonds. He received us very coldly

[70] Heveningham Hall was designed about 1777 by Sir Robert Taylor for Sir Gerard Vanneck, son of a wealthy London merchant and grandson of the paymaster of the land

and, keeping his hat on, asked us in. No notice need be taken of that kind of thing in England, the intention is good, the forms alone are lacking. We withdrew to put on our own hats, then we entered.

Sir Gerard's sister was at breakfast, we took tea with her, and the conversation became less frigid every moment. Sir Gerard talked a little, and we saw how well-disposed he was towards us and how his first greeting had given us quite the wrong idea of him. After breakfast we went over the house, which is superb and which I shall describe to you in some detail.

There was at one time a small, much older house,[71] which was extremely run down, though its site was agreeable. Ten or twelve years ago, Sir Gerard had all the internal walls knocked down and made his hall (or vestibule) out of the shell: everything else has been added; and in truth, in the middle of the handsome modern building, one would not doubt that the old one is there. This hall is 72 feet by 24, with columns and great altitude. It is extremely noble, magnificent, all clad in the finest possible stucco,[72] statues were lacking when I was there, but their provision will not be overlooked.

To the right of this superb room is the breakfast room, oblong, the finest proportions, large and hung with beautiful pictures; it is covered in a light blue paper, simple but elegant: the mantelpiece is of very well-carved white marble.

---

forces of the United Provinces. The sumptuous interior decoration was the work of James Wyatt, helped by one of Robert Adam's assistants, Biagio Rebecca. As Lazowski wrote in 1784, 'the house is magnificent, built in the grand manner, and makes a great impression.' Not the least valuable aspect of this July visit is that it supplies, as no other record does, a first-hand account, by reasonably sophisticated travellers, of the state of completion and details of the original colouring. Only the saloon, or drawing-room, in the south-east corner, was recorded as being 'pas encore fini'. Its decoration was in fact never finished: it remained the least grand and most 'liveable' room in the house. Wyatt designed the orangery, and Capability Brown the landscape.

[71] It seems to have been a house of about 1710, which Taylor gutted and used for his central mass, with 'the same Paris-inspired lines as Sir William Chambers's Strand front at Somerset House' (Sir John Summerson, *Architecture in Britain*, 1530–1830, 1953, p. 224). As to colouring, when I first saw the print-room in the 1950s, François 'blue' wall-paper had been replaced by a green one; but as we see with the shelduck at Snettisham later on, François 'blue' may have been our green. When I last saw the print-room in 1985, it was being entirely re-decorated: pink!

[72] Lazowski noted the scagliola columns, 'stucco columns imitating the antique yellow', but was not carried away, as many of us are, by this glorious room. He felt it was 'absurd' to have a room so large that it cut off one half of the house from the other.

139

From this room we went into another, small, papered in blue and with prints pasted straight on to it like pictures: a gay effect. It's a little room, but a pretty oval in shape. Here Sir Gerard dines when he's on his own. From here, we went through two other small rooms, then, turning back on our tracks, we crossed the hall and entered the dining-room.

I have never seen anything comparable with the perfect balance of the proportions of this room combined with the elegance of its decoration:[73] its dimensions are thirty-two (feet) by twenty-four; three large windows distribute a powerful daylight. I should still think it impossible to contemplate a more beautiful room if we had not immediately entered the library, which wiped it at once from my sight. This room is the masterpiece of taste. Doubling [he means 'paired with the dining-room, at the back of the house'] is a saloon, not yet finished.

The bedrooms are large and convenient. They are designed generally with only the bedroom; in accordance with custom here, some of them have a little sitting-room. The private staircases are numerous and all the conveniences are to be found in this house. I even went to see the kitchen, which is very fine, cleanliness supreme, and running water on all sides. The one inconvenience of this house is that the vestibule is so tall that it cuts the house completely in two, so that one wing has no communication with the other.

The exterior matches the interior in magnificence. It is built in the classical taste; twenty-three window-bays form the front, the ground floor is without ornament, but the windows are round-arched: the first floor is adorned with columns, very grand and all of the same order: the bricks are white and painted deep grey,[74] which looks pretty odd at close quarters but very well at a distance. The roof is flat, in the Italian way.

[73] Lazowski gave details: painted 'en camaieux ponceau', red, wild-poppy coloured painting, monochrome, in imitation of low reliefs – the reliefs in poppy-red, the background white. The library, Lazowski agreed, was magnificent, but not yet 'en livres'. 'Everything to do with ornament is charming, often in exquisite taste, but it belongs much less to any original English taste than to the antique taste borrowed in Italy and imitated and adapted to their own uses with a truth and an elegance that are stunning.'
[74] Lazowski calls it a 'grey-blue distemper'. He goes into detail about the arrangement of the Corinthian columns and the correspondingly rich cornice, the rustication at ground level (the French call it the *premier étage*, as well as the *rez-de-chaussée*).

The house is on a completely double plan, which makes it prodigiously large. The offices and outbuildings form another, smaller, building, almost in the rear. The stables also form a considerable block.

The position of the house is agreeable. On the slope of a hill exposed to the east[75] and backed by mature woods, it presides over an entire small valley, along the bottom of which a number of houses make a charming view; not too distant, nor too near, and the eye picks out details without effort; whichever way you look, the countryside is equally delightful. Soon, in the bottom of the valley, there will be a superb artificial river that should have (and I believe it will) a perfectly natural look. This is easy to make, for in the bottom there is a spring, from which the flow can be controlled, and also a pool a little lower down which will complete the river. Agreeable as the site is, I do not think it is the one on which this house should have been placed. The other side of the valley would have been better, to my way of thinking; you would have found equally delightful views and you would have avoided having immediately behind the house an almost vertical slope, which isn't very high but cannot help being very disagreeable. Sir Gerard has furnished the slope with a flower-garden that is as ugly as it is unsuitable. Apart from the fact that this slope blocks all the view from the windows of the saloon, it is so close that it must spread a lot of damp through the house, which does not stand on vaults.

As soon as we had viewed this superb house, Sir Gerard gave us horses to ride through the park with him. First we went through a wood – nice, but very small – then we crossed the valley in front of the house and came to another little wood on the crown of the hill opposite, from which we could see all twenty-three window-bays of the front in all their splendour. The simple, and noble, architectural design of this house shows – from all slightly distant points of view – to superb advantage (Pl. 28).

This last little wood was big enough and very dense; excellent, I should think, for game. The ride by which we crossed it is twenty feet wide and follows an easy contour without being straight: it is a grassy ride.[76]

[75] In fact it stands on a north-facing slope.
[76] Lazowski was tremendously impressed by the '16 miles of fine grassy roadway created for going by open carriage and on horseback over a superb countryside'. These woods were all terribly damaged in the great gale of October 1987.

141

The lodge is nearby. It seems to me to be built in exactly the right style: low, big enough, and clad all over with branches of fir and pine, fixed over the brickwork which they hide entirely. The curves of the window-heads are irregular, following the whim of the branch which happened to be in place over it. It is all very neat, and responsively rustic.

Our ride was one of about ten or twelve miles, always on paths of either turf or earth carefully sanded. The different view-points are agreeable and varied; everywhere the countryside that comes into view is covered with houses, farms and church-towers; all round, the land is well-cultivated, and the boundary hedges are (as far as the eye can see) well kept. In a word, the admiration that possessed me left no place for the minutest criticism,[77] and I was enchanted as I rode. As we returned over our tracks, right on the hill facing the house, we rode past the foot of a massive oak, the formation and the dark shadiness of which gave some idea of its antiquity. It is extremely massive and hollow, not very tall and with many branches dead; despite this, it shades an immense area and is planted in a good position. It is very remarkable that Queen Elizabeth, who lived at the time of our Henry IV and who owned this park, was in the habit of sitting at the foot of this tree to shoot the deer – her favourite sport. That shows you how old the oak is. Its girth is 35 feet, five feet above the ground.[78]

We returned to Sir Gerard Wanneck's only to leave as quickly as possible in order to spend the night further on our way and reach Bury the next day. We had a kind of extra breakfast of the best and most perfect fruit, and after thanking the master of the house and his sister for their kindness, we set off for Framlingham.

*   *   *

[77] He had already forgotten about the wrong choice of house-site, and that flower-garden at the back, both of which were very valid criticisms.

[78] We need not question the girth or antiquity of the tree, but the legend of Queen Elizabeth's visit springs from the undoubted fact that Lord Hunsdon owned the adjoining manor of Huntingfield, and from some slight similarity between the names Hunsdon and Huntingfield: the queen certainly visited him at his house at Hunsdon in Hertfordshire. Venerable oaks have a way of attracting legends: at Henham. not far from here, the 'royalist' Sir John Rous is alleged to have been concealed from the Cromwellians in a great oak: the trouble with this is that Rous was a member of the Parliamentarian county committee (see S.R.S. III, *passim*).

28. *Heveningham Hall, 1782. Thomas Hearne, engraved by W. Watts.*

29. *Framlingham Castle, 1785. Engraved by Godfrey, published S. Hooper.*
(Suffolk R.O., Local Studies Library)

The countryside is superb, its unevenness presenting pictures of infinite variety. We passed farms belonging to Mr Staunton, Sir John Blois, Sir John Rous, Mr Crawford, Mr Davy, etc.[79]

That is the district of Suffolk where the finest cows are, the best in all England for giving milk. The farmers with dairies there number perhaps forty or fifty. In their cows they set store by a good long body, a large carcass, a definite colour at the neck and generally a rich bay (red-brown) body, long udders and little legs – in fact, a fairly ugly animal.[80] They yield six gallons – a gallon is [blank] – of milk a day at the best time of the season.

All the farmers in these parts grow fields of cabbages for the winter-keep of their cows – eight or ten acres of them for forty cows. After the cabbage they have barley the same year on the same field.

The rotation of crops here is fairly generally: 1. fallow; 2. barley with clover; 3. clover by itself; 4. wheat; 5. beans, hoed twice; 6. wheat. Rent is from thirteen to sixteen shillings an acre.

At Framlingham we saw the church and the castle, as recommended, though there was nothing much to see. Someone told us at the castle (Pl. 29), in showing us the place where Mary Queen of Scots was for a long time,[81] that she had been brought into the world by a serpent – a popular belief held generally in this country, deriving from the enthusiasm that the English had, and still maintain, for their Queen Elizabeth.

---

[79] Young explains that they went to Framlingham via Yoxford, a distinct détour to the east: much more direct routes would have been by Peasenhall, or by Badingham and Dennington. Blois, Davy and *Crowfoot* held the Yoxford estates; Thos. Staunton at Sibton, and Rous at Dennington. Lazowski says they took the wrong road!

[80] He does not notice that they are universally polled – hornless – to reduce damage to horses and fences.

[81] Mary, Queen of Scots, was never at Framlingham, but Mary Tudor of England came to Framlingham at the critical moment of her accession in 1553: Lazowski, disgusted, wrote: 'Queen Mary Stuart was imprisoned in this castle and we hoped we might still find some vestiges of her rooms, for I was with a man equally passionate about her as I am: we were longing for details, but cruelly misled. An old woman led us to a murky recess in the thickness of the walls and gravely assured us that it was there that the queen was engendered of a serpent. There is no absurdity that religious fanaticism and antipathy will not produce: Queen Mary was catholic, the people of Framlingham are protestant: that explains everything.' Right explanation, but wrong Mary. Lazowski noticed that the walls were built before the invention of gunpowder, from the slits being wide enough for arrows but not for muskets!

144

After Framlingham, the road passes right through the district famous for fine dairy-cows. They are even finer than they were the other side of Framlingham. They feed all summer on grass, which they are careful to have in great plenty, and for that reason some fields rest fallow for five or six years; the cows sleep in the fields, which they don't leave, even to be milked. In winter they are fed on oat-straw; failing that, on the straw of wheat or barley, with some cabbage, which they relish as a great delicacy. During all the time of cold and snow they are kept in the farmyard and fed there, and never go under cover, and are always healthy. If you wanted to buy one, she would cost you seven or eight guineas.

Hereabouts the arable cropping is 1. fallow; 2. barley; yield five or six quarters;[82] 3. beans or clover; 4. wheat.

Soon after, we left this good land and the nearer we got to Stowmarket, the sandier we found the land.[83] The bad weather, which had scarcely left us at all during this little tour, showed us no mercy on our last day: it rained so much that we could hardly, to tell the truth, think about agriculture: the mist raised by torrential rain reduced visibility to scarcely a hundred yards. I was so fed up with it that, with my brother, I abandoned the cabriolet, which could not keep up with us, and we awaited our more leisurely companions in the inn, drinking good hot punch, which soon thawed us out after the cold and rain.

Stowmarket is a town at best no bigger than a small village, with scarcely three or four hundred houses,[84] but what makes it a town is its market. This town is placed right in the middle of the county, and so it is here that they hold the election of Members of Parliament when there are only two candidates.[85]

[82] Reading uncertain: looks like 'cinq ou six récoltes'.
[83] This can only refer to the Gipping valley sands and gravels, a narrow strip in the surrounding good glacial clays that Young called 'strong loam'. Young's 'Five days' tour', op. cit., suggests fruitful consultations with individual farmers in the Soham, Debenham, Wetheringsett, Stonham country which he must, I think, have inserted from earlier visits: they could not all have been fitted into this long, wretchedly wet English summer day.
[84] Nine years later, the Gipping was made navigable to Stowmarket from Ipswich, and by 1841 the population had doubled.
[85] He is referring to the election of the two M.P.s for the county: when there were only two candidates it was not a disputed election. With more than two candidates it would be held at Ipswich, the county town: see François' 'Fragment on government', pp. 73–4 above.

From Stowmarket to Bury (fourteen miles) the soil is so sandy that it is a serious handicap to agriculture. The chief product in the neighbourhood of Stowmarket is hops: near Bury there are few enclosures.[86]

Such is the summary of my tour in Suffolk made with the man who, perhaps in all England, was the most agreeable and most useful of travelling companions. This county, a very large one, owes its charm to the variety of things to be seen. There is every kind of soil, every kind of farming, its own breed of horses, an excellent breed of cows, great numbers of sheep – and I have forgotten to mention that they have black faces and legs, and superb wool. Can one disregard the attraction of the countryside that gives pleasure to the traveller and happiness to the inhabitant? This little tour gave me the most enormous pleasure: it was not merely that all I saw was new and interesting to me, every single thing was agreeable, and I was quite discontented on the sixth day to get back home.[87]

OF AGRICULTURE IN GENERAL

Agriculture is the mainspring and – looking at it another way – the end-result of a flourishing, well-peopled state. These two complementary propositions demonstrate both that England is well cultivated, and why.

Here, agriculture is held in the highest regard, everyone is involved in it, and the ordinary farmers are not looked on, as they are in France, as an inferior class created solely to feed the rich.

---

[86] François, perhaps rather tired of the journey, is less than accurate. Sandiness is not an obtrusive obstacle to farming between Stowmarket and Bury, and hops certainly grew down by the Rattlesden river at Abbot's Hall, Stowmarket: but Young recorded only 50 acres of them there, and 136 acres divided among nine neighbouring parishes (Young, *General View*, 1797, pp. 88–93).

[87] Arthur Young's comments must be recorded: 'Returned home, finishing a little journey, instructive from the variety of intelligence I received and pleasing from the conversation and politeness of my companions, who, I have no doubt, are convinced of the real importance of attending to the agriculture of the countries through which they may have occasion to travel.' François' next section demonstrates beautifully that Young's teaching and example had entirely succeeded.

Do not assume that what prompts this proposition is an admiration for the country where I happen to be, which causes me to see things other than they are and in a favourable light. If you glance for a moment at the form of government and the manner of life of the greatest landowners, you will see that fundamentals of agriculture lead them to an overall equality. Reality here shows this: the big landowner and the farmer have no differences between them except the degree of wealth. I am not speaking of the lords who sit in the Upper House; even more you will see that the respect they enjoy and the credit they have in their own county depend solely on the way they behave towards the gentry and the farmers.

The way the taxes are assessed gives most encouragement to farmers. The taxes they pay are heavy, but as the price of what they sell is proportionate, they profit accordingly. The tax to which they are subjected is on their land: they find the way to increase the yield of this same acreage, they do not have to pay more. A second tax they pay is for the poor. This is assessed on rent, but leases run for twenty years and in twenty years they can make considerable improvement for which they never have to pay tax.

Most of the gentry who live on their estates for eight months of the year have some of their land in hand, farmed by themselves; the right amount to occupy them, without risking ruin by faulty farming-practice. Some of them understand the business better than others, and they quickly expand and farm in a bigger way. So this art providential to the state is well regarded, and farmers enjoy a special consideration.

This circulation, so to speak, of people who go to spend two months in London and then as long taking the waters or staying with their friends, and return for eight months to their country houses, is, I reckon, the second reason for the good agriculture of England. Unquestionably, the first is the form of government. But why are the farmers prosperous and why do they pour immense funds into their farms? Because it is generally thought very honourable to be a 'substantial' farmer (a rich man with a large farm and a very extensive trade in cattle). The reason why farming is thought of as an honourable activity is that the highest in the land are engaged in it and that, although it may be for their own amusement, they try to make all the profit they can. This is also the explanation for the great and daily improvements in agriculture: large-scale experiments are made by these

147

amateurs, and if they succeed they are soon followed by the working farmers. You have no idea of the intelligence of all these farmers, and I mean even small farmers: I have seen a hundred of them in the course of our little tour of Suffolk, and around Bury, talking with Mr Young on the principles of their art, discussing new possibilities and reciting their own findings for three-quarters of an hour or an hour at a time; which always excited Mr Young's admiration, however accustomed to it he was.

I said that the form of government was the main basis of the state of agriculture in England. I wanted to discuss the equality that prevails through the influence of government and the way in which the taxes, fairly placed, bore severely on the rich and very little on the poor. But the greatest good the government confers, and the greatest it can confer in all states, is to do nothing at all: throughout this country, no rules, nothing forbidden, nor need of encouragement of any kind: the greatest of all encouragements, for any class of people whatever, is their own personal interest and the personal interest of a large collection of individuals constitutes the interest of the state.[1] Anyone can sell anything at the highest price he can get; traders travel about if they think they find it pays them to do so. No one meddles at all in their affairs, and England, to the eye of an impartial traveller, looks a hundred times richer than France.

It seems well established that the more a farmer pours money into his land in the form of improvement, the more money he makes; but, to do this, he must have a long lease, for with a short lease he can harvest only half the fruits of his labours. It is also very true that the more profit he makes, the more he is likely to learn, and so agricultural knowledge is the better off. Now, that is what they have in England and we do not have: in our country, a man who had money – even if he had made it in the same branch of trade – would not want to remain a farmer, he would move into town and act the little gentleman; in this country, when they have grown quite rich, they glory in the fact that a hundred

[1] François seems to have forgotten what he wrote about what was forbidden on Sunday. All this is the stuff of John Locke's writings on Civil Government, Toleration, etc. Whether or not he read them, François had clearly absorbed into his system the essentials of English political belief in the 18th century: 'For forms of government let fools contest; Whate'er is least administer'd is best.'

years earlier their grandfather occupied the same farm and had a hard time.

The farmers are so convinced that you must pour plenty of money into a farm on first going into it, that a farmer does not take up a lease unless he has in his pocket one guinea to lay out on every acre in his first year, whether in buying cattle, or in marling, etc.[2]

OF MR BAKEWELL

To give a striking example of the opulence of English farmers, of their aspirations to learn and of the expense they will go to in that cause, I will cite Mr Bakewell, who farms near Cambridge, who has become very famous by bringing to perfection all the breeds of animals that are useful in agriculture.[1] I saw him at Mr Symonds' house just as he was about to return home after a journey of three or four hundred miles through the best cultivated parts of England, undertaken solely to find out about the different methods others employed, about which they always give the clearest information: they are not afraid, as they would be in France, that if someone knew about their profits, a small increase in taxes would be imposed.

This farmer was accompanied by one of his friends, who was making the same journey for the same reason. They generally devote two or three months a year to making a journey to improve their knowledge; they are well mounted, and the two together spend a guinea a day.

Since I have spoken of Mr Bakewell as an example of the knowledge farmers acquire, I want to speak of him at greater length, for he is one of the most original men to meet in the kingdom.

He is a well-to-do farmer; his father left him his farm when he was a young man and he has had it ever since. From his youth he applied

[2] This is François' first reference to 'marling', the addition of marl, a chalky clay, to improve light land: a favourite theme of Arthur Young's.

[1] Robert Bakewell (1725–95) carried out his world-famous improvements in farm-stock at Dishley Grange, in the Soar valley, just north of Loughborough, in Leicestershire. In 1785, after writing this, François and the others visited Dishley and found that it was about 80 miles north-west of Cambridge.

himself to perfecting every kind of animal that could be useful to him, and after long research and great expense he has arrived at the greatest degree of perfection possible. He began by buying animals of all kinds, the finest specimens, and by crossing them arrived at a breed with all the qualities and perfections of all its forebears and without their defects. I may not have grasped it fully:[2] he bought supposedly the best cow and the best bull he could find, but arranged so that if the bull was tall and strong, with fine legs, the cow had a good head, well-made back, etc. It is known more or less which parts of the body will be affected by the father and the mother of the offspring, and arrangements can be made in consequence. After many, many attempts, his perseverance triumphed, and on the testimony of everyone who knows about such things, he acquired the finest breed of cart-horses, cows, sheep, pigs etc. His oxen have the propensity to fatten in less time than those of other breeders, because the cows that produced them were half-fattened when they calved; perhaps the bull was too. He has made a large number of bets on all this, and constantly wins. His sheep have the finest wool combined with length, such as sheep with fine wool don't normally have when intended for the butcher. They also have the advantage of fattening more quickly.[3] Finally, his pigs are large, with fat bellies and very short legs; they fatten well on potatoes, which others do not. They, too, fatten in a short time. He is now so sure of his facts that he will offer to supply anyone with an ox which will put on fat in its head, on its back, and even in those parts of the chest or the belly where they don't usually get fat. He even proposed to bet us that he would have some that would put fat on in their tails. All that is astonishing. I don't really understand it, but I believe it as I believe in Religion, because I have been told that you have to believe it, and that everyone believes in it. It often happens that a man who excels in whatever it is, is greatly valued by some people but by others not seen in the same light: it is not so with Mr Bakewell, who is highly regarded throughout England, and his breeds well-known and promptly hired.

[2] If François had not grasped it fully, that was perhaps because Bakewell took advantage of other people's experience but was deliberately careful of his own secrets (Young, *Farmer's Tour through the East of England*, 1771, I, p. 118).
[3] This was the great thing: other breeds took three or four years to get ready for market, his New Leicesters needed only two. No wonder he could let out his rams at the excessive prices François records in the next paragraph.

I say 'promptly hired' because he never sells what is most perfect in any breed, but lets out a horse, a ram, a hog, etc., for a summer, for the purpose of establishing the breed among those keen to do this. The price of hiring is excessive. He generally lets out rams of his finest breed at eighty or ninety guineas a summer. A ram can serve 140 ewes. The charges for other breeds are in proportion. This price is only for the most superbly bred. He sells the others that don't reach their top class, but which are still infinitely superior to any other in England. All this will seem to you inconceivable, and you won't believe it, but it is gospel truth.

Some time ago, those who hired animals of the breeds Mr Bakewell had brought to such perfection failed to pay up properly, none of the Scots he supplied paid up, etc., so that the continual and considerable expenses he incurred reduced him to bankruptcy,[4] though there was not the least blame on his part. In such cases the English are admirable, their charity is prompt and generous. His friends opened a subscription (or voluntary contribution) for him, and he at once received a thousand pounds sterling which enabled him to go on with his experiments. The duke of Richmond alone gave 500 guineas. So, without any meddling by the government, the generosity of individuals and their enthusiasm provide for the needs of the industrious person who owes his misfortune to no fault of his own. And now Mr Bakewell is much better off than he was, for he has been paid the money that was owed him and on account of which he went bankrupt.

This example I have given of English farmers is a little above their ordinary way of going on. They don't make journeys on which they spend half-a-guinea a day over two or three months, but they do gather all kinds of information from their neighbours and from those who have better results than they have themselves. The clubs where they often go provide the opportunity of instructive conversations, and I shall speak of them later. All the farmers are well mounted and most[5] enjoy the pleasures of the chase with the harriers three or four times a week. When you go to see them at home, you are well received, and they offer and open a bottle of wine that would cost three francs of our money.

[4] His bankruptcy was listed in *The Gentleman's Magazine* of November 1776, p. 531. Arthur Young had got into similar difficulties with his banker in 1770 (*Autobiography*, p. 53), but was able to avoid bankruptcy.
[5] *la plupart* is perhaps an exaggeration, but it may well be that most *would* have . . .

Their houses are always clean, always well kept, their barns in excellent condition, and they always manage to keep a small sitting-room excessively spick-and-span, and sometimes elegant, where they entertain their guests. The tables and chairs in this room are of well-polished mahogany, the fireplace is sometimes of marble but generally of carved wood.

ENGLISH FARMS AND SOME AGRICULTURAL DETAILS

English farming methods are as different from ours as the farmers themselves are different. All the land under cultivation is enclosed by ditches, with hedges on the higher bank of the ditch.[1] They divide their lands by this means as they wish, making the fields larger or smaller according to the relative goodness of the soil. This makes it possible for them to have many cattle in the fields day and night.

They never let their lands lie fallow, but the different methods by which they 'rotate' their crops depend on the local practice and on the intelligence of the farmers. They always find some means of getting some use from the soil, and when it is so poor that it cannot produce corn every two or three years, they sow grass, make a meadow and, by letting their beasts eat the crop thereby enrich the field with their dung.

Following this system, they accept that a field produces wheat only once in four or five years, but they compensate themselves for this slight loss by the quantity of cattle they keep.

The consumption of meat is very much greater in England than in any other country, without exception – all people eat it and, generally speaking, the Englishman is carnivorous. It is a great advantage to agriculture and the farmers know how to profit by it. Their livestock is the foundation of their farming; and the way they look after their stock is the mainstay of their wealth. The quantity of their cattle is immense, and their sheep, above all, are innumerable. In the summer, they are spread out all over the countryside, day and night, in fields that need

[1] He has not noticed that most of the farms he has seen in East Anglia are on heavy, water-holding boulder-clay; they need these ditches to drain them before they can grow good crops, whether arable or grass.

manuring, and in sheepwalks over commons. It is known that there are no wolves in England, a notable fact very favourable to farming.

The fields are well-enclosed, and shut off with sheep-folds from which the flocks cannot wander. In summer they are usually either in fields of sown grass or in hayfields or rye, for they are often sown solely for that purpose. In the autumn they are turned into the stubble-fields after harvest, to eat the stubble, which is always left very long, and the weeds: the pigs, too, go in so as not to lose the grain fallen during the harvest. In winter, the majority of cows, oxen and horses return to the farmyard where they are all together, always in the open. They are given great quantities of straw in cases of a kind, made of wood; they eat as much as they want, and the rest is spread to serve them as bedding. For me, it is delightful to walk about in the farmyard. Those who are nervous of animals can walk round the outside. You see a great quantity of oxen, cows, horses, foals and pigs, all there together, and in separate attitudes.[2] Their keep costs nothing very much – for a horse about a shilling (24 sols) a week. The other animals scarcely cost more. The sheep are the only ones spared this captivity: always in the fields, sometimes in sown grass, sometimes turnips.

The cultivation of the turnip is one of the most profitable: it is general in Suffolk. Other counties also cultivate it, but not so generally. The turnip has the property of giving moisture to the soil in which it is sown, also that of stifling weeds. It is a kind of round root, white and rotund, sown in June or July, the leaves appearing in September: they are hoed twice and kept in the ground all winter, to provide food for the flocks: their leaves stay green all winter, even through the frost and snow, and it is rare for either leaf or root to be frozen.

In fields where the soil is poor, the farmers have the sheep feeding on the turnips, through the winter, shutting the sheep into a field. The sheep eat them greedily. When there are fields that are absolutely impoverished on a farm, you put a flock on them in winter and cart in turnips and scatter turnips all over the fields. All kinds of animals like turnips so much that when a full cart-load arrives in the middle of a flock, they all follow it in order to eat any as soon as they tumble to the ground. Oxen, sheep and pigs are fattened on turnips, by being given them in great quantity.

[2] Here he anticipates Beatrix Potter.

Turnips grow well only in sandy country, improving the soil by making it moister and destroying weeds by their pungent smell. There are certain counties where they are not cultivated on account of the nature of the land; different substitutes are found, but in no country does one meet with any crop that has properties so advantageous to agriculture and is so easy to grow.

When the beasts have been fattened, most are sold in the country, the finest going to London. The oxen that are fattened all over England are not natives of any of the English counties but come at the age of fourteen or eighteen months from the hills of Scotland. They are distributed all through England to work there or to live for a couple of years, then be fattened and killed. They are called 'bullocks', and are smaller and grow fatter than those of English stock, which are not common.

Agricultural implements are not very different from ours, but they are a bit bigger and more convenient. Their ploughs are simpler. They are without wheels, in Suffolk and Norfolk at any rate; they are often of iron and, at the end by which the horses draw them, they all have a sort of small ratchet perhaps four or five inches long and with three or four teeth. The plough drives into the ground more or less according to the notch by which the horses pull.

Brand's Plough[3]

[3] For John Brand, of Lawford, and his famous first wrought-iron plough, see p. 115 above. Young, in his *Farmer's Tour through the East of England* (four volumes, written in 1770 and published the next year) noted that this plough was already in great demand. By 1785, Robert Ransome had taken out a patent for tempering cast-iron ploughshares. By 1803 he had perfected the ploughshare that did not need constant re-sharpening: S.R.S. I, *Suffolk Farming in the 19th Century*, 1958, p. 25.

The waggons, ploughs, harness, etc., are always'in good condition. Their horses, groomed carefully, have this peculiarity that their manes are cropped short and their tails to the first joint.[4] They assert that their horses would otherwise be unnecessarily overburdened and that, as there are few flies in summer, they have no need of their tails.

COMMONS ENCLOSURE

A traveller is bound to be surprised, in a country so well cultivated and so enlightened and where the good so generally obtains, to find so much common land as there is, even at the gates of the capital. These lands are for the most part enormously extensive and are no use for anything but the sheep of those parishioners who have a right to send them there: worse, they are sometimes so much overgrown with bracken that they are good for absolutely nothing. However, the traveller should try not to condemn without understanding, and not to ascribe to neglect what is merely irremediable.

These waste lands belong to a large number of proprietors, and it is necessary for them all to agree before an Act of Parliament can enable improvement: already there is difficulty enough. The Act costs a great deal, at least a hundred guineas. Then the last and most persuasive reason is that the prime mover can always be sure of making himself unpopular, because the poor have, from time immemorial, the right to cut the bracken and brushwood for firewood. People in this country fear unpopularity more than anything else.

These are the reasons why all the wastes are not at once put into cultivation. They are not powerful enough to prevent improvement little by little, and it is widely reckoned that, each year, in England, seventy parishes are cleared and enclosed. In a few years from now all will be in proper cultivation: everyone is agreed about this.

[4] François noticed this peculiarity of the Suffolk horse when he was describing them at p. 53 above.

A TOUR IN NORFOLK

Our little tour in Suffolk had been too agreeable and interesting for us not to be tempted to start off on another, in a different county. Norfolk, which is nearest, offered us some very interesting agricultural objects. We decided on a fortnight's tour there, and Mr Symonds was willing to come with us. Two cabriolets, known as *gigs*, and two horses, which we had just bought for our great journey, our projected tour of England,[1] were just what we wanted for this little tour; and the weather which had – as if by chance – been fine for a fortnight, seemed to promise us that all was set fair.

As prudent travellers do not embark on a voyage without biscuits, we did not set out without having a good number of letters to several gentlemen and farmers, whose property we should be passing, with a view to drawing from them as much instruction as we could.

We left [Bury] on 24 September, Mr Symonds and my brother were in one of our gigs, I was in the other with Mr Lazowski, and Mr Symonds' servant with one of ours followed in a third, so that the suite of carriages made our journey look more like an expedition for pleasure than one that had a purely useful aim.

The weather was very agreeable: the freshness of the heavy dew promised us a fine day: it was chilly in the shade, but the sun, already high above the horizon, seemed all the more encouraging.

Thetford, a dozen miles from Bury, was where we were going for breakfast: we arrived at nine. From Bury, we passed through a little village called Ingham where there are three substantial farms belonging to Lord Cornwallis: the road is quite good as far as that, but on leaving Ingham it becomes sandy and clinging because of the large quantity of shifting sand all too abundant in this area: besides, it is not made up and the very deep ruts are often highly troublesome. You cross the duke of Grafton's estate, remarkable for the great numbers of rabbits you see and foxes you don't see: this, together with the poor soil, gives little chance of agricultural prosperity. Also, all this country, which the road crosses for eight miles, is covered only with heather, reaching out of

---

[1] From 16 February to 26 April, 1785, they toured England in this same searching, observant way, and in 1786 Lazowski and Alexandre went to look at Scotland and Ireland. I hope to publish their findings.

sight in all directions; not a shrub, not a decent herb, except in the little valleys that one sees some way off, shallow and so hardly damp.

Thetford was formerly one of the principal towns of England. There was a fortress in the time of the Saxons: one still sees the remains, an artificial mound perhaps as much as a hundred feet high, perfectly round and symmetrically constructed; around it, some sort of redoubts had been made, dominating one another, and the countryside, and the town. A hollow road that one can make out provided access to the river running below. The fosses have the appearance of great depth; however, I noticed that the bottom was only at the level of the surrounding land and the rest was built up with transported earth. This building must have been a work of immense labour and I cannot think where they can have brought all this earth from.[2]

The town is practically deserted today. It stands in the shallowest of valleys on a little river that divides the two counties of Norfolk and Suffolk. As three-quarters of its houses are on the Norfolk side, I put the town in that county. I believe that you can count a mere three or four houses that are well built: the rest look poor and miserable. I must not forget to mention that Thetford is famous for setters:[3] almost all the rich in this place keep them, because the whole countryside round is very good for shooting – the heaths are full of game, and it may be found there at all times. There are many dogs of every variety of the best breeds.

After Thetford, the road continued across a country just as barren, and even drier, than the one we passed through in the morning: not a tree, no cultivation, everywhere sand, everywhere small tufts of heath-rushes[4] and bracken. A great part of this arid land is full of rabbits: the number amazes me. We saw them in multitudes, in broad daylight.

---

[2] We now know that this great earthwork is not Saxon but very early Norman. We remain as much amazed as François at the castle-building achievements of 11th-century magnates with such primitive earth-moving equipment and such a sparse population. As mounds go, Thetford is perhaps their most impressive.

[3] *Chiens couchants*: ?the original sleeping dogs. Lazowski describes a livelier Thetford than François: 'It lives now only by its markets, by its small river-borne trade, and by a fine brewery and a papermill which employ fifty persons daily.' He describes at rather too great length the working of the papermill. He also describes the castle in rather more minute detail than François.

[4] Perhaps gorse: see next paragraph.

They weren't afraid of noise, and we could almost reach some of them with our whips. I asked for an explanation of so prodigious a number. I was told it was an enormous warren, bringing in two hundred guineas a year to the proprietor, and let to a farmer. These rabbits have never heard gun-shots, and are not in the least timid.

The explanation of so enormous a number is simple. The farmer is careful to maintain all round a four-foot bank of turf sown with gorse,[5] which forms a boundary beyond which rabbits cannot go. Nor can they be caught, for the penalty is so disproportionate to the gain that no one would want to run the risk. The law looks on the rabbits of a warren[6] as property quite as sacred as the land itself, and breaking the law of property was pronounced a capital offence. For a few rabbits that sell very cheap, one wouldn't want to risk one's neck!

In some valleys watered by a trickle of a stream, I caught sight of fine trees and houses and cultivated lands, but not many. The dry sand blocks improvements, and I don't believe that anyone could succeed, in the end, in cultivating the twenty miles or so of wretched land we drove through that day.[7]

We were going on to sleep at Swaffham. We had come only eighteen miles from Thetford, but we stopped to give our horses a feed of oats and, while that was going on, we took a walk round. I continually admired the way, in all these little villages, the houses are clean and have a comfortable look that ours in France do not have: there is something – I can't define it – that presides over the arrangement of

---

[5] *jonc marin* is a plant François thought he could identify (see p. 134 above). Jonc normally means rush or reed or sedge. My first thought was that here he may have seen the native sandsedge, common in Breckland and on the sea-coast: *carex arenaria*. But he used the name to describe what is undoubtedly gorse (or whins as East Anglians call them) when he came to South Creake: see p. 177.

[6] Licences for warrens were granted to lords of manors (for a consideration) usually by royal charter, like markets and fairs: rabbits were introduced into England in the 12th century, and the 13th was the time of many such grants.

[7] At this point Lazowski gives a lyrical description of Mr Tasburgh's farm at Bodney, just short of Hilborough: François made no reference to it. Lazowski called it 'a fine, magnificent farm, a triumph over warrens and deserts achieved in the past 20 years'. Fields in good order. Fine vigorous trees. The manor-house old, but pleasant enough. Not much of a garden, but the stream and the trees shading the stream made it, for Lazowski at least, 'a romantic enough place'. Nowadays, it is spoilt by the adjacent Stanford battle-training area.

these houses and gives them the appearance of being better than they really are.

This village is called Hilborough. Among a dozen houses, one belongs to a man of affairs who may pass for one of the most adroit. While managing the estates of Mr Coke's uncle, he contrived, in a very few years, to amass nearly £40,000 sterling, and he is so artful that Mr Coke was obliged, on succeeding to his uncle's estates, to pay him money to be rid of him (Pl. 30).[8]

The rest of the way on this first day became a little less disagreeable as we drew near Swaffham. We saw, close to the town, some good enclosed fields and the soil looking a lot better.

Swaffham, situated in a large, very open, valley,[9] is reckoned to have about 2,500 people. It is built in the form of a triangle, in the middle of which is a sort of kiosk, a little temple-rotunda, well built and elegant in its design, which serves on market-days as shelter for the corn-merchants.[10] Its shape is circular and its diameter perhaps fifteen or eighteen feet: the roof, the same shape, is supported by thirteen columns. All the houses round the market-place are well built and struck me with their smart appearance: small white fences, posts well looked-after, the bricks and the neatly-painted doors give these houses something that one cannot get tired of admiring. This triangle of buildings makes up

[8] This refers to Hilborough Park House, then recently built and beautifully emparked just north of the church and beside the river Wissey. Ralph Caldwell, the Holkham agent, built it in 1779 of white brick, like Holkham itself. As it was expressed in the so-called 'Armstrong' History of Norfolk (1781), VI, Hundred of S. Greenhoe, p. 36: 'The earl died in 1759, and by his last will not only confirmed the enjoyment of those offices to Mr Caldwell during the term of his natural life, but appointed him and Sir Matthew Lambe, bart., devisees in trust of all his estates and effects, and the executors of his will.' It was Mr Coke's great-uncle, Thomas, the 2nd earl of Leicester, to whose enormous estates he succeeded. The Cokes had trouble with embezzling agents in the 18th century, as we see when the travellers reach Great Massingham. (See A. M. W. Stirling, Coke of Norfolk and his Friends, I, 1908, pp. 191–200.)
[9] Misleading: it stands at the crossing of three old roads on an eminence (for E. Anglia) about 250 feet above sea-level, between the little valleys of Wissey and Nar. See D. P. Dymond, The Norfolk Landscape, 1985, pp. 163–4, for a brilliant thumb-nail sketch of the town's structural history.
[10] Lazowski noted that this was where the farmers brought samples of their grain for the merchants to judge before buying. Lord Orford (see later) had had this market cross erected the previous year. It is still one of the most memorable small buildings in Norfolk. François fails to mention the crowning figure of Ceres with her sheaf of corn, a commodity that evidently sold better here in previous centuries.

159

the whole town: there are no other streets, so that at first sight you would think it bigger and more opulent than it is.

Market-day is Saturday. The trade is in goods needed for consumption by the local inhabitants, and some wheat, but only a very small amount.[11]

We were curious to see the church which was built by a pedlar who had, so the story goes, a very odd dream: he saw a churchyard and was assured that if he dug down a few feet he would find a treasure. Impressed with this good revelation, he went there next day and found two enormous coffers full of money, with a part of which he had the church built. It is one of those dreams that doesn't happen twice, and that one has to have experienced if one is to believe it. The church is certainly good, the bell-tower very tall, a square tower built entirely of freestone. The church was built in the days when the English were catholic, for one sees all round the outside of the building shields carved with two crossed keys (Pl. 31)[12].

Leaving Swaffham, we found our sand again, but what a difference! No more of those immense fields lying waste; all the fields are enclosed and well farmed; yet we could recognise here the same sand that on the road yesterday was so hampering to our horses. However, the make-up of the fields seemed already to have acquired more consistency, moisture and a slightly darker colour: in a word, they are beginning to be transformed through the care of the hard-working farmers of the

[11] Has he been misled by the size of the samples?!

[12] This magnificent church is dedicated to St Peter, hence the keys. As to the legend, what was certainly recorded in the remarkable Black Book, a great list of the church's benefactors, begun in 1454, was that among the most generous benefactors were John Chapman and Catharyne his wife, whose gifts included two great ships of silver (altar-vessels), 2 great songbooks, 2 great candlesticks, a whole suit of Cloth of Tissues (i.e. richly woven, probably in gold and silver): they also 'did make the north aisle, with glazing, pews and paving with marble and did give to making the new steeple in money, besides the foregoing, £120'. John Chapman was churchwarden in 1462. The name chapman is interchangeable in meaning with pedlar. This sumptuous benefaction might well have given rise to a popular legend. The legend was recorded (in very much greater detail than François' brief version) in a letter written by William Dugdale, the great antiquary, on 29 January 1652/3. All this is recorded in the invaluable *History of the County of Norfolk* by Blomefield and Parkin, VI, 1807, pp. 211–14 and 219. A late medieval wood-carving of a chapman, on the reading-desk, suggests that this punning emblem was used by the great benefactor in, or soon after, his lifetime (Pl. 31).

30. *Hilborough Park House, 1781. F. Martin, engraved by J. Page.*

31. *The Swaffham pedlar: a chapman, carved on the 15th-century reading-desk in St Peter's church.*

district. The enclosures are very large, some thirty or forty acres; one doesn't see enclosures as small as those in Suffolk.

The aspect of the country is nowhere agreeable. Never does the view seem able to open out, it is always unveiled between two slopes with no feature of the slightest interest. The turnips that we saw in great quantities all the way along are fine, and the clover which is left in the field after the harvest of the barley that was sown with it, is green everywhere and prolific.

After a two-hour drive, we arrived at a large village on the slope of a fairly big hill.[13] Its name is Castle Acre. There are many ruins to see, the remains of a very considerable abbey: I do not know what order of monks. The houses of the village are dirty and badly built and not even fit to be in France: however, one can see, some way away, some solid, good buildings which I suppose must be farms. At the foot of the hill on which this village stands, a stream runs, big enough to make the landscape pleasant, and the ruins make it picturesque. The most complete remains of the abbey are a large tower, probably a gateway and through which the road passes: it is square and built of stone.[14]

After Castle Acre, we found again the same good agriculture, the same enclosed fields, the same improved soil.

A FARM

At Rougham[1] we stopped partly to visit a farm and a gentleman-acquaintance of Mr Symonds, partly to feed our horses.

The farm was what first took our attention as we were driving past the front of it. Its great number of buildings showed us in an instant

[13] Not so high as Swaffham, only 150 feet, but the slope up from the Nar is steeper.
[14] It was a Cluniac priory, founded in 1187–9: the prior's lodging and the west front of the great church are among the best preserved monastic remains in these parts. François seems not to have noticed the ruins of the castle of the De Warennes: the little town is contained in its outer bailey. Lazowski, on the other hand, was much interested in the ramparts.

[1] Three miles north of Castle Acre.

that it belonged to Mr North, a cadet of My lord North's family.[2] This farm is so prodigiously large that its returns are £1,660 sterling.

Mr Symonds did not know the farmer.[3] He would have liked to meet the proprietor first, to secure a letter of commendation to the farmer, but as the double journey would have been four more miles we preferred to approach the farm without introductions.

I counted nineteen different blocks of buildings making up this prodigious farm; most of them are a considerable size. The farmer's house is in the middle; well-built, not sumptuous and with a good kitchen-garden, well kept and quite large.

[2] Lord North, George III's minister, was grandson of the *2nd* son of Dudley, 4th baron North of Kirtling: here at Rougham, Mr Fountain North was grandson of Roger, the *6th* son of the 4th baron: they were thus second-cousins. Roger, who bought Rougham in 1690, on his retirement from successful practice of the law, was the author of the *Lives of the Norths* (3 vols, 1890, ed. Augustus Jessopp), a famous and endearing picture of a most remarkable family. He was also the author of a treatise on music (John Wilson, *Roger North on Music*, 1959) and delightful writings on architecture that Howard Colvin and John Newman have edited and adjudged 'the most entertaining treatise on its subject in the English language' (*Of Building* in *Roger North's writings on Architecture*, 1981, p. xvi). On Saturdays he and a brother would go and quiz Wren as they watched St Paul's building. His own life here at Rougham, redesigning and remodelling the old house, with its Father Smith organ in the gallery and its collection of music and musical instruments, its 1st-floor library (an annexe for 1,150 volumes was built on to the north aisle of the church), its enlightened farming and woods and avenues, all reflects the idyllic family life of his childhood at Kirtling, near Newmarket, in his grandfather's day. Here at Rougham he and his son Roger (1703–71) are said to have planted ten thousand oaks – many of them surviving into our time. A spectacular avenue of limes leads east towards the house, which lies snugly just north of the beautiful church. Roger II was troublesome: for all his own careful upbringing, he flogged his son Fountain abominably, so that he ran away to sea and returned only on his father's death. He had been so unhappy that, by the time François and his party were here, he had pulled down the house and the library his grandfather established at the church, and gone to live at Hastings: the house was then remodelled from the old service buildings, and is still lived in by the Roger Norths. Here Roger I's dovecote survives, and in London, in the Strand, the distinguished Middle Temple Gateway he designed, making the best of a very narrow site. He is still very much alive in his writings. But François' account is valuable, coming as it does so soon after the destruction of the big house, and remodelling of its service block. It continues a most remarkable family.

[3] Lazowski names him as Mr Barton. He adds a characteristically detailed note on a sort of Dutch barn, open on all sides, '64 feet by 23, on two sides of which are stalls for the feeding of the bullocks, eight each side, an alley down the middle for bringing the cattle their food. The roof rises to a point in the middle and is thatched. The man looking after the bullocks had a little planked room of his own.'

163

After we had walked for some time, we met one of the foremen returning from the fields on his horse to organise dinner for the harvesters. We approached the man for some details on a subject so very interesting; here is all that I remember of what he told us.

The farmer has fourteen domestic servants employed by the year for indoor work, as well as three to do housework.[4] On top of that, thirty journeymen are always in regular employment; at harvest-time, which lasts five weeks, there are as many as seventy labourers whom he is obliged to feed on top of their wages of forty-five shillings. At other than harvest-time, he pays his labourers fourteen pence (*sols anglais*) in winter, eighteen in summer.

Seventy horses are at work on this farm, something we have no idea of in France. The land the farmer has in cultivation is vastly extensive: we were told 3,000 acres. Different parts of the farm are three miles distant from each other, which obliges the farmer to have two foremen who are paid more than the others and whom he can trust and who take his place. I said that today this farm renders £1,660 sterling: I must add that thirty years ago these same lands, altogether, produced no more than £400. The farmer has made improvements that one can hardly believe, and this is how.

At that time, all these fields were like those we passed through the day before, without hedges to enclose them and give moisture to this over-dry sand: the majority were even left fallow and yielded almost nothing. Since that time, it has been found that underneath a large part of Norfolk – that is to say underneath the sand that is all-too-plentiful in this county – is a bed of material entirely suited to enriching the soil: often it contains chalk, sometimes clay;[5] this bed lies one, two or three

---

[4] 'Domestic servants' means that they were young, probably yearly employed, farm-workers 'living in'. See Ann Kussmaul's book, noticed at p. 55 above.

[5] This is the famous marl that wrought such an improvement in the various light lands of E. Anglia, especially of Norfolk. William Marshall, in his two volumes on *The Rural Economy of Norfolk*, I, 1787, p. 16, wrote: 'The grand fossil manure of Norfolk is MARL; through whose fertilizing quality judiciously applied lands which seem by nature to have been intended as a scanty maintenance for sheep and rabbits, are rendered capable of fattening bullocks of the largest size, and finishing them in the highest manner.' He goes on to describe the whitish CHALK-MARL of central and north Norfolk, and the equally fortunate grey CLAY-MARL of eastern coastal districts: at pp. 150–7 he gives a full description of the whole process. One sees that Arthur Young's memorial to his wife was not just a back-handed compliment: 'She was the great

feet underground, and has to be dug out and spread over the surface for a year before the land is cultivated. Once this process is performed, it need not be repeated for another fourteen or fifteen years, and by treating the land in this way it becomes remarkably fertile by contrast with what it was before. It is to this discovery that the whole of Norfolk owes its good agriculture. All the fields are being cleared and enclosed, they are being cleared daily, and if it happens that there are some still lying fallow, it is because the marl has to be brought so far that the cost of marling these fields would be more considerable than could be recovered from improved production.

It is difficult for me to be precise about the cost of marling an acre, because that depends on the depth below ground of the bed of marl, and the distance from the prodigious pit that has to be dug to extract it; but generally it is reckoned at three pounds sterling an acre.

It seems as if, in this county from which Nature has withheld a good soil, she has given the inhabitants in compensation a great aptitude for agriculture. It isn't surprising that today farming should be at such a pitch of perfection, because the farmers are inspired by the success they have achieved. But what is surprising is that the very first ones should have had the enterprise to cultivate a sand which, on a quick inspection, looks so sterile.

But we must get back to the large farm and the method of cultivation: it is exactly the same as in Suffolk. The land never lies fallow: generally the cropping is divided into a rotation of four, starting every fourth year: 1. turnips; 2. barley sown with clover; 3. clover on its own, sometimes for two years; 4. wheat.

If they sow peas, or oats, it is instead of one of these crops, and the ordinary rotation is not changed.

On this farm there are two thousand sheep, fed in winter on the turnips and clover. Every year they fatten 520 of them, letting them eat as much turnip and hay as they like.

---

grand-daughter of John Allen Esq., of Lyng House, Norfolk, the first person, according to the Count de Boulainvilliers, who there used marl.' Presumably that was in the late 17th century. Marling had been practised in England since the 13th century, but by no means commonly. In Norfolk it was promoted from about 1730 by Lord Townshend: for the Townshend farming improvements see later, p. 171.

Thirty bullocks are fattened on turnips, hay and the ears of barley and wheat after they have been threshed. As for the cows, there is no great number, only enough for the needs of the house: eight or nine.

We were unable to see the farmer; he had gone to see his crops. We saw only his wife, a good and simple farmer's-wife who offered, and made us drink, a glass of wine to her good health. As it was exactly dinner-time, we saw in the kitchen a prodigious amount of meat and of cooked turnips, and the puddings made in linen bags almost as big, truly, as those we put powdered plaster into in France.

Mr Symonds' friend whom we went to see two miles from Rougham parish[6] and who is distinguished by a wide range of learning, confirmed everything that the man at the farm told us. He assured us that it was only in the last thirty years that the improved agriculture had come to this part of the county; and as for the increase in rental values, he gave us the example of a farm which, in Queen Anne's day, had been sold for £500 and now produced that same amount in rent. The capital had become the rent.

As this gentleman was going to dine in town[7] we could not stay long with him. We soon left him for Houghton, six miles away, where we were spending the night.

We passed through a place called Massingham, where we went for a moment into a farm to have a word with someone threshing in a barn, and ask him a few questions.

This farm belongs to Lord Orford,[8] who lives at Houghton. It occupies nearly two-thirds of the parish and may be as much as eight or nine hundred acres, of which the ground rent is ten or twelve shillings an acre.

The improvements here are new, made over the past thirty or forty

[6] Lazowski names him as Mr Jackson of Wisham, presumably Richard Jackson of Weasenham Hall (Blomefield and Parkin, X, 1809, p. 76). Was he the 'Omniscient Jackson' who died in 1787 and got a brief entry in the D.N.B.? The one surviving 18th-century memorial at All Saints, Weasenham, commemorates Elizabeth, wife of Richard Jackson, esq., but the date of the death of her husband remains blank. One may find a clue in the register of burials.

[7] King's Lynn is 15 miles west, Fakenham 7 north-east.

[8] George Walpole (1730–91), 3rd earl of Orford, nephew of Horace Walpole the famous letter-writer, who himself succeeded briefly to the earldom 1791–7. George was by this time (1784) intermittently insane.

years. The predecessor[9] of the present farmer made immense sums by improving all the land belonging to it. In his time it was let at eighteen shillings (*sols*) the acre.

There are two other farms in the same village. They are not so big: I don't know precisely how big, but in general all the farms of this district are a good size – seven or eight hundred acres: the buildings, similarly, are solidly built of brick, their massing in the middle of the fields is greatly augmented now, after harvest, by the enormous stacks of wheat and above all of barley raised all around. As they had an excellent harvest this year, the stacks were huge.

The parson of this parish is, so they say, the greatest fop ever, and for this reason very amusing. His parishioners told us that he always gets up in the pulpit with his hair powdered and beautifully dressed,[10] but he reads so fast and also preaches so loud that no one can understand a word he says: and they leave as well informed, they say, as they were when they went into the church. The manner by which he got his doctorate at Cambridge is unique. Having gone there to take his degrees, he was asked: Does the sun turn round the earth or the earth round the sun? The cleric, not knowing what to say and wanting to say something, adopted an emphatic manner and declared: 'Sometimes the one way, sometimes the other.' The reply seemed so ridiculous that they made him a doctor for this fatuous stupidity.[11]

[9] Probably the 'Mr Carr' referred to in Young's *Annals* as living at Massingham and having a long experience of marling.

[10] The rector of Gt Massingham in 1784 was undoubtedly the Rev. Cock Langford, son of a London estate agent. The only other possible hint of foppery I have found is that he died of an apoplectic fit, i.e. a stroke, as he was dancing at Lynn Assembly Rooms, 17 February 1789 (*Gentleman's Magazine*, 1789, I, p. 278).

[11] The trouble with this story is that Langford took no doctorate. François may have been confused by tales of the previous rector, 1731–70, the Rev. John Gardiner, LL.D. He and his son Richard seem to have been literally a pretty pair. Writing of the disreputable Richard Gardiner, R. W. Ketton-Cremer (*Norfolk Portraits*, 1944, p. 110) quoted this description of the father, the rector of Massingham: 'He is a very pretty man and they say his wife is a very pretty woman.' He undoubtedly had a doctorate. The son, a rogue, had to be removed (rather like Ralph Caldwell, whom we just noticed back at Hilborough, p. 159) from the post of Auditor-General at Holkham Hall: fortunately he was removed before much misappropriation could occur (A. M. W. Stirling, op. cit., pp. 191–200). This Richard was in orders, briefly (1748–51), and his fellow clergy were heard to say: 'What a *Jessamy* Parson we have got among us! a pretty *Sprig* of Divinity this!' (R. W. Ketton-Cremer, op. cit., p. 115). One sees how François might have been confused by the gossip in the charming village of Great Massingham.

Before reaching our inn at Houghton, we passed through the village, made up of ten houses built to the same pattern by Lord Orford. The inn is set at a distance, the last of the houses (Pl. 32).

HOUSES OF GRANDEES

The moment we arrived, we went to look at Lord Orford's house, a quarter of a mile across the park (Pl. 33).

The mansion was built and the park created by the famous lord Walpole, while he was Sir Robert Walpole, First Minister for thirty years and favourite of the King and Queen. If he did well by the affairs of the state, he did not overlook his own affairs, and particularly in the building of this house, on which he spared no expense.[1]

The stone itself, of which the entire house is built, is an item of the greatest expense: it is Portland stone. I don't know how many hundreds of miles it had to come.[2]

Lord Orford was not there but only some of his friends who had established themselves in the house and lived there at their own expense; a common practice here, which seems to me very convenient.[3] Lord Orford spends little time here each year himself; he finds it so big that it would be too expensive to live in all the year round; and yet he has lands in this county alone worth more than £7,000 or £8,000 a year.

[1] It is nothing less than a small palace.

[2] Portland stone was a good guess. But Houghton is built of a beautiful sandstone from the Aislaby quarries of N. Yorkshire, near Whitby, with their own jetties from which the sea-passage to Lynn is not more than 150 miles. (More impressive than the mileage is perhaps the tonnage.)

[3] François does not mention, and perhaps did not know, that Lord Orford had serious bouts of insanity in 1773 and 1777, from which he made only intermittent recovery. Horace Walpole, his uncle, rescued him from mismanagement, and the house from ruin, in 1774 – out of devotion to his own father, the great prime minister. In 1778, Horace rescued him again, but Lord Orford's response was to sell off the supreme glory of the house, Van Dycks and Rubenses, Poussins and Rembrandts, the best of Sir Robert's fabulous collection, to Catherine the Great of Russia, the empress who expressed her pleasure in the transaction by presenting the portrait of herself referred to by François. Horace expressed his sadness by describing his nephew and his cronies as 'a madman excited by rascals'. The pictures are preserved in the Hermitage at Leningrad. François was describing the saloon. It and the Stone Hall are two of the most astonishing rooms in England.

32. *The former hotel at Houghton.*

To the Right Honble the Earl of Orford.

Published as the Act directs, March 10th 1779, by M. Booth, Norwich.

33. *Houghton Hall, 1779, the home of the earls of Orford. Drawing by M. A., engraved by Page.*

We went over the whole house, seeing nothing but gilded panelling and doors.[4] It is all in the greatest degree magnificent, and the finest rooms follow one after another. If I were to describe each of them in detail, I should never finish, the recital would become boring, and it would take me a long time to do. It's enough for me to speak of two rooms that gave me the most pleasure. The one contains three history pictures and the portrait of the empress given by herself, a very elegant work, with a character of nobility that I prefer to everything: this room might be 50 feet by 30, and is proportionately tall. The other is the hall which is a cube of 42 feet, full of marble busts, some of which are Antique.[5] These vast enfilades of apartments that we saw on the *piano nobile* are full of the most costly marbles and gilding, executed by the best craftsmen of the time. But, totally magnificent as all this is, I cannot express what boredom this house induced in me. Although the cornices, doors, etc., are gilded in more than one place [and the doors?] are of such dark wood, this magnificence which has passed right out of today's taste is so oppressive that – forced as one is to admire it – one longs to get away from it.

The façades of both fronts are heavy and magnificent: the Order is Ionic, but spoilt by four ridiculous turrets placed at the four corners of the house above the cornice.[6] From the main front two wings curve forward like a horse-shoe, the wings connected to the main block by a colonnade.[7] One wing used to be a gallery of pictures Lord Orford sold, preferring the cash to the collection, unique in England, that he once had:[8] the other is a conservatory.

The park is very grand, perhaps seven or eight miles round. I don't know how many acres.

[4] The doors are of fine mahogany.
[5] Lazowski was greatly taken with the bronze Laocoön in the hall, 'de grandeur naturel'. But, like François, he was disposed to criticise: 'the park is without water, and very flat' etc.
[6] In Colen Campbell's original Palladian design, the four corners were meant to be crowned by pediments as at Inigo Jones's Wilton: but James Gibbs added four beautiful cupola'd stone domes in their place. Pevsner helpfully saw them as adding 'a continental warmth and opulence to the cool perfection of the rest' (*North-West and South Norfolk*, 1962, p. 207).
[7] Design traced to Palladio's Villa Badoer (*Burke's and Savill's Guides to Country Houses in East Anglia*, 1981, p. 139).
[8] It really was unsurpassed in England: Horace devoted a very unsatisfactory book to his father's collection, *Aedes Walpolianae*, 1752.

34. Raynham Park, 1783, home of Lord Townshend. Engraved by W. Watts.

From Houghton, we left on Sunday morning to go to Raynham, only six miles away, to see a fine piece of land improved by good farming and to see the house of Lord Townshend, to whom this estate belongs.

We made the whole journey, seemingly, in the middle of fields – the road itself little used and bad – but we could see, sitting at ease, as we passed through them, these fields improved by art and added to yearly by dint of hard work. Everywhere the same sand which becomes a little better the lower you go, everywhere the fields enclosed, but large fields (in general, fifty or sixty acres). We saw some good fields of clover and ray-grass, all that was left growing since the harvest.

Lord Townshend's house is built of brick with stone string-courses. The architecture is at once simple and noble: the interior is well planned, the ceilings are in the modern style, but the doors and the panelling are still gilded in the old way (Pl. 34).[9]

[9] It is surprising that he does not comment on the impressive, dominant situation of the house. Nikolaus Pevsner has called Raynham 'the paramount house of its date in Norfolk'. It was begun in 1622, and he is referring to the influence of Palladio here,

What is remarkable in this house is a collection of family portraits painted by the best painters, in military dress[10], and in the fashion of the day. The queen of France, Marie de Medici, is also there, painted by Rubens: it has an astounding effect, and I was full of admiration. There are pictures by Van Dyck, Salvator Rosa and the greatest masters. But one work, as beautiful as it is magnificent, and stirring the admiration of the connoisseur and ignoramus equally, is a *Belisarius* by Salvator Rosa. He is at the gate of Rome, blind and leaning against the ruins of a temple, superb carvings and columns lie tumbled at his feet, and you have before you the inconstancy of the fortune of the great man; in the distance, three soldiers.[11] The design and colouring could hardly be more perfect, and it makes the greatest possible effect.

This picture was given to Lord Townshend by the King of Prussia: the Prussian eagle naturally appears on the frame: the picture is perhaps 10 feet by 4.[12]

---

exactly a century ahead of Houghton. There is argument about the designer and it has been claimed as work of the great Inigo Jones. The likely explanation seems to be that the owner Sir Roger Townshend, who travelled in Italy in 1620, was the designer, with his master mason, William Edge. Nor can the influence of Inigo Jones be doubted. It is curious that François refers to the ceilings as in the modern style: they were, like Houghton's, the work of William Kent and of 'a magnificence that has passed right out of today's taste'.

[10] Lazowski, describing the portraits, adds 'at the time of the Revolt of the Netherlands'. One ancestor was knighted in 1588 for spirited conduct against the Armada, and his son in 1596 at the siege of Cadiz. His son married the daughter of a very distinguished soldier, Horatio, baron Vere of Tilbury. See J. C. Durham, *The Raynham Pictures*, 1926.

[11] In fact, they are cowering behind him.

[12] Charles, 2nd Viscount Townshend, was Sir Robert Walpole's brother-in-law. In the 1720s they were the two most powerful politicians in England, under George I, and in the first three years of George II. Then in 1730 Walpole felt able to ditch his brother-in-law and manage things (under King George and Queen Caroline) more or less on his own – as he did for twelve more years. Townshend, as Secretary of State for the Northern Department, naturally had close dealings with Frederick William, King of Prussia. His great achievement in those years was peace. After 1730 he retired to Raynham and earned his famous nickname – Turnip Townshend. It is very surprising that François makes no mention of that vegetable. Lazowski, on the other hand, wrote: 'You must know that this is the district where turnip cultivation was first tried out as a field crop, the grandfather of the present lord Townshend introduced them on to his estates and got the idea of the turnip crop established, both by his example and by his wealth and intelligence.' Turnip Townshend *was* the grandfather of 'the present' lord. In fact, two peasant farmers in the Waveney valley, at Weybread and St Olaves, were feeding their fat and dairy cattle on turnips in the early 1660s (Thirsk and Imray,

The park is perhaps four miles in circumference. In front of the house it unfolds beautifully, and the arrangement of the massing of trees on each side has a very fine effect. A fine green carpet over land that is not all regular and level, and in the distance is covered with masses of trees, creates all this delight. And there are masses of roe-deer which I always love to see.

They have tried to convert a marsh into a lake, but have made only a shapeless thing, without start or finish, very large but not pleasing.[13] All round the house is a pleasure-garden, moderately large and very agreeable.

The whole neighbourhood is very convenient for shooting: it's full of game. I saw pheasants and imagine there's no shortage of hares and partridges. Lord Townshend is a great sportsman and a great farmer, two qualities not entirely compatible: however they are compatible with a good reputation, for he is generally loved.

In the park he has sheep unlike those of the district, for they have white heads and legs, not black ones like the rest of Norfolk. They come from the west country and are fatter than the locals.

Lord Townshend has a very considerable fortune in lands in Norfolk, the best land in the county. As for the farming practice here, it differs very little from that at Rougham. Any difference that may exist is in the farmers, who all have some special ways of their own, rather than in anything to do with general custom.

As soon as our horses were ready, we set off again in the direction[14] of a very large farm belonging to Mr Coke and managed with the greatest intelligence: it is regarded as the clearest demonstration of the improvements effected in Suffolk.[15]

The weather, which had been only just passable on the previous days, on this day became very bad: it came over so black at noon as to deprive us of one of the greatest pleasures of our journey,[16] and soon

---

Suffolk Records Society, Vol. I, 1958, p. 20). Townshend's work in the 1730s was to get the idea known and widely accepted. In 1904, the Townshends fell temporarily on hard times and their great picture-collection was sold at Christie's: the *Belisarius*, valued at £5,000 in 1804, was sold for £273. In 1948, it belonged to the Sitwells.

[13] A just comment.

[14] Due north.

[15] One admits that François probably meant to say Norfolk.

[16] None of them says what this was.

afterwards the rain, which pelted down, completed our dejection.

In this deplorable situation, in all the rain and wind, we came to Dunton, the parish in which this great farm is established, occupying, indeed, the whole parish. None of us knew, nor had a letter for, Mr Case, the farmer. However, we stopped, and Mr Symonds went to ask if we might see the farm. In a short time someone was sent to find us, our horses were stabled, and the farmer received us with the greatest possible politeness; a little later we were served dinner, and we took our places at table as naturally as if we had already known the farmer.

Mr Case's approach is not just that of a farmer, he is affable, his manners polished, in the English way: that is, without much ceremony, which is all the more convenient because one can dispense with it oneself. His wife was there also – small and plain and, more unfortunately, deaf. She made us the warmest welcome she could. Her hardness of hearing prevented us from having very much conversation with her. It was the first time in my life that I had found myself dining in a farmer's house; what made it even more astonishing was that we did not know him: however, we were very soon at ease with him.

We ate hungrily the several sorts of cold meat and cheese, which was all they could give us at such short notice. We drank several kinds of beer and wine to the health of the farmer and the deaf lady, and soon afterwards we left with Mr Case to see the farm and some of his fields. The farm-buildings are immense, with stables, barns, etc. The barns are full of corn and, besides that, corn-stacks are ranged around the farm-buildings in great blocks: the stacks of peas and barley are taller and bigger than the other buildings of stone and brick. It is an astonishing sight and a pleasure to see such a fine harvest: it has been an excellent one this year.

The farm consists of 1,600 acres, all round the farmhouse and all linked together. Mr Case has fourteen servants[17] and twelve labourers working by the day all year round: on top of that, eighty team-horses, some for ploughing, others constantly used to cart the corn to Wells, a little town and sea-port nine miles away.

He has a thousand sheep and a hundred and eighty pigs, fed mainly on peas. His cows give him a good lot of butter which he sells in Fakenham market. What I mean to say is that he keeps many more

[17] This means that they lived in, not that they necessarily worked indoors: Kussmaul, op. cit.

174

than he needs for his own household: besides that, he feeds thirty more, for which he is paid a fixed price.

Harvest lasts five weeks, during which he has sixty-three labourers, paid between two guineas (forty-two) and forty-five shillings, as well as their food, which costs a prodigious amount. Those men eat meat three times a day, drink strong beer as often, and small beer whenever they are thirsty. Mr Case told us he has two bullocks killed each week and three sheep a day. One can judge the high cost laid out over five weeks!

He fattens a great many bullocks, but in the fields themselves, carting turnips and peas to them for fodder. He finds that pays, because they enrich the soil with their dung which they tread in with their hooves. All this land was uncultivated fifty years ago. It was Mr Mallett, Mr Case's father-in-law, who cleared it all and made the enclosures. At that time he paid two hundred pounds sterling a year: today his son-in-law pays eight hundred.

The fertility of this land is entirely artificial: the factitious vegetable bed is perhaps no more than eight or ten inches deep, and a few years of bad management would make it as impoverished today as it was before. The rotation of their crops is: 1. wheat; 2. turnips; 3. barley and clover; 4. clover that is cut the first year, left for the second and sometimes the third, to be grazed by the flocks.

Sometimes the order is changed: they substitute this: 1. peas; 2. wheat; 3. turnips; 4. barley with clover; 5. clover on its own for two years.

Those are the two rotations of crops throughout Norfolk: they are general, with little difference in practice between different places or the different farmers.

When we had seen over the farm, we returned to the house, where we took tea and coffee, for Mr Case was reluctant to let us go without that: then we got on our way, the farmer himself mounting his horse to show us the road and then conducting us to our inn at Fakenham, only three miles from Dunton.

There was still, before he left us, the pleasure of talking politics with him for an hour over a bottle of port, and then he went back into the night.

There is a weekly market at Fakenham, of little account. The town itself is small, with nothing to note.[18]

---

[18] This seems ungenerous. Lazowski at least says 'assez bien bâtie'.

On the 27th, after a good breakfast, we left our inn to go and see a farm belonging to a Bury gentleman, who had written to his farmer that he was to tell us everything we might want to know.

On our way we saw the farm we had heard about from Mr Symonds' friend near Rougham,[19] and that was worth in rent today as much as it would have sold for in Queen Anne's day. It was called Sculthorpe, and belonged to a parson.[20]

The Bury gentleman's farm we were making for is at West Barsham:[21] about forty years ago, his uncle, Mr Morley,[22] cleared 1,400 acres which he divided into four farms, for each of which he built a house, a small one but big enough for the job. The stables, sheds, etc. are on the same scale.

In the time when it came to Mr Mallett,[23] the whole property was worth no more than £80 a year. He inherited, from another side, an estate valued at £2,000, which he sold and used the money to improve this one, to marl, and make hedges, etc. The upshot was that in the last years of his life he was farming this same land at £800 a year. It is on the same footing today.

The farmer we saw, on one of the four farms, was engaged in marling his land for the second time, but he was sorry to see that the improvement was less than when he marled the first time: from which he concluded that the lands would fall in price at the first leasings, and that there would be in that a sort of revolution in the farming of the district.[24]

[19] Mr Jackson of Weasenham: p. 166 above.
[20] Lazowski names him, Mr Jones. In 1751 the Jones family acquired Cranmer Hall (built in 1721) and lived there till after World War II, when Sculthorpe became a great airfield.
[21] Half a mile from Cranmer Hall.
[22] A retired Guards officer, according to Lazowski. He succeeded Charles Morley, a Doctor of Medicine, in this manor, known as Wilkin's, and died without progeny (Blomefield and Parkin, op. cit., VII, 1807, p. 46).
[23] He was the father-in-law and predecessor of Mr Case at Dunton, see above.
[24] Two years earlier (*The Rural Economy of Norfolk*, II, 1787, pp. 102–107), William Marshall was discussing the rise of rents and 'the scarcity of money' as the main source of 'the poverty of the present farmers'. He recorded the discussion in January 1782, and it is clear that François' very rosy picture was by no means universally applicable, even in Norfolk. It is to be hoped this West Barsham farmer read, and took comfort from, William Marshall's very comprehensive section on marling (I, pp. 150–57) when the book appeared: it suggests that he needed to mix the marl with farm-yard dung to get better results.

The rotation of crops here is more or less the same as at Rougham, Dunton, etc. If there is any difference, it exists solely in their sowing wheat very rarely. Their main crops are barley and turnips. They prefer to grow good turnips and use three-quarters of the amount of manure that they would need for wheat, and the turnips are more useful to them as fodder for the sheep and cattle that are fattened throughout the district.

We ate at this farmer's house a little cold meat, drank some glasses of watered wine, and smoked. Then off we went again in the direction of a village called South Creake,[25] where Mr Laurens of Bury had procured us an introduction to a rich farmer of Lord Townshend's.[26] I was sad to see on the way a long strip of common which really ought to have been cleared: it is especially odd that the examples of neighbours have not resulted in its improvement: at present it is prolific in nothing but gorse.[27]

We stayed only an hour with Mr Glover. His farm belongs to Lord Townshend and is about 3,000 acres; but over and above this enormous acreage he manages another farm by himself, which belongs to him and is larger still.

I cannot give any very precise details of this farm because the farmer would tell us almost nothing; when, by force of questioning, we got a reply from him, it seemed that it was in spite of himself. His wife, who was there, wanted to respond in more detail; but when she ventured an opening phrase, the husband always found some way of interrupting her, and changing the subject: so that all I know is that he has 1200 sheep and that he fattens a large number of bullocks. He showed us the yard in which he keeps them. It is very large, and surrounded by a rack into which the turnips are tipped. The farmer prefers to have the dung in the yard than to spread it gradually over the land, leaving the animals themselves there to fatten on the fodder that is brought to them.

[25] Some three miles north-west of West Barsham.
[26] Mr Glover, see below.
[27] This common on the eastern edge of South Creake is still called Short Whins. Whins is the traditional East Anglian dialect word for gorse, *Ulex europaeus*, which strongly suggests that this is what François meant by *jonc marin*. See also pp. 134 and 158 above. Here the whins have been replaced by conifers.

He has eighteen servants and as many day-labourers. At harvest-time, for five or six weeks, he has a hundred labourers to whom he gives about two guineas as well as food and lodging. Their food-bill is as heavy as Mr Case's: three sheep a day, two bullocks a week, three pints of strong beer a day and as much small beer as they want. Nor do the puddings work out any cheaper: every weekday they have currant pudding, only on Sundays no currants. The harvesters eat five times a day, twice on bread and cheese, three times on meat (one of these, in the evening, on a hot joint), which adds further to the expense.

You see how little we managed to extract from this cautious farmer.[28]

I forgot to say that this great influx of people into this county for the harvesting comes down from Scotland and in from other parts of England because here they are better paid than elsewhere. What has to be said about the Scots is that they do their work perfectly well, but they love to quarrel. From up there where they live, to the farms where they go to work, they go on foot, carrying a bag filled with bread by their wives. That is all they eat on the whole journey, and they drink a little small beer or some milk. Returning home, they do the same thing, in order to bring the money they have earnt intact. In English towns they are easy to recognise by their clothes; they always wear jackets but no trousers, only a little cloth skirt down to the knees; their bonnets are well made.

We passed through a little village where a brother of Lady Spencer lives as rector.[29] He has done some very agreeable tree-planting.

We slept at Burnham Market, a large country-town,[30] badly built, and where it rained all the time we were there. The inn is not a good

---

[28] François was clearly irritated by Mr Glover's closeness. Lazowski came away, characteristically, with a mass of observations, considering that they were at South Creake only an hour: details about marling, turnips, labour, 'superb barns, redbrick, general around here', *hangars* [Dutch barns], much about ventilation. 'The threshing-floors of these barns are always boarded, not clay like most of ours . . . The least expert person can tell if the grain is threshed on boarding or clay – it looks permanently grey in the latter case.' After all this, he complained that the farmer was disinclined to open up, so that all information had to be extracted 'by finesse and importunity'.

[29] The village was North Creake, the rector Charles Poyntz, brother of Georgiana, wife of the 1st earl Spencer, who had died in October 1783. As his son and successor was married, the rector was technically brother of the dowager Lady Spencer.

[30] Not really large – not more than a thousand inhabitants, but with a large (disused) market-place.

35. Mr Curtis's Farm, Summerfield, Docking.

one: I arrived dying of hunger and scarcely managed to appease my appetite. The next day's journey was one of the worst of our tour, the rain falling in torrents and the wind equally troublesome. We break-fasted at Docking, then pulled up at a magnificent farm occupied by Mr Curtis, for whom we had a letter (Pl. 35).

This farm belonged to a lady whose name I have forgotten and who died not long ago.[31] She cleared and enclosed her farm herself, and it gave her as much pleasure to make it agreeable to the eye as fertile to the farmer. The farm has 400 acres surrounding the house on all sides

[31] The farm was Summerfield, in earlier times Southmere-field, a couple of miles north-west from the village. Catherine Henley inherited the estate in 1743: her husband died five years later. Blomefield and Parkin (X, 1809, p. 364) say: 'Mrs Henley found the lands here ill-cultivated, destitute of wood and spring water, and proverbially called Dry Docking. By her constantly residing in, and by a benevolent and sensible attention to the various interests and wants of, the place, both have been consulted and provided for. In different parts of her estate above 140 acres have by her been planted with various kinds of wood: and four wells sunk between 180 and 190 feet deep; exclusive of one in the centre of the town for the common use of the inhabitants who are daily reaping the advantages.' An inscription in copper at the corner of Well Street and Brancaster Road records that Mrs Henley gave the well, 212 ft deep, in 1760.

179

and is framed by a plantation of evergreens which is perhaps a hundred or a hundred and twenty feet thick. These trees create valuable moisture in a sandy soil. All the roads are well laid out and the cross-roads planted carefully: the hedges are shaped in a particular way. In short, it all bears the stamp of this lady's care.

The farmhouse is attractive and extremely presentable, with no expensive objects or luxuries. But I call it luxury in a farmhouse when extreme trimness prevails. The barns and stables are vast and well-built (Pl. 35). In the middle of the yard is an immense pond – more like an ornamental water than a drinking-trough. We saw, beyond the well-filled barns, a great many stacks of corn to signal an excellent harvest. Barley has been as abundant here as in other parts of this county, and the wheat more than doubled the expectations of the farmer, for we saw six stacks, each of which held 200 combs. A comb is [blank].

Behind the farmer's house is a small kitchen-garden and, further away, a small wood planted entirely for the pleasure of it, with little walks and landscape features that make it very attractive.

The farmer is young, very open, and has a most interesting appearance. He has an extremely large private income and is one of the best fox-hunters in the whole county. He keeps two or three hunters, among them one which cost him a hundred guineas and whose portrait he had painted for twenty guineas.[32]

---

[32] I print in full Lazowski's vignette of this farm: it brings out well the similarities and differences of interest and touch between the two, besides naming the painter of Mr Curtis's hunter. 'It is one of the most attractive farms imaginable, and you can be sure there couldn't be a second in England. It was built about forty years ago by a lady whose house was in Docking village, and who wanted to have an agreeable and useful farm.

'You drive by a large stretch of turf, closed by a fine plantation of evergreens, the farm-house trim and commodious ahead, the stables to the left, yards and barns arranged so that all is built over and makes a fine effect. Beside the house to the right, a piece of water of about 2 acres, shaded by a double line of trees, the water clear, the shape circular.

'He has 10 servants and as many day-labourers. He reckons he needs a plough for every 200 acres and 4 horses per plough, because the teams change 3 times a day. He has a waggon for every plough, and five horses per waggon, and so he has forty horses quite apart from his saddle-horses, of which his favourite has been painted by favour of Stubbs, a London painter of horses, and for which he gave 20 guineas – a picture of 2½ feet by 1½ feet: I mention this to give you an idea of English farmers and I doubt if one could cite a parallel in any other country.'

180

Everything about this farm is in first-class condition. To strangers, what is remarkable and what is revealing, through the revenue it produces, is that the more one makes useful embellishments[33] in a farm, the more one recovers the outlay.

We stayed only a very little time at this farm and, after seeing over it and talking with the farmer, we set off again, making for the home of Mr Styleman, a cousin of Mr Symonds, where we were expected for dinner.[34] We found him a most original man, a real Englishman, full of

[33] *embellissements utiles* seems like a contradiction in terms, but one sees what he means.
[34] The Stylemans lived at Snettisham Old Hall, a fine Dutch-gabled house of the local rich carstone, and of perhaps Elizabethan structure, much remodelled by them in the 18th century. (It is now a Sue Ryder Home.) The manor was conveyed to Nicholas Styleman of Snettisham for £1,000 in 1710 (Elizabeth M. James: 'The Old Hall, Snettisham, and the Styleman Family', *Norfolk Archaeology*, XXXVIII, 1983, pp. 343–57). Lazowski noted that Mr Styleman had handed his estates over to his nephew, reserving an annuity for himself and his wife. 'He lives now in a small, very agreeable house, surrounded by several acres of meadows, either natural or artificial.' This 'small, very agreeable house' is now known as 'The Hollies', the residence of Dr Shaw (Pl. 36). With its stable yard it faces south: initials 'N.S.' and '1757' in the gables show that Nicholas Styleman added a new north range to the house that year. To the south, across the meadows, now covered with suburbia, the Stylemans built a delightful rusticated carstone hexagonal gazebo beside the fast little stream bubbling down from Shernborne: the stream is still popular with mallard (and muscovy duck), and the walk beside it is a public footpath. The rustic cottage is now the home of Mr and Mrs Reynolds: it was Mr Reynolds who suggested to me that 'The Hollies' was probably Mr Styleman's home in 1784. Lazowski continued: 'Mr Styleman has made use of a former pasture, through which runs an attractive stream, to create a most agreeable covered walk. This winding walk was planted about 20 years ago, and at its densest it is already tall. I saw a *cyprès à feuilles d'acacia* [a contradiction: could it have been a *robinia pseudoacacia*?] seven or eight feet in diameter and about 24 feet tall. Beside a massive *plein* [is he using the English word, plane?], he has built an octagonal pavilion containing a sort of saloon, or sitting-room, and a lodge for a family who look after all sorts of tame birds that they keep on the walk: the cornice of the octagon serves as pigeon-house. We saw two ducks called *sterlockes* [presumably *shelduck*] which live in the north and winter in England, where they sometimes nest: but although relatively tame, so that they don't fly away, they don't nest in such a state of domestication as this.' [His description of the plumage tallies with no known duck – 'thinner than our duck, the neck longer, deep in their plumage is a beautiful blue, and in the wings and tail the feathers are a yellow-red: red feet.'] The name *sterlocke* remains the best clue: and as we saw in the print-room at Heveningham, 'blue' for François may have been what we see as green; shelduck do have a lot of plumage that could be 'yellow-red'; and not all of them spend the autumn moulting in Heligoland or Bridgwater. Lazowski also describes two dark grey geese, with wings and tail tipped black: he called them 'Scottish geese', perhaps because they were known to fly south over Scotland. 'This stream covered with many species of aquatic birds added a lot of gaiety and life to this enclosure . . . No need to worry about

good-nature; no polite formalities; at his house, you do as you please, but he makes no engagements and it is as if you are at home; ask, and you have it; don't ask, and you don't have it. We were asked to dinner, but we also supped and stayed the night (Pls. 36 and 37).[35]

The conversation was continuous and delightful and ranged over a variety of topics. In general, his ideas are very unusual. He is well-educated but not like anyone else: everything he knows takes on an original quality, without losing anything, becoming singular. The same

---

the mess produced in this aviary, the family living in the pavilion is busy all day, washing and sweeping, so that the pleasure is not spoilt by all the droppings.'

[35] Lazowski was even more taken with Mr Styleman than François: 'Ever since I came to England, I have looked out for Englishmen of the old school as described in the novels, with exaggeration perhaps, but with truth . . . Mr Styleman is one of them, and in all my life I never met a more original character. Do you remember Western, in Fielding's novel, *Tom Jones*? He is Mr Styleman, to the life, so that after two hours with him you think Fielding must have copied him. He no longer hunts, but he has all the prejudices of Western, and to a greater degree, for he is better read and better informed than Western . . . He is an ardent Jacobite and zealous partisan of the Anglican church; he is attached to the Stuarts because the house of Hanover is foreign; he is Whig and ready to die for the Republic [Lazowski presumably means "Revolution", of 1688, which must have seemed like a sort of Republic to Bourbon France]. He loves the laws of England, fanatically, but he seems even more sensitive to their abuses, however necessary they may be . . . He lives in the country all the year round and has thus acquired his taste for agriculture and for natural history: but he mixes in with that his political prejudices, and so believes that enclosures are necessary for the perfection of agriculture but is opposed to them on the grounds that the commons are beneficial to the people . . . Open and frank, he is incapable of dissembling, and his natural goodness is evident in everything. He is at table with a Frenchman who doesn't speak; he must be surprised at this, and reflect on it; his fair-mindedness aided by his good nature does not take this silence amiss; he is so far from thinking it a result of either some disagreement or natural pride that he gets angry with his neighbour for speaking because the Frenchman didn't speak to him in his language, and then added that he would wager his fortune that he is a good fellow. He was interested in the feelings of an unhappy foreigner among people he didn't understand. With his rough appearance, he is sensible to the beauties of poetry, but it had to abound in characters and images, so that Dryden is his poet, and he read us some passages. His wife has lived in the great world and he shows her great consideration and shares her views. [Her name was Catherine Henley (Elizabeth M. James, op. cit., p. 357), almost certainly the daughter of the benefactress of Docking.] I must mention one last trait. He had never seen us before: at seven o'clock he was astonished at the way we kept on our riding-boots and the way we didn't feel easy about joining Mme. Styleman in our slippers: for himself he went to put his own on, and by the end of a lively conversation he was lying stretched out near the fireplace with a dog sitting on his stomach, and I must tell you that he had an enormous belly which added not a little to his character. He insisted on our staying overnight, but when we left next morning at eight o'clock, he had not got up.'

36. *The Hollies, Snettisham, home of Mr Styleman.*

37. *The Round House, Snettisham.*

easy-going atmosphere that prevailed during our stay spared us the formalities of taking leave. When we left next morning, we saw no-one about, and promptly set out for Lynn.

As soon as we reached Lynn we found Mr Young. He had very kindly agreed to come to introduce us to Mr Coke, the owner of the finest house in England which we badly wanted to see. The town is built in flat country beside the river Ouse, which enters the sea two or three miles away; the streets are narrow, winding, badly paved and scarcely levelled out, though that could very easily have been done. The church is a good size but has nothing to commend it.

The market-place is large and pleasing, overlooked by some very good buildings, including Mr Hogg's house, which is truly grand and handsome (Pl. 38). He is a very rich merchant for whom, while we were there, a most unusual and delightful event occurred: he was able to see from his windows twenty-five of his own vessels all ready to set sail.[36] The port is nothing very great, consisting of the river-channel which has been widened, strengthened and deepened. The course of a small tributary of the Ouse forms a small part of the harbour.[37] I think the port could hold 250 merchant ships. It was nearly full when we went by, but I was a little sad not to see a single French ship. Among all these vessels, I noticed that one was built in a peculiar way and asked its function. I was told it was built for whaling. Lynn sends out five of these. Each is manned by a crew of forty-five and carries on its deck six long-boats, very lightly built, for launching into the sea. Their voyages last eight or nine months, and they catch one, two or three whales. It is known that in a single voyage the merchants cover the cost of fitting out the vessel and sometimes the cost of its construction.

Lynn does a tremendous amount of business, sending a large number of vessels to the North, and some to America, but its most considerable branch of trade is coasting. At Lynn, a great amount of the inland

[36] He is describing the Tuesday Market-place, a noble space of about 3 acres. In 1784–5, the year of Stephen Wilson's mayoralty, Stephen Hogg was admitted freeman of Lynn, as apprentice to George Hogg senior, deceased, and George Hogg junior, merchants (*Calendar of the Freemen of Lynn, 1292–1836*, Norfolk and Norwich Archaeological Society, 1913, p. 263). The sailing of Mr Hogg's fleet was presumably timed to coincide with the annual Mayor's Feast.
[37] The river Nar formed a small, curved natural jetty called the Boale, or Ball, at the south end of the harbour.

38. *King's Lynn, the Tuesday Market on market-day c. 1790. The Hogg family's house, on the left of the picture, is now Barclays Bank. (King's Lynn Museums)*

navigation of Midland England emerges: this port is the entrepôt of all the commodities that converge here and that are shipped on to London and thence abroad. All the coal for parts of Norfolk, Suffolk, Northamptonshire, Cambridgeshire, etc., indeed for a very large part of England, passes through Lynn.

A FEAST AT LYNN REGIS

We arrived in this town at the precise moment of its celebrations. The election of the mayor was the occasion.[1] The mayor at Lynn is the same as the alderman at Bury, the head of the corporation, and elected each year. On election day, the new mayor gives a great dinner, ball and supper, according to old custom; all the nobility of the district come, and strangers are bidden. We were invited. After a procession in the town and a service in the parish church, we were seated at table. There were three: one for the two mayors,[2] at which all the men sat; alongside, in the same room, the women's table, with the two mayoresses at the head; and in another room another table for the young men and women who were unmarried. Although our place naturally was at the table of the innocents, in order to do honour to strangers, the mayors put us at their table. I was next to Lord Walpole.[3]

The dinner was magnificent, masses of meat, plenty of game although it was still scarce at the start of the season, there were puddings[4] in abundance, also venison, for one gathers it is the dish the English rate most highly. ·

When the dessert came, a cup given to the corporation of Lynn by King John was brought in; it is singularly well fashioned for the time when it was made; it is gold, enriched with two emeralds and two very

---

[1] In fact the election was in August: the feast celebrated the new mayor's swearing in, at Michaelmas.
[2] The new mayor and the outgoing mayor, as Lazowski explains. He says about 300 people sat down to this dinner in the Guildhall.
[3] François is politely silent about his strange table-neighbour: one supposes they spoke of Houghton without enthusiasm on either side, which might have eased the conversation.
[4] *Poudains*, presumably meat puddings.

fine topazes:[5] the foot of the cup and the cup itself can be turned without coming apart. It is filled with port, and the custom is for two to drink from it. The two mayors drank first, one holding the cup by the middle of the foot, the other giving the cup a half-turn. Thus the custom. Thus one drinks in pairs. The cup went first round of the men's table, then that of the women and then that of the young people.

Much is drunk, that too is the custom; and, what is more, it goes on for a very long time. Then we danced: the ball was a very brilliant affair. It was at the ball that we made the acquaintance of Mr and Mrs Coke, who had the goodness to ask us to stay with them at Holkham.

This record of our Norfolk tour never got finished, because at Holkham we were too busy enjoying ourselves to find time to write. I think there would be little point in doing it now, from memory: I could give only inaccurate recollections. The most interesting part of this trip is traced out – descriptions of farms, and of trade. The rest, which has escaped me, is only descriptions of houses and towns. Yarmouth is the one place I regret not having properly noted: it is the English Dieppe.

So we went to Holkham, and from there to lord Buckingham's house,[6] to Norwich, Yarmouth and then back to Bury, very glad to find ourselves in our home territory again, though we had had infinite enjoyment from the tour.

[5] It is now seen to have been made *c.* 1340, not at the time of King John, but it is still marvellously well fashioned, with exquisitely finished enamel panels framed or mounted in gold. Reading this hair-raising account of its customary use as a loving cup, one is not surprised to learn of enamel and gilt repairs in 1692, 1750, 1770 and 1782, and one is relieved to read that the mayor's feast lapsed at about the end of the century. There is now no sign of emeralds or topazes! I doubt if François invented them. (The cup was shown at the Royal Academy's great winter exhibition, *Age of Chivalry*, in 1987, item 541, *Catalogue* entry by Marian Campbell, illustrated on pp. 435–6. The discontinuance of the feast was recorded in William Richards, *History of Lynn*, 1812, 2 vols., p. 1154.) Marian Campbell (Mrs Ramsey), of the Department of Metalwork at the Victoria and Albert Museum, thinks it not impossible that the four gilt balls on the lid-knob are replacements for those four gems: they are certainly not original.
[6] Blickling. François pardonably referred to Lord Buckinghamshire as Lord Buckingham, who was someone else.

At this point, François remembered he had meant to give his father his observations on the useful part played by clubs, and indeed pubs, in English life. So with Clubs, Mélanges *come to an end. His plan, you remember, was to write in no other order than as subjects came into his head. However, it is clear that he was unhappy about his failure to complete notes of the Norfolk tour, of Yarmouth especially. It may not surprise readers to learn that Lazowski wrote very full notes on Lynn, Holkham, Norwich and Yarmouth. I therefore propose to end this volume with edited extracts from Lazowski (translated) to round off the Norfolk tour that pleased them, according to François,* infiniment. *But first his appraisal of clubs. It is extremely interesting for what it says about the early and effective spread of the Friendly Societies in Suffolk and, as he believed, across England. Clearly it was not strong enough to cope with the distress of the agricultural depression at the end of the Napoleonic Wars, and it was only in 1875, ninety years after François' account was written, that the Suffolk Provident Society was established (Thirsk and Imray, S.R.S. Vol. I, 1958, p. 155), alongside the smaller clubs, the Independent Order of Oddfellows, Ancient Orders of Buffaloes, Frothblowers, etc. François was writing for the information of his father, the duc de Liancourt, and Suffolk may feel it played, through this next passage, a small part in the establishment in Paris, in 1818, of the still flourishing* Caisse d'Epargne et de Prévoyance: *the duc was its joint founder and first President.*

CLUBS

Clubs are established in England in every province of the realm, in every town and every country district. It is perhaps one of the most sensible institutions, the best mark of confidence felt in society and in general, apart from the benefits they produce in the country districts.

The London clubs are well known to the French. It is not of them I want to speak in making my fine panegyric on clubs. Those in the capital are nothing more than associations for debauchery and expense, etc., places where one ruins oneself and where one retires to indulge in the most sensual luxury. The most miserable of men – according to Boileau and Voltaire – those who are devoted to wine and gaming and women, are the most zealous supporters of the London clubs and preach their merits on every occasion: but they haven't a hope of persuading anyone that they meet there solely to discuss public affairs;

they have all the newspapers there, but they don't go there in order to read them; they read them there as they would do anywhere, through habit. How many families there are who curse these clubs, where one goes to pieces naturally, so to say.[1] For the rest, one must not expect more of clubs than of any other forms of association: when there is a great deal of luxury in a town, with many people leading disorderly lives, they all naturally seek each other, and will find each other, whether at a club or anywhere else.

To be admitted to one of these societies you have to be introduced by one member and accepted by all – either through a majority of votes, sometimes two-thirds, sometimes three-quarters; or, in other clubs (the most famous), the vote must be unanimous: if one member declines to vote for you, you are rejected. The ballot is conducted with beans, each person having a white one and a black one. You can have meals at the club, and there is gaming. There are clubs of this kind in almost all English towns.

Clubs of a more useful kind, and which are more widespread though less well known to strangers, are associations of people who are experts and amateurs in the same art or useful science. They fix a day of the week, or sometimes the month, and spend the day together discussing the progress of whatever it is they are meeting to promote. They gather at an inn, arrive in time for dinner, talk at table until seven or eight o'clock, tea and a light supper make the evening pass rapidly, and one is sorry to leave. Time seemed short: not a moment's boredom.

I confess I have been present sometimes when the conversation has not been on the objects of the club, and that hunting and women are often subjects of discussion among working-farmers and gentlemen-farmers who should have had their minds on the plough. But sometimes they get back to their fields, and pride themselves on always having some achievement to quote which shows them to have done better than their neighbours. It is a happy life and, meeting often in this way the individuals of a district, or of a county, are bound together closer than by the ties of humanity. I must also observe that these regular meetings of little societies spread money around, put the innkeeper in a position to have very clean rooms, even a touch of luxury in his establishment.

[1] François had clearly formed an unfavourable opinion of London clubs. He had already disparaged them in his early account of London, p. 15 above.

In towns where the clubs are run at a level of considerable expenditure, the large inns do very well; so do the butcher and the traders, etc., so do the cultivator and the merchant; so, in the end, does the country itself. That much more so because those who go to these clubs do not reduce correspondingly their daily outlay at home. Don't dismiss my idea as trivial: I am sure that if one could make a study of the amount of money put into circulation by clubs of this kind one would see the great benefit that they bring to a country.

The third sort of club is more useful to the small working-farmers, the kind we call peasants. The meeting-place is also the inn, but that of the small village, or the last inn in town. They meet for dinner once a year. The price of the meal is fixed, high enough so that it could be cheaper, but not so high that it will ruin the mass of the members. It is always at table that the English do business, it is then that they are happiest and freest.

These clubs are spread through all parts of England; every country district enjoys their advantages. In the inn chosen for the meeting there is a box with two locks and a little slot to take the money of all the club members. The innkeeper is always one of the members and holds one of the keys; a local worthy has the other.[2]

As I say, there is no end of such clubs. There are some that admit members at 20, others at 30, until they reach the age of 50 years; the members of each club pay into their coffer a sum calculated on the probable length of human life and going towards the three or four shillings a week the club pays out to each of its sick members. If a peasant is ill all he has to do is send his wife to the club for his allowance. Naturally, his illness must be bad enough to prevent him from working. He is paid three or four shillings a week all the time he is ill.

---

[2] This is why they were generally called Box Clubs. Arthur Young listed 219 of these clubs in Suffolk in 1797 (*General View of the Agriculture of Suffolk*, pp. 262–6), with 7,709 members, an average of 35 in each club. They were not spread among 219 places: Lowestoft, with its fishing industry and porcelain factory, had eleven Box Clubs. They are sometimes known as Friendly Societies, or Mutual Benefit Societies. Their part in Suffolk life would reward research. The one general study of the subject starts after the 18th century: P. H. J. H. Gosden, *The Friendly Societies in England, 1815–75*. One person's benefit is vividly illustrated in Ann Kussmaul's admirable edition of *The Autobiography of Joseph Mayett of Quainton (1783–1839)*, Buckinghamshire Record Society, 23, 1986.

It is an admirable thing that peasants, rough fellows who need manual work to earn their living, have enough confidence in the honesty of a society to put a portion of their money into the common fund and to feel sure of getting great help in return if need be. This confidence is general; no-one gives instances of its betrayal, either by those asking for money without being genuinely ill, or by those responsible for administering the fund not making a proper distribution of the income. This gives rise, I find, to sad reflections on our country.

François thought of adding a piece on English inns. He wrote the title, Des auberges anglaises, *and here his manuscript stops.*

A TOUR IN NORFOLK

continued from the unpublished 'Letters to a Friend' by Maximilien de Lazowski. We begin with those of his notes on King's Lynn in which he supplements significantly the observations of his pupil François.

LYNN

The river, as broad as the Seine at Rouen, carries ships of 3 to 400 tons: they cannot sail beyond Lynn: the river-channel is difficult and pilots are needed between Lynn and the sea: Castle Rising's castle is a useful landmark, and one threads the channel with a bearing on the castle. The navigation is protected in the north by a battery of twelve 18-pounders. This battery in any other position would not last ten minutes against a 30-gun frigate, but can adequately defend this passage because the channel zig-zags and is so narrow that no warship can get into position to fire a broadside at it.

The river water is perpetually salt, and in flat land like Lynn's formed by the deposits of the sea there is no possibility of fresh-water springs, yet fresh-water is supplied in a most ingenious way that could be adopted in most towns. In the south, a considerable stream runs towards the river, and there a water-wheel has been established to work two pumps by which the water is lifted to the height of a vast round reservoir lined with lead (Pl. 39).[1] This reservoir, which I measured

---

[1] Like the defence-works, these water-works were in the north, on the Gaywood river, and were known as the Kettle-mills (see pl. 39). Subsidiary pumps were added in the south, but Lazowski is clearly describing the Kettle-mills. They were in open country to the east of Pilot Street, beyond which everything is now a series of industrial eyesores.

*39. King's Lynn, Kettle Mills, or Waterworks. Aquatint by J. Hassell.
(Wm. Richards,* History of Lynn, *II, 1812)*

very imperfectly, may be sixteen feet tall by twelve in diameter. At the
bottom of the reservoir two stop-cocks are opened on alternate days and
supply water to the whole town: one half of the town today, the other
half tomorrow. In case of fire, one can close one stop-cock and open the
one supplying the part of the town where the fire is.

Conduits in all the streets carry water to every house: the consumption
of a large family costs only 17 shillings a year: the few people who are
not supplied with water to their houses pay a very reasonable rate for
drawing water at stand-pipes in the streets at certain hours of the day:
each house has its water-tank, proportionate to its consumption and to
the price paid. The machine that raises the water is simple, and there
are few places where one could not procure clean water by such means.

The town was fortified in the old days, and from the ruins of its
ancient wall it appears to have been larger. One can still see earthworks
raised at the time of the troubles under Charles I, the trenches and
ditches dug by Cromwell's army when they besieged and took the town.
It is now wide open.

There follows a detailed account of the new whale-fishing in Greenland, the lowering of the boats, the harpooning of the whale, the uses of whale-bone and whale-oil: the fishing dangerous (last year five fishermen perished), the navigation difficult but safe: the economics of whaling.

There are 90 Lynn vessels, but as they each make an average of ten trips a year, that equals 900 ships! Some do as many as fourteen, but others go further afield, to Malaga, or to the Baltic . . . The ships are busy transporting the grain harvested in this part of Norfolk and in those parts of Suffolk near the navigable rivers. They export annually 75,000 quarters of all sorts of grain and bring in coal to those parts: the coal imported from Newcastle is, on an average year, 120,000 chaldrons, each chaldron weighing a ton and a quarter. The remaining imports are iron, hemp, peas, tar, timber and planks from Sweden and Russia in the Baltic, the iron almost all from Sweden: a great many of these boats leave almost in ballast, for the county's industrial products are exported through Yarmouth.

I said all these imports spread into the counties bordering the water-ways: this inland navigation is conducted in flat, covered boats called lighters:[2] there are 300 of them operating every year: they are sailed with proportionately fewer hands than other ships – six of them are towed one behind the other and need only three or four men to handle them.

Lynn has its shipyard: they reckon the cost of building a ship is £6 a ton, but that is only for the carcase of the ship: the rigging and every-thing that's needed to equip it comes to £1,200 for a ship of 300 tons.

We owe our connections in Lynn to the friendship of Mr Young. He arranged for us to converse with the merchants, especially at a supper which he arranged for this purpose.

The second day at Lynn was spent going to look at the embankment of Captain Bentinck:[3] it is a sea-bank about six miles long, which he planned and directed himself, and by means of which he reclaimed a thousand acres of good earth from saltmarsh, and built five farms which

[2] Lazowski called them *ligsters*: I suppose they were what we call barges or narrow-boats.
[3] Young's account appeared in *Annals of Agriculture*, II, 1784, p. 353: 'An embankment against the sea, of the late Count Bentinck.'

he has let at £1,000.[4] For travellers whose ambition is not to miss seeing anything useful, especially in agriculture, in this county, you will agree that this visit was well worth our trouble, which was not negligible: we covered 15 miles on foot, much of the journey in the rain . . . Captain Bentinck had begun another project, a canal alongside his sea-bank, but which has been halted by his death . . .

At the dinner and ball at Lynn we were presented to Mr and Mrs Coke, the owners of Holkham, of which we had heard such marvels. Ordinarily one is able to see this house only on a Tuesday, but Mr Coke most obligingly invited us to come and spend a few days with him to see in our own time his house and estates – an invitation we had no difficulty in accepting. Holkham is 22 miles from Lynn, to the north-east.

HOLKHAM

Holkham is perhaps the most agreeable house in England. It is built of brick, but the earl of Leicester who created all this had the bricks specially made and would use only those that were an absolutely identical shade of white: the rest were sent to London[1] . . . So the house seems from its colour to have been built in freestone. The architecture is extremely elegant, the whole composition of an extraordinary lightness, and the rightness of the proportions such that you view the details and the whole with equal pleasure, unable to say which aspect you find the most arresting . . .

[4] One of these, Bentinck Farm, south-east of Terrington Marsh in Terrington St Clement, still has his name: the low bank is still visible above the even lower land.

[1] Thomas Coke, 1697–1759, the builder of Holkham (it was building 1734–61) was a friend of Lord Burlington and William Kent and spent his formative years, from 15 to 21, in Europe and especially Italy. Holkham, with its great collection of books and manuscripts (including an incomparable collection of the works of Livy), as well as statuary and pictures, is a monument to his scholarship as well as taste. From Vitruvius he learnt that bricks were better building material than marble. No fewer than thirty different moulds were needed for each unit of 'rustication'. He was something of a brute as well as a scholar, a leader of cock-fighting in England. He was created earl of Leicester in 1744. His only son and heir, a great disappointment, predeceased him in 1753, and in 1759 his title became extinct. His estates passed to his daughter Anne; married to Wenman Roberts, who changed his name to Coke, and whose son Thomas William was the famous agriculturalist, 'Coke of Norfolk', host to Lazowski and the La Rochefoucauld boys in 1784. He was created 'Earl of Leicester of Holkham' in 1837.

The entrance is in the north front, which is given great lightness by the rustication running the whole length of the ground-floor basement: above the rustication there is just one storey, with big windows, the main one Venetian, giving a very pleasant effect, but I don't want to go on any more trying to describe the architecture: you need a drawing to get any idea.[2]

You enter the hall, from which you reach all the other rooms: its proportions are 70 feet by 46, by 43 in height, and it is clad in red-veined white marble from Derbyshire.

You are faced by a grand stone staircase set in a semicircular apse, and what is most incomparably magnificent in this house is the mixed cherry-pink and white in the marble of the hall which quite shocked me. *After describing the superb Corinthian columns ranged round the hall at the level of the top of the staircase, and the corridors formed by these colonnades, he passed straight ahead from the staircase into the saloon.*

This word saloon does not carry the same meaning as *salon* in France: it is a ceremonial room for state receptions: in France we have no comparable room. It is 40 feet by 28, by 32 in height. From there into the drawing-room,[3] which we would call the *salon*: 30 feet by 22 by 24: it leads into an octagon 21 feet in diameter and 32 high, which in turn communicates with the Statue Gallery, 60 feet long by 21 and 23 feet high. The statues, all in niches, are antique and in white marble. This leads on to a second octagon, which communicates with the rest of the

---

[2] The architecture was doubtless in the minds of Coke, Burlington and Kent since their studies in Italy twenty years before the Holkham building began. Cinzia Maria Sicca has lately shown how some elements of Kent's work here derive from Renaissance Rome, in particular from Giulio Romano's own house there, of *c*. 1530 (*Architectural History*, 29, 1986, pp. 138–45). But there is no question that the essence of Kent's great design is Palladian, nor that it was actively approved in every detail by Coke himself. When *The Plans and Elevations of the late Earl of Leicester's House at Holkham* were published in 1761, Matthew Brettingham (1699–1769) claimed to be the 'Architect' on the grounds that he 'had conducted the laying of every brick.' The design is palpably Kent's, including the triumphal arch that provides the south entrance to the park, its rustication very effectively done in the local flint. In 1747 Brettingham's son, Matthew, was in Italy collecting, very successfully, a good deal of Holkham's antique sculpture.

[3] They have turned into the *west* drawing-room, and are going round the reverse way to that which Pevsner describes as 'a route probably followed by more than two centuries of visitors' (*North-West and South Norfolk*, 1962, p. 202).

house.[4] The library is handsome and contains a good collection of books: Mr Coke was unable to house them all and has made a kind of gallery above, in a sort of passage, where he has found room for a great many books and manuscripts.

I forebear to give you a description of the interior of this house: I have said enough to give you a view of the general way in which their rooms and apartments here are fashioned on a much grander scale than with us: as for the convenience of their interior arrangements, that is another thing: here there are 150 *lits de maître à donner*[5] and in all more than 300 beds.

It is not one of the most magnificent English houses,[6] but it is one of the most elegant; and above all, one of the best provided with every kind of comfort and convenience. A machine in the yard, set in motion by a horse for three-quarters of an hour every two days, raises water into good lead reservoirs on the roof which supply all necessary water in each apartment and generally throughout the house. What with that great convenience and every refinement in its distribution, everything is provided for living in the English manner; and what is perfect is that you can live in great luxury, like a nobleman, in this house, and yet you can live here on a relatively middling income.

The furniture in general is good, and more magnificent than elegant: there are few rooms in which you do not see pictures by old masters.

The stables are separate from the main building as they are everywhere in the country: they are fine but not distinguished as a building: they are largely covered by a wood.

The gardens, or rather the park, is not what it should be: many new plantations have been begun, and when finished they will cover 2,500 acres.

From the south side of the house, there appears to be a great sweep of country, but it is an illusion: a long stretch of fine grassland separates the house from a great mass of planted trees: the mass is cut through in the middle, and another avenue leads to an obelisk of white brick, in

---

[4] Well, it leads either to the north dining-room and back into the hall, or to the guest wing. They returned through the Statue Gallery and first octagon to the (S.W.) library wing.

[5] Presumably guest-beds.

[6] The late Sir Nikolaus Pevsner concluded that 'the interior of the house is more consistently palatial than that of almost any other house in England'.

imitation of freestone, and 80 feet high: the pedestal seems out of proportion at 1½ or 2 feet wide: it runs up to an obtuse point and bears no inscription.[7] At a mile beyond the obelisk, in the same line, is a sort of triumphal arch, serving as gate-lodge, and on one side and the other of the arch great plantations are disposed which announce that you are approaching a great house.

The woodland which, as I told you, backs the stretch of grass in front of the house, covers the space between it and the triumphal arch, because the land dips very often and that where the triumphal arch is built is only slightly raised, so that from the house the height of the trees seems to occupy the whole distance between the wood and the arch – which is in fact part of the farm.

All this land, or at least much the greatest part of it, will one day be part of the park: it is only a matter of time.

The view to the north of the house is much richer and more varied, more agreeable, owing entirely to the strip of water I shall tell you about.

This strip of water lies to the north-west of the house and fills an old creek of the sea, quite a deep valley for its size. West of the water is an eminence, planted with trees, and a certain distance behind this wood is another, much taller, eminence on which a church has been built.[8] This forms the happiest possible eye-catcher from the house. There is virtually no distance between the two eminences, and the perspective is such that the church seems to crown the wood. To the east of the water, and almost in line with the wooded hill, another plantation is made on land that is shaped rather like a funnel.[9] Nothing could be more striking, or create a better effect, than these two framers of the view, a concave edge to the west, a rather convex edge to the east, the water in the middle with the shadow of one or other of the plantations at every moment of

---

[7] It was erected in 1729, the first of all the new buildings at Holkham, and was naturally based on an antique model. It stood on a slight eminence.

[8] Lazowski makes it sound like another piece of garden furniture, and indeed it had been reclad, probably by Brettingham and William Ingram. But it is a most interesting medieval building, dedicated to St Withburga; and Holkham's first Anglo-Saxon name was Withburgstow. When the church was severely restored in 1870, remains of an earlier, probably Anglo-Saxon, tower were found.

[9] Was it, perhaps, a decoy? But he describes the *terrain*, rather than the plantation, as funnel-shaped.

the day; and the church, which crowns the whole prospect, is part of a picture painted with bold, impressive strokes. It is with the right blending of the shape of their land and their plantations that the English establish one of the chief attractions of their parks, but the landscape must be gradual, gentle, otherwise the hand of the designer obtrudes and all illusion vanishes.

In front of the house, someone has planted trees in clumps of varying size but similar shape, giving an unfortunate, slightly shocking, sense of regularity. And there is a naked patch to the east, which jars. These defects are about to be corrected: some of the clumps will be absorbed into a wood which will run eastwards irregularly and with gaps to give variety.

The sea lies beyond the plantations but is not visible from the house: the plantations and [sea-defence] embankments, however inadequate, block the view of it. However, you do enjoy a view of it from the imperceptible rise on which the obelisk is built to the south of the house; and I promise you, the picture is superb, for the sea concludes majestically the landscape I have just described to you.

I have said nothing of the kitchen gardens that cover eight acres, of differing soils. I must hurry on to the subject of Mr Coke's methods of cultivation, for to a great love of the countryside itself he joins a love of agriculture, in which he is prodigiously well informed.

But first I must tell you that all this land, even that on which the house is built, was covered by the sea forty years back: while we were at Holkham, we learnt that some days ago a ship's captain had come to see this fine country over which he had sailed forty years earlier: he had anchored in the creek now occupied by the ornamental water.[10]

We omit the long descriptions of Coke's famous farming methods, for they are described in equally great detail elsewhere.[11] Thomas Weaver's painting, of c. 1807, not only shows him with some of his marvellous South Down sheep, but

[10] Lazowski was wrong about the house: the north-west wing replaced the old manor-house of Hill Hall, which Leicester occupied until it made way in 1757 for the last unit of his great new building. But it is quite likely that the skipper of the vessel had anchored in the creek.

[11] In E. Rigby, *Holkham and its Agriculture*, 1818, and in A. M. W. Sterling's delightful book, *Coke of Norfolk and his Friends*, 2 vols., 1908, especially in chapters XI, XII and XIII; more recently in R. A. C. Parker, *Coke of Norfolk*, 1975, and Susannah Wade-Martins, *A Great Estate at Work*, 1980.

40. Coke of Holkham with his sheep. Painting by Thomas Weaver c. 1807.

also illustrates the carefully planned relationship of the house with the church in this unvoluptuous landscape (Pl. 40).

In coming to Binham, we have left on our left Wells, a little sea-port engaged in exporting some of the corn of the county. The port dwindles daily as the navigation becomes difficult by reason of the amount of sand silting up the mouth of its river. Having missed Wells, we made a detour of some miles to go to Blakeney, a new small port[12] formed by a creek opposite Cley, which is another port formed by a stream running in a narrow valley which empties into the tide.[13] From a village, Blakeney is becoming a little town, not solely developed through trade, but an overall change, including several good newly-built houses. This

---

[12] Not at all new but going back to the early Middle Ages.
[13] *marée*. This is the Glaven estuary. We saw earlier that none of the party seems to have known the word *estuaire*.

little place has twenty little boats belonging to it, occupied only in the coastal trade and the transport of the corn of neighbouring parts. We didn't visit Cley: we could see it well enough to say the town is quite strung out, built to the north-west along a low ridge: the boats are moored along the line of the town, sheltered from the south and south-east winds, also in the lee of a ridge which faces the contrary winds. These three ports export the grain of this part of the county between Lynn and Norwich: they import only goods needed for internal consumption.

This is the most picturesque part of Norfolk. The soil is extremely poor, sand and gravel; extremely uneven, often folded into little hills that are either isolated or in a group and some wooded: but what is so attractive is a number of streams that wind in the little valleys which give the grass a brilliant green and which water many clumps of maritime trees: the contrast with the brown of the little hills is pleasant.

Holt, where we pulled up, is a small market-town, well-built, it has a gay, rather prosperous air, its farms in much better condition than those around Cley: all are enclosed.

We had planned to go as far as Aylsham, and to see in passing the house and park of Lord Buckingham, at Blickling, but black night descended before we got to Blickling so that we had to sleep there[14] to be able to see the park next day.

[14] Presumably at Aylsham. John Hobart, the 2nd earl of Buckinghamshire, was directly descended from the Henry Hobart who bought the house from Anne Boleyn's family and had this great house built in 1616–24 by Robert Lyminge, the architect also of at least part of Hatfield House. It passed to the National Trust in 1940, and is their Headquarters for East Anglia. There was a considerable rebuilding, in the style of the original, by Thomas Ivory, an eminent Norwich architect, over the twenty years 1765–85, immediately before the La Rochefoucauld visit. Until 1725, the structures of the medieval house occupied the north side.

BLICKLING

This estate belonged to Anne Boleyn's father,[1] and her statue and that of Queen Elizabeth are carved on either side of the grand staircase: I am not sure whether Anne Boleyn was not born here.[2]

The house was built in the time of James I, and thus in an old style, but part of the interior has been modernised, and some very convenient apartments made. The library, 100 feet long, is fine and contains a fine excellent collection of books.[3] The present Lord Buckingham[shire] has created and furnished a superb drawing-room[4] on a big scale, noble and beautifully proportioned: I mention this room only to tell you that it has one wall of tapestry given to him at the time of his embassy at St Petersburg by the present Empress. It shows Peter the Great on horseback and in uniform at the battle of Poltava: the portrait has a natural grandeur. It is worked in wool in the manner of the Gobelins tapestries, and although one couldn't say it was as well made, as precisely drawn and coloured with the accomplishment of the best tapestries, it must be admitted that it is superb; and one can't imagine how such a craft has managed to take root under a sky and in a climate so sombre and among a still barbarous people.[5]

The park is beautiful and presents a variety of pictures: it is well stocked in general with trees of very fine size,[6] the artificial lake is extremely beautiful, curving out of sight behind a well-tree'd hill, so that you enjoy a perfect illusion; the other bank is level and partially

[1] Indeed it was acquired by her great-grandfather, Geoffrey Boleyn, and although there are monumental brasses in the church to three female Boleyns, 1458–85, their main home was Hever Castle in Kent, and there is only the inevitable local legend to link Queen Anne Boleyn, executed in 1536, with Blickling.

[2] The life-size carved wooden figures in niches beside the staircase, representing Anne Boleyn and her daughter Queen Elizabeth I, show Anne in the most up-to-date fashion of Lord Buckinghamshire's day, and the La Rochefoucaulds': her plinth asserts that she was born here.

[3] In fact 120 feet – the Long Gallery – and fortunately enhanced by 12,000 books from a Lincolnshire house, Nocton, that was later destroyed by fire.

[4] *salon*: I think drawing-room is what he meant here: it is now the Peter the Great room. Its most recent appraisal is by John Maddison, *Country Life*, 31 March 1988.

[5] Buckinghamshire was ambassador to Catherine the Great from 1762–5; the tapestry was woven in St Petersburg in 1764. Lazowski writes with the sadness of a Pole of Russian barbarity.

[6] Near the house, some fine old turkey-oaks survived the great 1987 gale.

wooded, the view of the water through the trees, increasing the sense of perspective, creates another most agreeable picture. Opposite, above the hill, someone has raised a kind of artificial mound, very steep. One imagines that the earth for this mound came from the excavations of long ago, for creating the lake.[7] The labour must have been immense: it is planted with a dense mass of shrubs and a kind of belvedere is set up on top, from which the eye swoops down on the whole country over a considerable distance.[8] The land on which the mound was erected was already high enough to command a view over the surrounding country. The countryside is uneven and was very early enclosed: there are great numbers of big trees in these enclosures and, as you survey them horizontally, there are many places where they form a mass and present a view of Germany, of immense forests with patches of cultivation, and houses, bell-towers and the houses of farms that can't be seen: in these openings, nothing could be more delightful than the selection and the making of this view: it is quite unlike any view of England and makes a tremendous effect.

On the other side, to the left, the land is absolutely flat and so even that Lord Buckingham[shire] tried to establish race-tracks for horses. Although there are fine groves, the view is depressingly uniform, and an attempt has been made at a diversion by building a house with a tower above it.[9] The house has a room for taking tea, and you climb up to the platform of the tower and enjoy a superb view very different from the one from the other side, the land rises insensibly, the eminences increase, but always presenting different amphitheatres dotted with villages and handsome country houses. This whole view spreads round in a semicircle, so that you can, at the same time, pick out the details and enhance the whole.

Leaving this edge of the park, you plunge into a wood of magnificent forest trees, in which someone has put together a cabin on the edge of

[7] The lake was created more simply, by damming the beck from Silvergate, just before it reached the river Bure.

[8] The belvedere was replaced by a tall cylindrical water-tank, now disused, and effectively screened by yew-trees. The view from the top is now obscured, even in winter, by the height of the surrounding very mature trees – several beeches must be 100 feet high.

[9] It has handsome Gothic windows and niches, is still called 'the Racecourse Tower', and is still well-maintained and inhabited.

41. Blickling, The Ladies' Cottage, drawn by Humphry Repton, ?1781.

quite a steep gully, with great trees growing upright and semi-prostrate and making the place picturesque (Pl. 41).[10] The cabin is built like a simple cottage, with straw seats, two prominent deal shelves all round the walls, furnished with all the pottery necessary for milk and tea and making a simple meal, but as plain and as unadorned as you could find in the homes of the people. It is that yellowish pottery that you know of, and that the English import from Flanders: it looks neat and goes well with the cabin.

In front of the cabin, in an open space, some ruins have been put together, statues and urns set up and spread very effectively over a slight natural elevation. At one side is an apparently modern urn containing the ashes of one of Lord Buckingham[shire]'s children, as you read on an inscription on the pedestal. One of the sides of the pedestal is inscribed with some perfectly chosen lines of Milton.[11]

[10] Known as 'the Ladies' Cottage', it dilapidated and now shows only footings. But Humphry Repton's drawing shows it beside its steep cleft, as charming as when they saw it in 1784.

[11] Later, a mausoleum was built here for the family remains: the mausoleum survives but the remains have been removed.

You see from these details that this park, without any great reputation, is none the less an agreeable place.[12]

It is only ten or eleven miles from Blickling to Norwich, but we had planned to go some miles out of our way to see a portable barn, take its measurements and find out how to build one; but we stayed too long in the park and so I was not in too strong a position to do what I wanted. Considering that something unknown in France and useful in itself is much more necessary to see than fine estates – which after all we have, in all sizes, and which after all we can never put to our own use like this portable barn – no obstacle should have prevented me from seeing it. I will see to it that I procure a drawing or at least an exact description to give you.

The little town of Aylsham is pretty and well-built with gay, well-maintained and well-gardened exteriors, and the houses that are scattered over the countryside are all more or less decorated up.[13]

We omit a paragraph about old enclosures, well-tended turnips, and carrots too thickly sown.

NORWICH

The nearer you get to Norwich, the richer the countryside becomes, because of the increasing number of fine houses with beautiful parks. This gives the superb country more the appearance of a town in which large gardens belong to all the houses than merely a countryside. Norwich, which closes the view, completes a beautiful picture, which would have an even greater effect if it were not so extensive.

You have heard often enough that Norwich is the largest English town after London . . . What will surprise you, as it does me, is that Norwich has preserved its old wall, without building outside.

It is estimated that Norwich has 40,000 inhabitants of whom two-thirds are employed in the factories . . . Like all ancient cities, Norwich

[12] It had a great reputation with Arthur Young, who had written fourteen years earlier, in his *Tour of the Eastern Counties*: 'This partial view of the lake (for the branches of the beech hang over the water and form an horizon for the scene) is strikingly beautiful. You will dwell on it with uncommon pleasure.' As a rule he reserved such lyrical language for the cultivation of carrots. His love of scenery could not always be suppressed on his tours through England and Europe.
[13] *ornées*

42. *The old Norwich theatre, 1758.*
(T. L. G. Burley, Players and Playhouses of East Anglia, *1928)*

is badly planned and built. It is not that there are no good or beautiful houses, but a well-built house on a bad site or in a narrow street can never appear more than very moderate.

It has a company of actors which tours Cambridgeshire, Essex and Suffolk at various times of the year.[1] I can't tell you about the playhouse: we haven't seen it but it is quite large, and as it is fitted up in the English way, you can be sure it is very ordinary (Pl. 42).

This town has the advantage of being almost in the middle of the county, and having very good soil all round it, cultivated by a large number of labourers and providing fully for the town's great consumption. It stands in an area where grain of all kinds is abundant, where all breeds of livestock are raised, where malt especially makes a good price, since it is exported from Norfolk to Scotland, and in quantities to other parts of England. The town is therefore in the excellent position of being the mainstay of agriculture by its great consumption and of being

[1] See T. L. G. Burley, *Playhouses and Players of East Anglia*, Norwich, 1928.

maintained in turn by its advantages, the good price and the ease of access of all its provisions: notice that this applies not only to the town but to the countryside up to eight or ten miles round, where some of its workpeople live.

An inestimable advantage is everything that Norwich derives from its river and from its proximity to Yarmouth. The river Yare is navigable for boats of 40–60 tons. It is by water that Norwich receives all its provisions in grain, etc., and all its coal, of which the consumption is considerable; for its dyes and the preparation of cloths, all the ingredients of the dyes; its wool, arriving spun from different parts of England and Ireland; in a word, all its consumption requirements and all the raw materials for its manufactures. All the manufactures themselves are taken the twenty miles to Yarmouth, and through that port its merchandise is exported to all parts of Europe. This dispenses with all need of waggons. I don't need to emphasise so considerable an advantage: you can imagine the immense saving in the cost of manufacture . . . the permanent indisputable advantage in the markets of Europe.

Norwich is crossed by the river Yare, which ceases to be navigable above the town. The water of this river supplies the dyeworks as well as the human needs of the town. It is the same system as Lynn's: the main pipes run through all the streets, in each street there is a key to open the pipes and supply water to the different houses in the street, the key is covered by a sort of iron man-hole cover, opened and shut as required and over which the carriages pass. The cost to the inhabitants of this abundant water is not great. The very considerable large inn where we were staying pays only three guineas a year: it's more or less the same rate as Lynn's.

The poor rate is enormous: eight shillings and fourpence in the pound on the rentable value of the house. There can scarcely be any other example of such a tax. It amounts in all to £18,000, but it is not often so much. Manufactures were so enormously diminished in the last two years of the war[2] that talks had to be held with large numbers of workmen; and as the rate was already so much increased they preferred to make loans, which now have to be paid off. The rate remains enormous: in an ordinary year it is five shillings.

[2] The Peace was ratified in March, 1783.

This rate maintains two Houses of Industry, containing thirteen hundred poor people. The other poor, who need only relief and help, receive, in proportion to the size of their families, and their need, a certain money-payment weekly. That way they distribute £2,500 a year.

We went to examine in close detail one of these workhouses. It is a very ancient building converted as well as possible to this use, but it really is not convenient, immense though the building is.[3] The different partitions are too small, the lights, the windows, are neither large enough nor numerous enough, and in consequence, despite the care and attention given to maintaining cleanliness as laid down by the rules, the air is unhealthy and there is a perpetual stench.

The girls are occupied with sewing and general housework, or with spinning for the use of the tradesmen of the town; the boys generally go out to work and the manufacturers or workmen who employ them pay the price of their labour towards the economy of the house. Married men either have separate rooms when they have children or live in the big rooms with boarded partitions: there is proper attention never to separate the children from their fathers and mothers until they are of an age to be occupied with the others in various ways.

The children learn to read and write and great care is taken to instruct them in the principles of their religion stripped of anything approaching intolerance or superstition.

The two houses share the poor between them in a way which, designed to give them more facilities, serves also to maintain their customs: in one are all the girls up to the age of fifteen and all the boys over that age, until they are ready either to earn their living without any help, or to go into an apprenticeship or to sea: in the other are the girls over fifteen and all the boys under that age.

The poor are well looked after and clothed according to their needs, though the durability of clothes is limited by the passage of time; they are well-nourished, eating three times a day, with meat three times a

---

[3] An Act of 1712 established three workhouses for the whole of Norwich: one in New Hall, which had been the great church of the Black Friars and is now in public use as St Andrew's Hall; another in the remains of the duke of Norfolk's palace in Bridge Street, now occupied by a multi-storey car-park for 1,000 cars; the third, called the Infirmary, stood further out to the north, on the right just beyond St Austin's gates (Francis Blomefield, *History of Norfolk*, III, 1806, p. 432).

week; on the other four days, milk products and vegetables; there are two meals a day when they have only butter or cheese, but at all meals and every day they have small beer.

It costs about £7 a year to feed each poor person, but the maintenance, etc., of the house is not included in that sum.

Each house is administered by a general manager,[4] on whom turns all details and all order. It must be confessed that it is impossible to have a simpler, or a more economic, administration, but the lay-out, the structure of these houses for so large a number of poor people – whatever care one may take – will always ensure that these establishments fall short of achieving their object. For the rest, I am not giving as much detail as I would if I did not intend to write you a particular account of the working of the Poor Laws in England.

Apart from these two houses, there are five other establishments in Norwich. The Great Hospital,[5] or more properly the County Infirmary for it belongs to the county of Norfolk and not just to the town, has no funds but has been built and is maintained by the voluntary subscriptions of the inhabitants of the county: it has cost, to build and furnish entirely, seven thousand and some hundreds of pounds sterling. Nothing could be cleaner or simpler: there is no finery or show, only comfort and good care and scrupulous cleanliness.

It is intended for a hundred people, half of them men, half women, and the detailed management rests with a matron: everything is well planned and organised, she has one man-servant and six women, who can be supplemented according to need, but when it is necessary to watch patients through the night, women nurses are taken on and paid according to the number of days they have been employed.

The sick are kept in large, well-aired rooms, provided with ventilators, the bedsteads are of iron and the curtains of linen so that they may be washed as often as need be.

---

[4] The Master.

[5] The Great Hospital is the name of the Hospital of St Giles in Bishopgate Street, lying to the east of the cathedral and immediately north of the Close. It was founded in 1249, embodied St Helen's church as part of the hospital and is one of the most remarkable buildings in Norwich. But Lazowski is describing not it, but the Norfolk and Norwich Hospital founded, out on the London Road, in 1771 'for the relief of the sick and lame poor'. It was an early beneficiary of Norwich's triennial music festival, founded in 1824.

Four doctors serve the infirmary by the month,[6] but they come together to consult upon grave illnesses. An able surgeon is paid to come daily and as often as necessary and to perform all operations. The apothecary and his apprentice live in. The infirmary stands outside the walls of the old town, with a lot of land adjoining, enough for pasture and fodder for some cows and for a horse needed for service.

I never in my life saw an infirmary so clean, so well managed with so little means, in which there is no more odour than there is in the home of an individual who cares about cleanliness, and where the buildings are so well adapted to the needs without the least excess.

The large administration is composed of governors drawn from the number of subscribers: they issue the notes by which the sick are admitted; on which subject I am pleased to be able to tell you that there is no distinction between foreigners and nationals: it is enough to be poor enough to have need of the help of the hospital.

The second of these houses is a hospital for 40 men and 20 women who are fed and looked after in the house: these are old people and cripples. This hospital is for the town, and is full of people whose lives have been good and who have worked in the cloth manufactury.[7] The third hospital is intended to house, feed and instruct in a trade 36 boys: the fourth for 36 girls. Finally, there is an institution set up and maintained by subscription in the town to clothe and instruct in a public school, built uniquely for this purpose, 400 children.[8]

The cathedral is a big and very heavy Gothic building which seems to have been built by the Saxons [details of length, breadth, circumference of cloister, etc. Lazowski had no time for any serious appreciation of church architecture, even cathedral architecture]. I shall tell you nothing of this building, it has nothing of particular distinction. The bishop's house is also ancient, slightly modernised, vast and joined on to the cathedral: intermediate buildings have been pulled down.

We were in Norwich on the day of the Sessions. For the October Sessions it is customary for the entire county to come to Norwich, a rallying point for all sorts of people: those who are ambitious come to

[6] gratuitously.

[7] This reads like an uncharacteristically sketchy reference to the St Giles Hospital, the real 'Great Hospital'.

[8] This was the greatest of the Norwich Charity Schools which were even more numerous than Lazowski noticed.

win, or to maintain, popularity, the others to see their friends, and in general for love of public assemblies; the party politicians are also much in evidence at the public assemblies.

The ballroom, which they call the assembly-room, is very fine, spacious and elegant. A grand vestibule separates it from two magnificent rooms, one of them occupied by parties of whist:[9] in the other, cotillions were generally danced.[10]

It would be difficult to come across a more brilliant or more numerous assembly: I scarcely know of towns in France with anything of this kind.[11]

I wanted to tell you everything I thought necessary about Norwich before coming to its manufactures which, for two centuries, have been steadily increasing, but which have never known so much activity as there is today.

The American War, properly speaking, did it little harm, though Spain's entry considerably diminished the trade: you will remember that the manufactures of Sudbury in Suffolk and Colchester in Essex experienced the same revolution. This is not only because Spain imports a large amount of English cloth, for so does America, but because the prohibition was rigorously observed in Spain whereas in America, despite the laws against importing English goods, they imported a great many: the habit, the language, preference, etc., proved stronger than laws.

Now the Norwich manufactures are livelier than before the war. *Over 1,500 words of intricate and abundant detail about manufacturing methods and the whole economy of Norwich are here omitted.*

[9] *With.* It was sometimes also called whisk in the 18th century, and the French naturally had trouble with its pronunciation.

[10] Lazowski writes as though the banquet-room, across the vestibule from the ballroom and equally handsome, was then in use as two rooms.

[11] Outside Bath, and perhaps York, the same may be said of England. Norwich's Assembly House is the work of its excellent architect Thomas Ivory (1709–79), who designed a house in the entrance court of the Great Hospital in 1752, and this as a speculation in 1754. It has his initials on the down-pipes, and beautiful plasterwork within. He was also building the Octagon Chapel for the Presbyterians, 1754–6 (S. J. Wearing, *Georgian Norwich and its Builders*, Norwich, 1926). The years *c.* 1750–80 seem to have been a hey-day for Norwich: Lazowski was seeing it at a good moment, as he recognised.

I forgot to mention the castle. It is an ancient fortress built by the Saxons,[12] on a mound which commands both town and country. The building is square and was flanked by towers: nothing remarkable. Nowadays one climbs it to enjoy a very extensive view.

From Norwich to Yarmouth you have in view, nearly all the way, the plain through which flows the Norwich river, often extremely broad. Ten or twelve miles from Norwich you enter an immense plain traversed by the river Thurne.[13] The greater part of this plain is flooded and marshland. The river waters, it is true, have little movement, but dykes and locks will convert the marshes and poor pastures into excellent meadows.

On this Norwich to Yarmouth road we saw for the first time the dibbling,[14] that is to say the planting, of wheat. The process is the same as for peas: the plough cuts and turns over the turf of the artificial meadows, a man armed with a sort of pike[15] in each hand walks along the furrow making two holes, side by side, in the turned-over turf, and children walk behind with the seed-wheat in little panniers, dropping one or two grains in each hole: then the harrow, with its teeth adjusted accordingly, follows behind, filling in the holes.[16]

The land here is all enclosed and the arable farming much as it is between Aylsham and Norwich: the soil clayey.

YARMOUTH

You come in from the north, for you have to cross the river Thurne [Bure] and go a long way out of your original direction, the Breydon

[12] It has been left to the 20th-century antiquaries to be able to determine the difference between Saxon and Norman architecture.

[13] It is really the river Bure, which meanders down from its source near Melton Constable to join 'the Norwich river', the Yare, at Yarmouth. The Thurne is a tributary of the Bure, joining it at the village of Thurne.

[14] His word seems to be *driller*, and drilling *was* a new way of planting wheat: but the process he describes here was dibbling. Both processes were described and warmly recommended by Young, *General View of the Agriculture of Suffolk*, 1797, pp. 47–52. By 1797, drilling was not catching on so well as dibbling, probably because the drilling machines were expensive and complicated.

[15] This 'dibble' is a sort of iron rod with an egg-shaped tip, the size of a pigeon's egg, and a wooden handle at the other end, like a spade-handle. It is described as something new in the Attleborough area in 1781 (Wm Marshall, *Rural Economy of Norfolk*, II, 1787, p. 39). Plate 5 shows dibbling being demonstrated at Liancourt in *c.* 1802.

[16] Young recommended rolling, rather than harrowing, at this stage.

marshes blocking the direct route and forcing you to go north of these almost-islands that increase daily through the deposit of sands by the sea.[1]

This town is divided into two towns, the old one and the new one on the opposite side of the river; in Suffolk, but ruled by the same town officials (except that they are in different parishes). They are joined by a wooden bridge, which opens in the middle to let boats through.

Although Yarmouth is a town of considerable importance through the extent of its shipping, it has nevertheless fallen from its ancient opulence since so many other towns have increased their trade. There are 14,000 inhabitants. The town has a corporation and sends two members to Parliament.

The market place is very fine, with trees, and very spacious, but what distinguishes Yarmouth from all other English towns is its Quay: it is superb (Pl. 43). The distance from the bridge to the South Gate is 5014 yards (a yard equals three feet): the width of the quay is in some places as much as 103 yards.[2] Beyond the South Gate, the quay continues even further for the little boats, but the side of the quay is not walled beyond the gate.

The Norwich river, augmented by the Bure[3] which joins it above the town, flows from the bridge due south[4] until it passes the fort which I will tell you about: once past the fort it turns due east and pours itself into the sea. Just where the river turns to enter the sea, there is a sand-bank that cannot be passed by ships of more than 150 tons without their being unloaded and lightened. The navigation of this river is extremely difficult: the bottom is of such shifting sand that sometimes the channel changes every week: so all vessels employ

---

[1] Lazowski's grasp of this strange geography was sketchy, but as late as 1826 Edward Mogg, the editor of *Paterson's Roads*, was hoping that 'the spirit of improvement so evident at Yarmouth will ere long extend itself to shortening the very circuitous road to Norwich.' A year or two later, the Acle–Yarmouth turnpike shortened the journey by four miles cutting out Burgh St Margaret and Caister-on-Sea.

[2] Lazowski, for all his pains, has come a puzzling cropper: the quay was, as he says, as much as 103 yards in width, or even a little more, near the South Gate: but the distance from the bridge to the South Gate was precisely 1200 yards, approximately two-thirds of a mile, a very respectable length. The South Gate was pulled down in 1812, but long stretches of the town's medieval wall survive.

[3] He called it the Thurne.

[4] He said north, as he did at Lynn: one has two choices.

43. Yarmouth Town Hall and Quay, undated, by J. P. Neale (1780–1847).

coastal pilots, of whom there are always six stationed in the fort, where they moor their boats. They take soundings in the river so that they know where the channel runs. Several times a week, the sea brings sand along the coast, and to keep the mouth navigable it has been found necessary to construct a jetty, which is extended every year.

All the coast to the north of the river-mouth is flat, and easy for an enemy landing. To prevent that, a fort has been built and three redoubts, a mile apart, to the north.

The fort itself is an ancient, irregular fortification, without bastions. The platforms, on which they could put a battery of forty guns, are raised about 20 feet above sea-level and also command the surrounding land. The parapets, four feet thick, are of brick, and in good condition. To the north, where a landing is possible, a redoubt, arrow-headed in plan,[5] has been added, with 12 pieces of cannon with fire-power enough to flatten all the land around: south of it, the fort is surrounded by double ditches, palisaded and well maintained: it is not very roomy,

[5] It is odd that such a shrewd military observer did not use the French word for 'an arrow-head redoubt' – a *redan*.

213

could hold only a feeble garrison, and provided no shelter, that I could see, against a bomb.

Going north, we passed the three redoubts a mile apart, each with 12 pieces of cannon and a small wooden building for the look-out in time of war. Supposing the last of these redoubts were to be captured, one could turn the others and the fort by going a little higher, crossing the river where one might well come under the fire of the redoubt near the town only for the space of a short sprint.

On the Suffolk coast a mile to the south-west of the river-mouth, an equally strong redoubt has been placed on a fairly high point. The coast here rises gently from the beach and becomes vertical cliff, so they fear no attempt on this side; but they have built this redoubt to take in rear any ships that could open fire on the fort from either the north-east or the west. Neither the redoubts nor the fort possess a single mortar.[6]

Yarmouth has 250 boats belonging to the trade of the place, from 100 to 150 tons, though only 50 boats are in the latter class. Eighty are employed in the herring fishery, which the Dutch share with them. They come to Yarmouth with what they need in the way of salt for their fishing; and, ten days before our arrival, they had left the port in 100 vessels, to start their fishing.

Each Yarmouth vessel was expected to catch 10,000 barrels of herring – a barrel is 800 – and they reckon that about 500 lbs of salt are needed for 10,000 herring: they bring their salt from Liverpool: it is very fine.[7]

They don't salt their herring – only the Dutch do that: they smoke them in kinds of drying-houses,[8] kept entirely shut, in the bottom of

[6] Admittedly, the French had only lately been at war with Britain in the American War and became so again in very different circumstances a decade after this visit, but to record so professionally the defences of your hosts in letters home seems unfriendly, despite much evidence to the contrary in all these records. Two decades later, Napoleon, into whose family Alexandre married, planned to land near Folkestone. Reading Lazowski's report of his reconnaissance at Yarmouth, one understands Nelson's hunch that Yarmouth was where they would disembark; and that is worth remembering as one salutes him on his column here, between the old town and the river-mouth.

[7] They probably *did* salt them, before putting them through the elaborate smoking process. These drying-houses were known as 'fish-houses'.

[8] David Butcher of Lowestoft, author of a classic study of *The Driftermen* (Reading, 1979), tells me 10,000 barrels must have been the prodigious annual catching capacity for the bigger vessels only.

which they light several fires of great pieces of oak which give off little flame and much smoke.

As soon as the herring are unloaded, which the ship does as soon as it has a full load, in order to get back to the fishing-grounds, – as soon, I say, as the herring are unloaded, the women wash them well by putting them in a rush-basket and then plunging them into a great tank of water and shaking them about; they are then threaded on to wooden spits and suspended in the fish-house I have mentioned, where they stay for a fortnight or three weeks.[9]

The port is frequented by 400 vessels, English and foreign, every year.

Each vessel pays ninepence a year on its freight to the maintenance of the jetty, the lighthouses, etc., and a shilling for the ship's mooring on the quay, whatever its freight.

At Yarmouth there is a hospital solely for the fishermen: they must be more than fifty years old to be admitted: each has a little room, and whether or not he is married the room is the same: they are given 2 shillings and 6 pence a week, and the majority still earn something, whether by making short, easy sailing trips, or by filleting mackerel: those employed on the herring fishery earn about £500 a boat.

The poor rate is alarming: 10 shillings in the pound. I have never managed to understand the explanation of so exorbitant a tax.

At Yarmouth, at the end of summer, people come for the sea-bathing: it is the town's brilliantly festive season.

LOWESTOFT

This is a small town on the same coast, with no port but an excellent roadstead for shipping, a sandy bottom, and shelter from off-shore winds, for there is a tall shoreline [cliff, also two vital offshore shoals].

It is a fishing town with 24 vessels in the herring-fishery. Each ship is manned by twelve men, the fishermen are paid four guineas for the whole catch, the master gets 12 shillings a last, the first mate 9, the

---

[9] The best contemporary description of all this was given by Edmund Gillingwater, *Historical Account of Lowestoft*, 1790, Section III, especially pp. 95–6. As Lazowski noticed, there were important differences between the processing in Yarmouth and that in Lowestoft. The best recent books are by David Butcher, op. cit. and Robert Malster, *Lowestoft: East Coast Port*, Lavenham, 1982.

second 8: in an average year the vessel takes 20 lasts. A last is 10,000 herrings.

They prepare the herring in two ways. For consumption in England, the herring are smoked for only ten days, but for export abroad they are smoked for three weeks at least. The roof of the smoke-house is open at the highest point, by means of tiles which open on each side. They attribute to this arrangement the superiority of their herring, which are usually sold at 10 shillings a last more than those of Yarmouth. The usual price of their herring is 4 shillings a hundred. They are all exported to the Mediterranean.

The wood used for smoking is chiefly oak. Elm is equally good.

This town has also a factory producing porcelain for everyday use, employing 90–100 workers.[1] There are two glazing-ovens[2] in which only coal is burnt. The fire is kept burning for 28 hours to bake the porcelain, but the porcelain is kept in the oven for three days in all, to allow it to cool gradually.

Skilled workmen earn 14 shillings a week: painters earn a guinea and a guinea and a half. Young workmen doing minor jobs get 7 or 8 shillings a week. Up to half of this porcelain is exported to Holland, and thence reaches France under the name of *Porcelaine des Indes*, which it resembles.[3] It is very cheap. Cups painted with blue designs cost threepence, those with a gold rim only sixpence.

The roadstead at Lowestoft is lit at night by a lighthouse (Pl. 44). It is defended by two redoubts.

---

[1] Geoffrey A. Godden, in his effectively embellished work, *The Illustrated Guide to Lowestoft Porcelain*, 1969, p. 1, wrote that the Lowestoft factory 'never employed more than about seventy workpeople', and added: 'my personal belief is that only twenty to thirty persons were employed at the factory.' There is no reason to doubt Lazowski's general figure, which was clearly gained from a personal visit, though probably not from a head-count. The point is worth establishing if we are to form an accurate picture of the major industry that produced the beautiful porcelain as well as the cheap goods for the Dutch market.

[2] He uses the technical word *réverbères*, and I owe its translation to Griselda Lewis: Sheenah Smith thinks this refers to a slow-cooling kiln for the biscuit firing, and a glost or glazing oven.

[3] This Dutch (and indirectly French) market is said to have led to the decline of the factory. Francophile Dutch had brought Holland into the American War in 1780–3. G. A. Godden, p. 7, quotes as a cause of failure Pichegru's famous conquest of Holland across the frozen dykes in the winter of 1794–5: 'amongst the British property destroyed was a quantity of Lowestoft China at Rotterdam, in value several thousand pounds . . .

44. Lowestoft porcelain mug, showing the Lowestoft lighthouse described by Lazowski.

Seabathing is also done here from a little hut, mounted on a track which takes it into the sea, and attached by cable to the beach. Outside the hut, a platform is lowered. It is covered with canvas in the form of a tent, under which you bathe.

The ware was sent weekly in hogsheads by way of Yarmouth.' The factory closed *c.* 1802. Sheenah Smith was able to use the Lazowski material through Mrs Marion Bell, a correspondent of the late Jean Marchand. Her masterly article in the *Connoisseur*, February, 1977, observed: 'There is more information packed into Lazowski's short but detailed report than the optimistic researcher would hope to find over a period of years.' Her own research substantially confirmed Lazowski's reliability.

On the road to Bungay we stopped to look at a house of industry built for 25 parishes, I think, in the Hundred of Wangford.[4] It is very well run, with 200 poor, but in the winter 300.

Towards Bungay, the farming improves: they raise cattle, sow hemp, and this is the first time I have seen it in this part of England. They cultivate turnips here on a big scale. On their poor lands they grow buckwheat; and they cart an abundance of muck to enrich their wheat.

Bungay is a market town, small, well enough built, only a few miles from Beccles, another town, with quite a considerable population. I have nothing to tell you about Beccles, where we slept.

Through Harleston, a little town extremely nicely built and apparently prosperous.

Here the soil begins to get damp and clayey, pasture predominates, and you see that you are approaching the heavy lands of Suffolk by the Suffolk cows you meet. The farms are not large but they have a large proportion of their land in pasture, and keep a great many cows. I noticed several fields planted with cabbage for winter-keep for the cows; but the cabbages were poor, not weeded – in short, badly cultivated.

From about six miles this side of Bungay, the road follows the river Waveney which separates the two counties of Norfolk and Suffolk. The river flows in an infinitely agreeable valley. We are back in Suffolk, returned from our excursion. I have introduced you to many of our actual experiences. It is high time for me to have a rest; and for you too, no doubt.

We know from Alexandre (tome IV) that they were keen to get back to Bury in time for all the fun of Bury Fair. Once the Fair was over, 'our plan was to make our big tour through England'. But in his tome X he wrote: 'After being ill in Bury, and delayed two months in the town by a second illness, our preparations were finally made for as long a journey as possible.' In the end, they toured widely through the midlands and the north and the south-west in February, March and April of 1785, observing all the way. In 1786, Alexandre and Lazowski made an excursion into Scotland and Ireland. Those travels are the making of another volume.

[4] Shipmeadow Workhouse was built in 1765–7 by the 27 parishes of Wangford Hundred incorporated for the purpose under Gilbert's Act of 1764. It cost £4,000 to build (Suffolk Record Office, ADA9/AB1/1 fol. 37), not 'about £8,500' as Mrs E. Mann wrote in her edition of the diary of an inmate, 1837–45: *Proceedings, Suffolk Institute of Archaeology*, XXIII, 1939, pp. 42–9.

Index

François equipped his *Mélanges* with a very full Table of Subjects, which appears on pp. vii and viii above.

219

Bristol, Frederick Hervey, 4th earl of, 26
Bristol, John Hervey, 1st earl of, 18n.
Brown, Lancelot 'Capability', 36, 139n.
Buckinghamshire, John Hobart, 2nd earl of, 187, 200n., 202
Bunbury, Sir Charles, 75–6
Bunbury, Henry, xxii n.
Bungay, 218
Bure river (Norfolk), 211n., 212
Burlington, Richard Boyle, 3rd earl of, 195n.
Burney, Fanny, xxxiv–xxxv
Burnham Market (Norfolk), 178–9
Bury St Edmunds, Alderman, 73n., 186; billiard room, 98–9; dancing, 42; the Rochefoucaulds in, 16–17, 97–8, 187; engravings of, xxii n.; French emigrés in, xxxiv–xxxv; labourers' wages, 55; in Middle Ages, 81n.; post-horses and horses for hire, 96–7; prosperity 96n.; religion, 66, 67; Suffolk Assizes, 81

Caldwell, Ralph, 167n.
Cambridge, 95
Cambridge University, 91–5
Campbell, Colen, 170n.
Canning, Richard, 128n.
Canterbury, 5
Capel St Andrew, 135n.
cards (see also whist), 128, 133n.
Carlyle, Thomas, xxxiv
carriages, cabriolets, 96, 156; charettes, 4; curricles, xxii n; gigs, xxii n., 156; post-chaises, 95–6, 97; Tilbury, 51
Castle Acre, 162
Castle Rising, 191
Catherine the Great, Empress of Russia, 168n., 170, 201
Cattawade Bridge, 125n.
cattle, 126 and n.; Bakewell's, 150; bullocks, 132; cows at Dunton, 174–5; cows on Rougham farm, 166; dairy cows, 144, 145; fattening, 175; fodder, 166, 153, 172n., 175, 177, 218; grazing, 136; polled, 144n.; quantity of, 152; Scotch, 154; on South Creake farm, 177; Suffolk, 126n., 218; winter quarters, 153
Chadacre, 107n.

chamber pots, 23
Channel crossing, 3
Chapman, John, 160n.
charity, 151
Charles I, King, xvii
Chastullé, Adélaïde Pyvart de, xxxvii
children, 207, 209
Christchurch Mansion, Ipswich, 132n.
churches, Holkham, 197, 198, 199; King's Lynn, 184; London, 7–8; Mistley, 119; Norwich cathedral, 209; St Paul's Cathedral, 11–12; St Peter's, Swaffham, 160; Westminster Abbey, 13
cider, 18
cleanliness, English, 33; farmers' houses, 152; François first notices, 4; Heveningham kitchen, 140; inns, 132; London, 8; Norfolk County Infirmary, 209; prisons, 90; spinster's house, 125; weekly house washing, 19; workhouses, 207
Cley (Norfolk), 199, 200
clocks, 135
clothes, 4, 43, 178, 207
clubs, Box Clubs, 190–91; discussion, 189–90; London, 15, 188–9
coaches, 3, 5, 6
coal, 4, 112, 206
cock-fighting, 45
Cockfield Hall, Yoxford, xxxv n., 133n.
Coddenham, 126n.
coffee-house, Ipswich, 128
Coke, Thomas William, later 1st earl of Leicester, and 1784 General Election, 76; books, 196; Rochefoucaulds make acquaintance of, 187; and embezzling agent, 159; his farm, 173; love of agriculture, 197
Colchester, 111, 113–14
Coldham Hall, Stanningfield, 27n.
common land, 155, 177
constables, 87–8
Cornwallis, Charles Cornwallis, 1st marquis and 2nd earl, 103, 105, 156
cosmetics, rouge, 43
cows, see cattle
Cranmer Hall (Norfolk), 176n.
Creake, South (Norfolk), 177; North, 178n.

Martlesham Creek, 132n.
Mary, Queen of Scots, 144
Mary Tudor, Queen, 60, 144
Massingham (Norfolk), 166–7
Mayer, Luigi, 127n.
mayor, election of, 186
meals, breakfast, 21; club dinners, 190;
    dinner, 22, 24, 111n., 186; dinner-time
    at Rougham farm, 166; Dunton
    farmhouse, 174; harvest labourers', 55,
    175, 178; of Scottish labourers in
    transit, 178; times of, 100; West
    Barsham farm, 177; workhouse, 207–8
Melford, Long, 109–10
Melton, xxxv n., 133
Mistley (Essex), 115, 117, 119–20, 122,
    124
Mure, Hutchinson, 100, 102–3
Mutual Benefit Societies, 190n.

Nacton, 20n.
Napoleon I, Emperor, xxxvii, 214n.
Nar river (Norfolk), 184n.
Nares, Sir George, 83n.
navigation, at mouth of Bure, 212–13
Nayland, 112
Nelson, Horatio Nelson, Viscount, 214n.
Newmarket, races, 46, 49, 50–51
newspapers, 21
Newton, 112n.
Newton, Sir Isaac, 94
North, Fountain, 163n.
North, Frederick, Lord North, 76, 163
North, Roger I, 163n.
North, Roger II, 163 and n.
Norwich, Assembly House, 210n.; castle,
    211; cathedral, 209; Catholic bishop,
    67; city wall, 204; company of actors,
    205; exports and imports on Yare, 206;
    hospitals, 208–9, 210n.; poor rate, 206–
    7; prosperity, 205–6; water supply, 206;
    workhouses, 207–8

Oakes, James, woolmerchant of Bury,
    28n.
Ord, Craven, 86n.
Ord, John, 16, 67n., 86n.
Orford, 134n.

Orford, George Walpole, 3rd earl of,
    159n., 166, 168, 170, 186
Ouse river (at Lynn), 184, 191
oxen, *see* cattle
Oxford University, 91–2

Palladio, Andrea, 171n.
parks, Blickling, 201–2, 204;
    Heveningham, 141; Holkham, 196–7;
    Houghton, 170; landscaped, 34, 36;
    Raynham, 173; Rigby's at Mistley, 122;
    Woolverstone, 127
pictures, xxiv; Luigi Mayer's
    watercolours, 127n.; family portraits at
    Raynham Park, 172; Townshend
    collection, 173n.; Walpole
    collection,168n., 170; Stubbs' portrait
    of a hunter, 180 and n.
pigs, 150, 153, 174
Plamplin, John, 107n.
Playford, 132n.
poor rate, 206, 215
poor, the, 207–9
poor-law unions, 20n.
porcelain factory, Lowestoft, 216
Poyntz, Rev. Charles, 178n.
prisons, 81, 86–7, 90
profanation of the Sabbath, 56–7
Punch, Suffolk, see horses

rabbits, 156, 157–8
Ramsholt, 134n.
Ransome, Robert, 154n.
Rattlesden river, 146n.
Raynham Park (Norfolk), 171–3
Rebecca, Biagio, 139n.
Red Towers, Melton, Woodbridge, 133n.
religion, 58–66; Anglicanism, 60–61;
    baptism, 61; burial of the dead, 65–6;
    confession, 61; confirmation, 61–2;
    death, 63–4; *dévots*, 65; English beliefs,
    64–5; marriage, 62; ministers, 65;
    religious toleration, 66–8; Roman
    Catholicism, 66–8
Rigby, Francis Hale, his house, grounds
    and farms, 119–20, 122–3
roads, 95–7, 109, 128, 156, 180, 211
Rochester (Kent), 5
Rosa, Salvator, *Belisarius*, 172

trade, Ipswich (*contd.*)
  and n.; London, 7; Lynn, 184, 186, 193;
  malt, 205; silk, 110–11; wool, 110–11
transport (*see also* carriages), post-horse,
  5–6
travellers, quantity of, 96
trees, Blickling, 201, 202, 202–3; in
  Cambridge college grounds, 92–3; fruit,
  35, 122; Heveningham oak, 142;
  Holkham, 196, 197, 198; Lombardy
  poplars, 134n.; Raynham Park, 173; in
  Rigby's gardens, 120, 122; Summerfield
  farm, Docking, 180
Turner, Nathaniel, of Ipswich, 130n.
turnpike, 212n.
Tusser, Thomas, 125n.

Vanneck, Sir Gerard, 138–9, 140, 141
Voltaire, François Marie Arouet de, 26

wages, harvest labourers', 54–5, 164, 175,
  178; servants', 20; silk workers', 111;
  weavers', 114n.; women servants, 55
Waller, Wm., of Sutton, 134n.
Walpole, Horace, *later* 4th earl of Orford,
  xxiv, 166n., 168., 170n.
Walpole, Sir Robert, 1st earl of Orford,
  168, 172n.
Walpole, Hon. Thomas, xxi, 15
Walton, Henry, xxiv
Wanneck, Sir Gerard, *see* Vanneck
Wantisden, 135n.
water fowl, 181n.
water rates, 206
water supply, 191–2, 196, 206
Watson, Richard, 95n.
Waveney river, 218
weather, agreeable, 156; bad, 173–4;
  Bristol, 16; Colchester, 114; mist, 145;
  rain, 145, 178; Suffolk, 16, 113;
  unpleasant, 107–8; winter, 30, 98
Weaver, Thomas, 198

Wedderburn, Alexander, 1st baron
  Loughborough, 84n.
Weedon, Mr, of Ramsholt, 134n.
Wells (Norfolk), 174, 199
Wells, 179n.
Wenyeve, John, 88n.
whist, 23, 107, 210
William I, the Conqueror, 7, 9
William II, Rufus, 9
Wimper, Mr, of Alderton, 134n.
wine, 18, 23, 174
Withepole House, Ipswich, 132n.
women, at public balls, 42, 43; hunting,
  40; in kitchens, 33; London life, 14;
  shooting, 41; wages, 55
Woodbridge, 126n., 132–3, 136; nurseries
  at, 133n.
Woolverstone, 127
workhouses, 207–8, 218
Wren, Sir Christopher, 9n., 10, 11, 13,
  163n.
Wyatt, James, 139n.

Yare river, 206
Yarmouth (Norfolk), 187, 193, 206, 212–
  15, 217n.
Young, Arthur, agriculture, 137;
  Autobiography, xxi–xxiii, xxiv; at
  Chadacre, 107n.; de Liancourt family
  and, xx, xxvi; discussions with farmers,
  125–6, 148; and duc de Liancourt's
  part in Revolution, xxxiv; farmer, 138;
  financial difficulties, 151n.; in France,
  xxxii–xxxiii; his home, 28; on Lazowski,
  xxi–xxiii; Lazowski and, xx; at Lynn,
  193; Mme de Genlis and, xxxiv;
  reputation and character, 27–8; Leslie
  Stephen on, xx n.; Suffolk tour, 109;
  travels on foot, 134; visits farming
  acquaintance, 130; his wife, 28; works,
  xx–xxi
Yoxford, xxxv n., 133n., 144n.

Angel Hill, in St Edmunds Bury, December 1774, engraving, second state: the gig has gone, the Angel has been given its present front elevation, and the more elegant figures in the foreground, added by Mr Bunbury. (St Edmundsbury Museums Service)